System Programming

with C and Unix

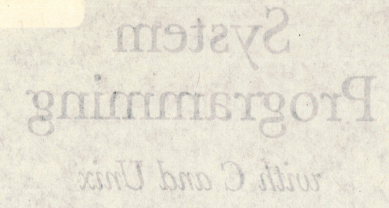

System Programming

with C and Unix

Adam Hoover

Clemson University

ADDISON-WESLEY

Boston   San Francisco   New York
London   Toronto   Sydney   Tokyo   Singapore   Madrid
Mexico City   Munich   Paris   Cape Town   Hong Kong   Montreal

Editor-in-Chief	Michael Hirsch
Acquisitions Editor	Matt Goldstein
Editorial Assistant	Sarah Milmore
Managing Editor	Jeffrey Holcomb
Production Supervisor	Heather McNally
Art Director	Linda Knowles
Cover Designer	Elena Sidorova
Cover Image	AbleStock / Index Open
Online Product Manager	Bethany Tidd
Marketing Manager	Erin Davis
Marketing Coordinator	Kathryn Ferranti
Senior Manufacturing Buyer	Carol Melville
Production Coordination, Text Design, and Composition	Windfall Software
Copyediting	Yonie Overton
Proofreading	Rick Camp
Indexing	Ted Laux

Many of the designations used by manufacturers and sellers to distinguish their products are claimed as trademarks. Where those designations appear in this book, and Addison-Wesley was aware of a trademark claim, the designations have been printed in initial caps or all caps.

The programs and applications presented in this book have been included for their instructional value. They have been tested with care, but are not guaranteed for any particular purpose. The publisher does not offer any warranties or representations, nor does it accept any liabilities with respect to the programs or applications.

This interior of this book was composed in Minion and Stone Sans using the ZzTEX typesetting system.

Library of Congress Cataloging-in-Publication Data

Hoover, Adam.
    System programming with C and Unix / Adam Hoover.—1st ed.
        p.   cm.
    Includes index.
    ISBN-13: 978-0-13-606712-2 (alk. paper)
    ISBN-10: 0-13-606712-3
    1. Systems programming (Computer science).   I. Title.
    QA76.66.H66 2009
    005.4′2—dc22

2008052700

Addison-Wesley
is an imprint of

PEARSON

www.pearsonhighered.com

ISBN-13: 978-0-13-606712-2
ISBN-10: 0-13-606712-3

4 5 6 7 8 9 10—DOH—18 17 16 15 14

Contents

Preface

The goals of this book are to teach the reader about system programming tools and resources, and to make the reader a better programmer. Consider the following questions: What is a library, and how is it used? What is a debugger, and how does it help during program development? What are scripting languages, and for what sorts of programming work are they useful? What are system calls, and when are they useful? Why would someone ever want to run a program from a shell instead of using a graphical user interface? These questions are addressed by the study of *system programming* as outlined in this textbook.

In addition to the concepts of system programming, this text explores the lower-level data types: bits and bytes, bit operations, arrays, strings, structures, and pointers. This material is covered with an emphasis on memory and understanding how and why these different data types are used. Understanding code at the memory level can help clarify even the most difficult programming concepts. It is common for a student to be less comfortable with these topics than with other basic programming concepts, such as loops and conditionals. Coverage of the lower-level data types is intended to reinforce an introductory coverage obtained previously. The goal is to advance the programming skill of the reader from the intermediate level to the advanced level, to the point where these topics are well and comfortably used.

Who Is this Book for?

The material in this text is intended to be used for study in a single-semester course in system programming. It was written to follow an introductory programming course. A colloquial title for this book might be *Second Semester Programming*. It is intended to precede the study of more advanced topics in programming such as data structures, algorithms, operating systems, and compilers. While it is not necessary to sequence these studies in this manner, the study of system programming will enhance the ability of a student to effectively implement the more advanced topics. There is a strong emphasis in this text on improving the practical programming skills of the reader, which should benefit a student in subsequent courses of study. For an audience with stronger programming skills, the earlier chapters could be covered briefly to allow more time for system topics. Although the book is written for a single-semester course, it contains enough material to customize study to the level of knowledge of the audience.

A Note to Instructors

Each chapter contains numerous code examples throughout the text demonstrating the concepts under discussion. All the examples have been thoroughly tested through repeated use in classroom instruction. They are also available for download at the publisher's web site, http://www.pearsonhighered.com/irc. They are intentionally short so that they can be coded, displayed, and discussed during classroom instruction. The author typically uses a laptop with a projector to execute many of the code examples during lectures, modifying and testing them in different ways to demonstrate the concepts. Students are encouraged to bring laptop computers and execute examples or short problems from each chapter's "Questions and Exercises" during class periods. These interactive techniques tend to engage students, and this text is designed to facilitate that type of instruction. However, these techniques are not required to use this text. The examples are short enough to warrant other types of display during lectures, and an instructor can use them with confidence, knowing that they do indeed execute as demonstrated in the text.

Certain chapters in this book present multiple examples of the topic under discussion. For example, scripting languages are demonstrated through shell scripting, Perl, and MATLAB®. All three languages do not need to be covered in depth, but seeing several examples clarifies the overall purpose and use of scripting languages. The same approach is taken for libraries (the examples are C standard, curses, and X) and system calls (the examples are processes, signals, and sockets). This coverage allows an instructor flexibility in labwork and in customizing the course, depending on which examples are emphasized.

In this book, Unix refers to any Unix-like operating system, including Linux, Mac OS X, BSD variants, Solaris™, HP-UX, AIX®, and so on. The author used Linux to develop the examples while writing this book, but they should work on any Unix or Unix-like system.

Supplements

The following supplements are available to qualified adopters of the textbook:

- An extensive set of lecture slides (in PPT and PDF), including all the figures from the book;
- Source code for all the example programs in the book, ready to compile and execute;
- Instructor's Solutions Manual containing solutions to all end-of-chapter questions and exercises;
- An additional appendix on software licensing.

To obtain supplements, please visit www.pearsonhighered.com/irc. Instructors seeking a password for instructor-only material can contact their local Pearson Education representative or send email to computing@aw.com.

How Is this Book Different from Other Books?

The focus of this book is on the concepts of system programming; it is not intended to serve as a complete reference for any of the topics it covers, such as text editors, shells, libraries, scripting languages, system calls, and program building. Such a text would be inordinately large and unwieldy, and good references for those topics are already available. This book puts all the system programming concepts together, providing a *textbook* perspective on systems-level problem solving.

Acknowledgments

The author would like to thank all those who reviewed versions of this manuscript during its development:

- Hussein Abdel-Wahab, Old Dominion University
- Brian D. Davison, Lehigh University

- Christopher R. Fischer, University of Delaware and Hologic, Inc.
- Gene Fisher, Cal Poly University
- Richard Fox, Northern Kentucky University
- Cindy Fry, Baylor University
- Patrick T. Homer, University of Arizona
- Sam Hsu, Florida Atlantic University
- Benjamin A. Kuperman, Oberlin College
- Natalie A. Nazarenko, SUNY College at Fredonia
- Bill Reid, Clemson University
- Bob Rinker, University of Idaho
- Nicholas A. Russo, University of Chicago
- Melissa Smith, Clemson University
- Tom Way, Villanova University
- Tilman Wolf, University of Massachusetts

Their efforts and feedback were of tremendous value and helped shape the final text. A special note of thanks to reviewers Melissa Smith and Bill Reid, both of whom used this material for instruction during its development. Finally, a note of thanks to the author's wife and children, Adair, Austin, and Gabrielle. The book is done; let's go hiking.

Adam Hoover
Clemson University
October 2008

System Programming

with C and Unix

System Programming

with C and Unix

1

Introduction

1.1 • What is System Programming?

Computer systems are made up of hardware and software. Software generically refers to the programs running on the computer. While both hardware and software can be modified or upgraded, it tends to happen more often with software. In fact, the major reason to have software is to provide the ability to change the instruction stream executed on the computer. This means that it is often *expected* that new programs will be written, or old programs will be modified or evolved, during the life cycle of a computer system.

Given this expectation, it is natural to look for methods to allow the computer system to support program development. A number of tools and resources have evolved over the last 30 years to assist program development. These include standard libraries (also called system libraries), system calls, debuggers, the shell environment, system programs, and scripting languages. Knowledge of these tools greatly enhances the ability of a programmer. While it is important to learn the details of some specific tools, it is more important to understand when and how to best use a tool. A number of good reference manuals can provide detailed information on a specific language or tool. This book is intended to provide a broader understanding of the concepts in system programming.

We may define system programming as the use of system tools during program development. Proper use of these tools serves several purposes. First and foremost, it saves a great deal of time and effort. Using system libraries saves a programmer the time it would take to independently develop the same functions. Using a debugger saves an enormous amount of time in finding and fixing errors in a program. Common tasks, such as searching for text within a set of files or timing the execution of a program, are facilitated by the existence of system programs.

Second, system tools provide opportunities for program development that are otherwise extremely difficult to come by. System calls provide access to the core functions of the operating system, including memory management, file access, process management, and interprocess communication. Some standard libraries implement complex functions that are beyond the capability of most programmers. For example, the math library includes trigonometric functions and other real-valued operations that require iterative methods to reach a solution.

Third, consistent use of system tools promotes standards, so that code developed for one computer system is more easily ported to another computer system. System libraries provide a layer of abstraction, implementing the same function calls on multiple computing systems. An application can call a system library without worrying about the details of the underlying hardware. In this manner, the application can be ported as long as the destination system possesses the same system libraries. For graphics, this has become increasingly important as the number and variety of hardware display capabilities has expanded.

Knowledge of the basic system file structure assists in program management. A Unix computer system typically includes well over 10,000 files related to system operation (this does not include user data files). Over time, a standard method for organizing these files has evolved. There are common places for libraries, system programs, device files (connections to hardware), applications, and user data.

Finally, there is the shell environment. The shell environment is rich with options, capabilities, and configurability, to the point that it is overwhelming to novice programmers. However, once some proficiency has been gained, the shell is a powerful tool for any serious system programmer. It offers tremendous flexibility in process control, system management, and program development.

This text was written with three goals. First, it supports teaching about the tools and concepts of system programming. Second, it should help the reader elevate his or her programming skill beyond an introductory level. Third, it provides a rigorous regimen of programming exercises and examples that allow the reader to practice and develop the skills and concepts of system programming. To help achieve these goals, example code pieces and programs are provided throughout the text. Each chapter ends with numerous questions and exercises that can be undertaken to strengthen understanding of the material.

Besides the concepts of system programming, this text explores the lower-level data types: bits and bytes, bit operations, arrays, strings, structures, and pointers. This material is covered with an emphasis on memory and understanding how and why these different data types are used. It is common for a student to be less comfortable with these topics than with other basic programming concepts, such as loops and conditionals. The coverage of the lower-level data types is intended to reinforce an earlier exposure to these topics. The goal is to advance the programming skill of the reader to the point where these lower-level data types are well and comfortably used.

1.1.1 Required Background

This text assumes that the reader has a basic understanding of programming, such as variables, loops, conditionals, and control flow. For example, the reader may have completed a single semester of study covering an introduction to C programming. If the reader studied a different language, such as Java or C++, then Section 1.5 can be studied to provide background on the equivalent C syntax. The text also assumes that the reader has a working computer system, with a C compiler, text editor, shell, and debugger already installed. The reader is assumed to be familiar with the basic operation of the computer system, such as navigating a directory or folder hierarchy and executing programs. Lastly, some shell knowledge is also assumed, such as that obtained from an introductory programming course.

1.1.2 Why Unix?

The majority of the material presented in this text can be studied on any computer system, using any operating system. However, it would be naive not to recognize the two most prevalent operating systems at the time of this writing:

Microsoft Windows™ and Unix.[1] For reasons about to be explained, this text advocates the study of system programming concepts on a Unix system. Note that this discussion centers on which is to be preferred for *study*. There are other ongoing debates as to which operating system has the better business model, better development, and other issues. The interested reader is directed to seek other sources for discussion on these debates.

The Windows operating system is designed to simplify computer usage. A Windows computer is essentially a closed system. The system is designed to be turnkey, in line with the business model of providing the typical user with a system that is as easy to use as possible. This design strategy necessarily obstructs getting "under the hood," to keep the typical user from doing something harmful to the system. In addition, Microsoft publishes limited information on the internal workings and design of Windows. This is also a business policy to protect their design from competitors. Finally, Windows is monolithic, not allowing for various parts of the system to be disconnected or swapped for alternatives. Once again, this is a business decision; Microsoft wants to sell its products and only its products, so it makes its system fully integrated. It is straightforward to understand the business motivations for the closed design, scarcity of published details, and non-modularity of Windows. However, the very properties that aid the typical computer user can be frustrating for the student studying system operation.

Unix, on the other hand, and specifically Linux, has different design principles. It is open source, so that all details of its inner workings can be studied. It is completely modular, so that any system component can be swapped for an alternative. For example, the Linux kernel is developed completely independently of the desktop environment. Within the kernel, a Linux computer operator has many choices as to how to configure the operation of the system. The kernel itself can be swapped or modified. One could argue that these properties prevent the more widespread adoption of Unix by typical computer users, who are not interested in this flexibility and openness. However, it is these design properties that make Unix an attractive choice for a student studying system operation.

Throughout this text, the examples shown are taken from a computer running the Linux operating system. For the most part, these examples can be run just as easily on a Windows or other Unix system. There are some important design issues that differentiate Unix/Linux and Windows, such as the multiuser versus single-user nature of the systems. These differences will be discussed in detail at the appropriate places. Beyond these considerations, deep down under the hood, the system concepts are largely similar.

---

1. In this book, Unix refers to any Unix-like system, including Linus, Mac OS X, BSD variants, etc.

1.1.3   Why C?

Selection of a particular programming language is an old debate in computing. For application development, the debate still rages. For system programming, however, very few experts argue for a language other than C. The reason is simple: C is closest to the hardware. All programming languages provide various levels of abstraction to assist in program development. For example, the concept of a named variable, as opposed to a numeric memory address, tremendously simplifies program development. Out of all the commonly used programming languages, C provides for the least abstraction and hence is closest to the hardware. Most single C statements translate simply to machine code. The available data types in C tend to reflect what the hardware directly supports. Accessing memory via indirection (pointers) provides the programmer with the ability to access all parts of the system.

Historically, the development of the Linux kernel, as well as the development of the original Unix operating system, was done in C. Most system software is developed in C. Device drivers are almost always written in C. An indirect benefit of being close to the hardware is speed. Code written in C tends to execute faster than code written in other languages. For a programmer who intends to work on system software, or who intends to develop code that closely interacts with hardware (peripherals or the main system), studying concepts using the C language provides opportunities to develop the most practical skills.

This choice does not preclude the study of other languages or advocate learning only C. Other programming concepts outside the scope of this text may be more readily studied and implemented using another programming language. However, it is the opinion of this author that a firm understanding of the programming language closest to the hardware better supports an understanding and proper use of a more abstract programming language.

1.2 • The Three Tools

The three main tools of a system programmer are a shell, a text editor, and a debugger. Familiarity with these tools increases programming skill and decreases the time it takes to get programs working properly. The following serves as an introduction to these tools and their interdependency. The real trick is in knowing how to use all three together. Noticeably absent from this list is a compiler. A compiler is a powerful tool that can certainly aid in program development. However, the compiler as a tool is addressed more fully in Section 6.1 during a discussion of program building.

1.2.1 Shell

It is assumed that the reader is familiar with basic operations in a shell, such as generating a file listing. There are a number of good books and online references that provide the necessary details to operate a specific shell. Appendix B offers a list of common commands. This section is concerned with *why* a shell should be used, and how a shell assists with program development.

A shell is a program that allows the user to run other programs. A shell is usually executed in a terminal. Historically, a terminal was a simple display and keyboard that was connected to a computer, providing a text-only interface to the computer. Today, most operating systems provide a graphical interface in which multiple virtual terminals can be run simultaenously, each running a separate shell. If a specific terminal is reserved for system administration or error messages on behalf of the entire computer system, then it is sometimes referred to as a console. In practice, the words shell, terminal, and console are often used interchangeably.

Most Unix systems provide several methods to start a shell. Some systems provide a shell after login, without the benefits of a graphical desktop. On other systems a shell must be started manually through a menu or mouse click interface. Once started, a typical shell looks like the ones shown in Figure 1.1. Commands are entered into the shell through a text-only interface. The shell informs the user that it is waiting for its next command via a prompt. In the figure, the prompt is ahoover@video>, which is the user name and machine name. Some shell configurations show the current directory or other information in the prompt. Throughout this text, the shell prompt will hereafter be shown as ahoover@video> to promote clarity.

A typical command is the name of a program, which starts execution of that program. For example, both the shells in Figure 1.1 show the execution of the ls program, which provides a listing of files in the current directory. Many of the programs run in a shell have text-only input and output, similar to ls. However, it is also possible to run graphics- (GUI-) based programs from a shell. For example, Figure 1.2 shows the result of typing xclock at the prompt; it starts the xclock program.

This method for starting programs may seem strange to those familiar with today's desktop approach to running programs. Clicking on an icon and perusing through a pull-down menu are typical operations used to run a program. Why then start a program, the shell, just to run other programs? The answer is flexibility. The desktop mouse and menu operations provide limited options in how a program is run. Typically, the desktop and menu shortcuts run a program

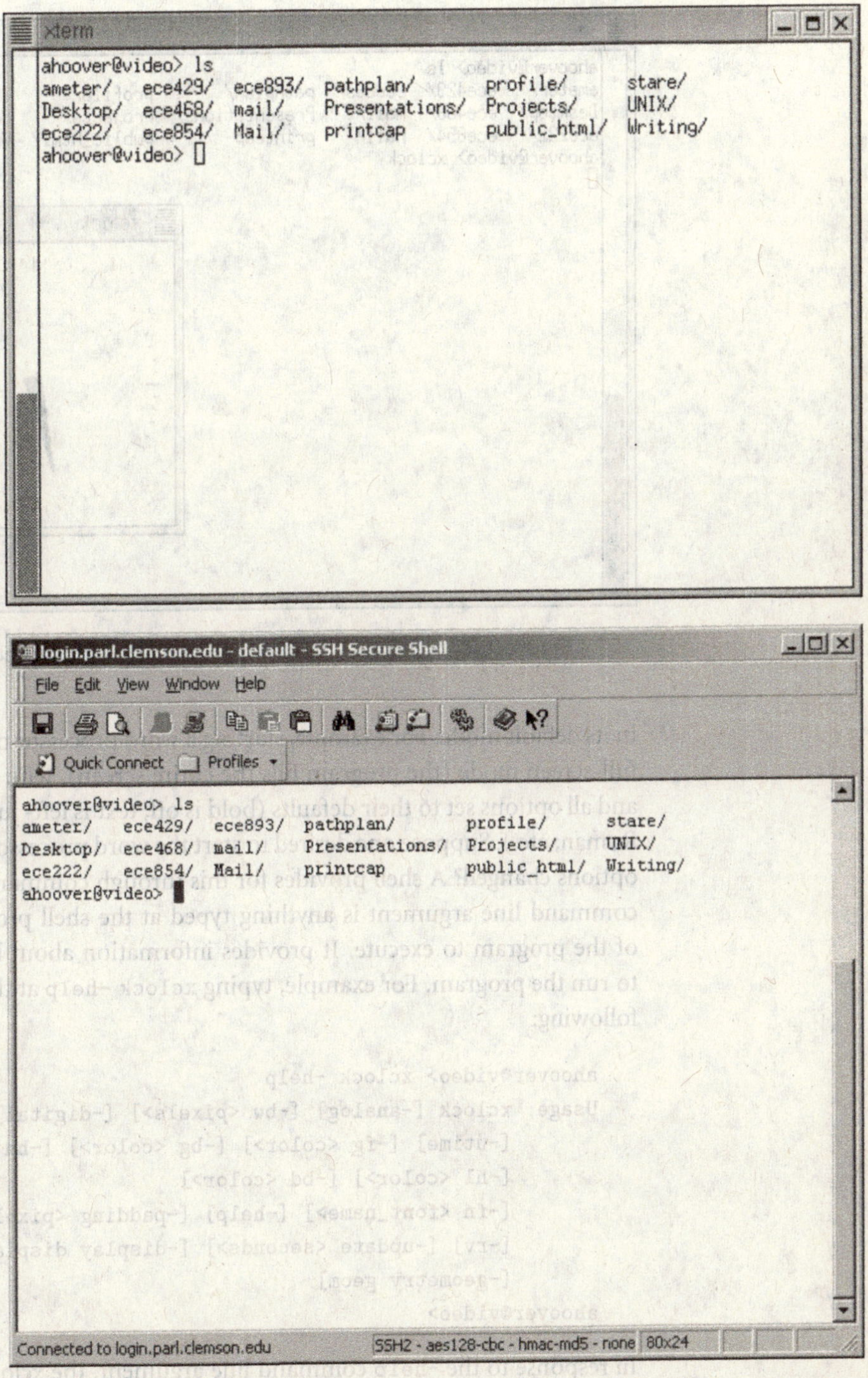

```
xterm                                                          [_][□][X]
ahoover@video> ls
ameter/    ece429/   ece893/   pathplan/      profile/     stare/
Desktop/   ece468/   mail/     Presentations/ Projects/    UNIX/
ece222/    ece854/   Mail/     printcap       public_html/ Writing/
ahoover@video> []
```

```
login.parl.clemson.edu - default - SSH Secure Shell           [_][□][X]
File  Edit  View  Window  Help

[toolbar icons]

  Quick Connect   Profiles

ahoover@video> ls
ameter/    ece429/   ece893/   pathplan/      profile/     stare/
Desktop/   ece468/   mail/     Presentations/ Projects/    UNIX/
ece222/    ece854/   Mail/     printcap       public_html/ Writing/
ahoover@video>

Connected to login.parl.clemson.edu    SSH2 - aes128-cbc - hmac-md5 - none  80x24
```

Figure 1.1 Two examples of a shell, running in different terminal emulators.

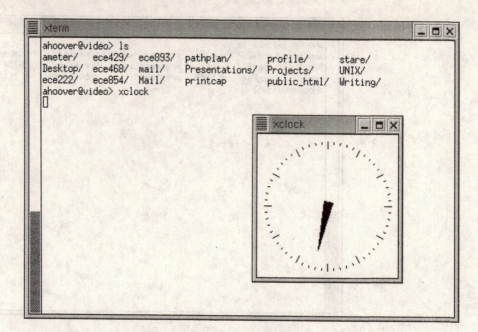

Figure 1.2 Starting a GUI-based program by typing its name in the shell.

in its default mode. For example, starting a word processor opens the program in full-screen mode (the program fills the entire screen), with an open blank page, and all options set to their defaults (bold is off; text is left-justified; font is Times Roman; etc.). Suppose one desired to start the word processor with some of those options changed? A shell provides for this through command line arguments. A command line argument is anything typed at the shell prompt after the name of the program to execute. It provides information about how the user wishes to run the program. For example, typing xclock -help at the prompt yields the following:

```
ahoover@video> xclock -help
Usage: xclock [-analog] [-bw <pixels>] [-digital] [-brief]
        [-utime] [-fg <color>] [-bg <color>] [-hd <color>]
        [-hl <color>] [-bd <color>]
        [-fn <font_name>] [-help] [-padding <pixels>]
        [-rv] [-update <seconds>] [-display displayname]
        [-geometry geom]
ahoover@video>
```

In response to the -help command line argument, the xclock program displays its usage and then quits. The usage explains all the command line arguments

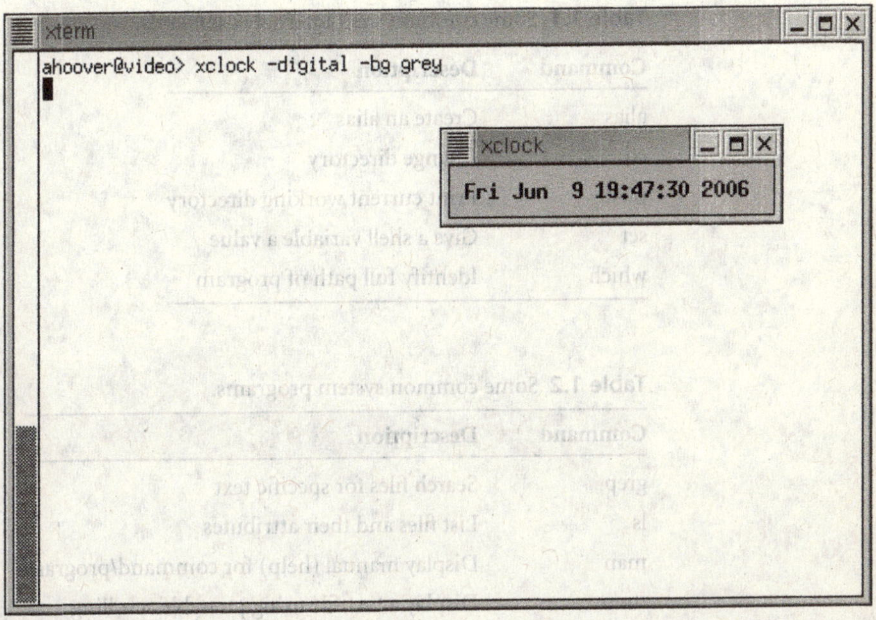

Figure 1.3 Command line arguments change the way a program is run.

that can be used when starting the program. For this particular program, most of these arguments change the way the clock is displayed. For example, `xclock -digital -bg grey` causes the program to run as displayed in Figure 1.3.

The control and flexibility offered by command line arguments is often useful during program development and system administration. While many programs can be reconfigured while running, selecting options through menu interfaces can take time. Configuring the program at startup through command line arguments can save a great deal of time, especially if a program is run multiple times, such as during development.

A variety of shells have been developed over the years. Some examples include `sh`, `csh`, `tcsh`, `ksh`, and `bash`. On a Windows system, there is a very simple shell called `console`, sometimes called `DOS console` or `command prompt`. The shells differ in their intrinsic capabilities. Besides having the ability to run programs, and provide command line arguments, a shell has a list of internal commands that it can perform. For example, most shells have the ability to set up aliases for commonly typed commands. In the `tcsh` shell, typing

```
ahoover@video> alias xc xclock -digital -bg grey
ahoover@video>
```

Table 1.1 Some common shell internal commands.

Command	Description
alias	Create an alias
cd	Change directory
pwd	Print current working directory
set	Give a shell variable a value
which	Identify full path of program

Table 1.2 Some common system programs.

Command	Description
grep	Search files for specific text
ls	List files and their attributes
man	Display manual (help) for command/program
more	Display a text file using pausable scrolling
time	Measure the running time of a program
sort	Sort lines in a text file

causes the shorter command `xc` to become an alias for the longer command
`xclock -digital -bg grey`. This can be quite useful when one is running the
same command over and over, for example during program debugging. Table 1.1
lists some common internal commands for shells. All these commands are common to all the most popular shells (notably excluding the Windows console,
which is intended to be only a limited shell). Unfortunately, different shells implement some of these internal commands using different syntaxes. For example,
to create the same alias using the `bash` shell as given in the above example for the
`tcsh` shell, one would type

```
ahoover@video> alias xc="xclock -digital -bg grey"
ahoover@video>
```

Most advanced programmers select a single shell with which to become proficient. Luckily, most of the shells are similar enough that proficiency with a particular shell allows a programmer to work adequately in any shell.

In addition to the internal shell commands, there are a number of programs
pre-compiled and ready to run on most Unix systems. Table 1.2 lists some of the
commonly used programs. These programs are called system programs because

they generally provide capabilities to manipulate, explore, and develop programs for the computer system. For example, ls is a system program that provides a listing of files in the current directory. Perhaps the most important system program to begin using is man. It accesses a manual of help files stored on the local computer system. Usually, there are individual "man pages" for all programs, and often for support files for the more complex programs. There are also man pages for all the functions within the various libraries on the system. These man pages usually come installed by default on a Unix system, but they are also posted many times over on the Internet, and can be found using a web search engine. It is also possible (and recommended) to find tutorials and other help via the Web on using a particular shell.

The purpose of both shell internal commands and system programs is to assist the system programmer. It is not terribly important to remember whether a particular operation is a shell command or a system program. Sometimes the operations are listed all together. The important thing is to become comfortable with the common operations that save time and effort. These programs are revisited in Section 5.3.1 during a discussion of pipeline chaining, and Appendices B and C provide longer lists.

1.2.2 Text Editor

The second tool considered here is a text editor. The basic operations of a text editor allow the user to write and edit code, save it to a file, and load it from a file. These operations are not much different from those supported by a word processor. In fact, it is possible to use a word processor to write code (although it is not recommended). However, there are additional features that a text editor can provide, beyond what a typical word processor provides, that are designed to support programming. For example, Figure 1.4 illustrates the finding of matching parentheses. Using the text editor vi, if the cursor is on an opening or closing parenthesis, pressing the percent symbol (%) moves the cursor to the matching parenthesis. Pressing it a second time moves the cursor back to where it started. The same keystroke matches opening and closing braces (the symbols surrounding blocks of code) and square brackets (the symbols used for array indices). For the text editor gedit, bracket matching is enabled through a menu option. For the text editor emacs, the bracket matching feature can briefly move the cursor to the opening bracket every time a closing bracket is typed, animating the grouping. Some text editors also provide color coding to highlight matching brackets and their enclosed blocks of code. Whichever text editor is used, the bracket matching feature can be quite useful in tracking down logic errors on expressions, flow errors on loops, array usage, and other bugs.

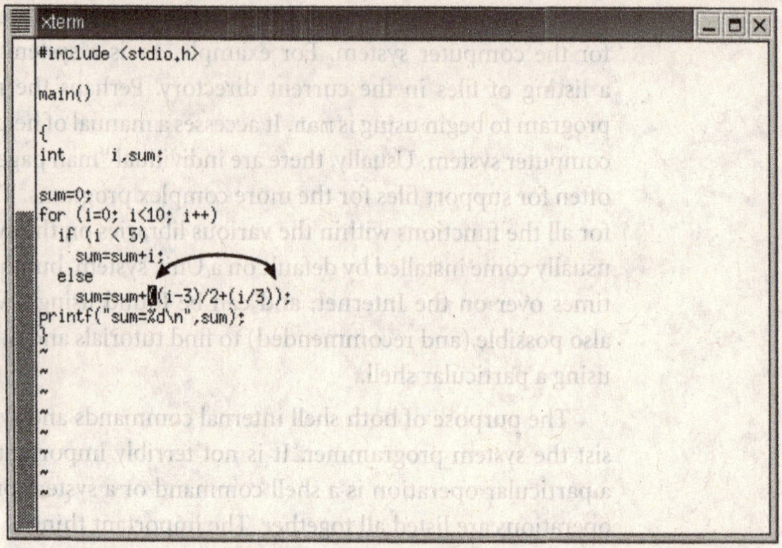

Figure 1.4 Using a text editor to identify matching parentheses.

Perhaps the most important features a text editor can provide to a programmer are the ability to display the line number of the program for the given cursor location, and the ability to move the cursor to a given line number. Figure 1.5 illustrates an example. Using the text editor vi, the keyboard sequence CTRL-G displays the line number. The keyboard sequence :N[CR] relocates the cursor to line number N. Using the text editor gedit, this feature is provided through menu options. Using the text editor emacs, the keyboard sequence [ESC]GN relocates the cursor to line number N (assuming a commonly configured installation). Whichever text editor is used, it is important to learn these operations. They allow a programmer to use line numbers to communicate with a debugger. The programmer can tell the debugger to pause program execution at a given line number. The debugger can tell the programmer at which line number a given error occurred. In this manner, the programmer can work with the debugger to focus on the relevant line of code.

As a programmer becomes familiar with a given text editor, other useful features will be learned. The ability to search and/or replace a given string is often helpful in debugging variable usage. The ability to cut and paste a word, line, or block of code is often useful during code writing. The ability to arrange indentation helps support good coding practices. Some text editors support color coding of keywords as well as of code blocks.

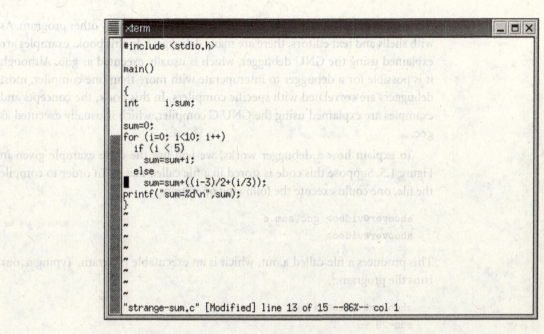

```
xterm

#include <stdio.h>

main()
{
int     i,sum;

sum=0;
for (i=0; i<10; i++)
  if (i < 5)
    sum=sum+i;
  else
    sum=sum+((i-3)/2+(i/3));
printf("sum=%d\n",sum);
}
~
~
~
~
~
~
~
~
"strange-sum.c" [Modified] line 13 of 15 --86%-- col 1
```

Figure 1.5 Using a text editor to identify or find a program line number.

Not all text editors share all features. The text editor vi relies upon keystroke combinations to access features. The text editor emacs uses a combination of keystroke and menu operations. Newer text editors tend to rely more upon menu operations since they can be easier to find. It is beyond the scope of this book to delve into all the features for various text editors. One can easily find an online manual as well as online feature guides for all the popular text editors. The important thing to realize is that whichever text editor is used, a programmer should dedicate some time to becoming comfortable with those features that support programming.

1.2.3 Debugger

The debugger is perhaps the most important tool for a system programmer. It allows a programmer to observe the execution of a program, pausing it while it runs, in order to examine the values of variables. It also allows a programmer to determine if and when specific lines of code are executed. It allows a programmer to step through a program, executing it one line at a time, in order to observe program flow through branches. This section describes how a debugger works; the process of debugging is addressed in the next section.

The debugger is itself a program, which is executed like any other program. As with shells and text editors, there are many debuggers. In this book, examples are explained using the GNU debugger, which is usually executed as gdb. Although it is possible for a debugger to interoperate with more than one compiler, most debuggers are correlated with specific compilers. In this book, the concepts and examples are explained using the GNU C compiler, which is usually executed as gcc.

To explain how a debugger works, we will use the code example given in Figure 1.5. Suppose this code is stored in a file called sum.c. In order to compile the file, one could execute the following operation:

```
ahoover@video> gcc sum.c
ahoover@video>
```

This produces a file called a.out, which is an executable program. Typing a.out runs the program:[2]

```
ahoover@video> a.out
sum=29
ahoover@video>
```

The program is executed, running until it ends, at which time the shell prompts for another command. In order to use the debugger to run the program, one must follow a sequence of operations:

```
ahoover@video> gcc -g sum.c
ahoover@video> gdb a.out
(gdb) run
Starting program: /home/ahoover/a.out
sum=29
Program exited with code 07.
(gdb) quit
ahoover@video>
```

We will discuss each of these steps in detail.

First, when compiling, we make use of the command line argument –g. This tells the compiler that the executable file is intended for debugging. (Other compilers use similar flags or options.) While creating the executable file, the compiler will store additional information about the program, called a *symbol table*. The

---

2. This assumes the current directory is included in the PATH environment variable; otherwise ./a.out must be typed.

symbol table includes a list of the names of variables used by the program. For our example, this list includes i and sum. The program is also compiled without *optimization*. Normally, a compiler will rearrange code to make it execute faster. However, if the program is intended for debugging, then any rearrangement of the code will make it difficult to relate which line of C code is currently being executed. When compiling for debugging, it is normally desirable to turn off all optimizations so that program execution follows the original C code exactly.

One can see the effects of compiling for debugging by looking at the size of the executable:

```
ahoover@video> gcc sum.c
ahoover@video> ls -l a.out
-rwxr-xr-x   1 ahoover  fusion       4759 Jun 19 18:53 a.out*
ahoover@video> gcc -g sum.c
ahoover@video> ls -l a.out
-rwxr-xr-x   1 ahoover  fusion       5843 Jun 19 18:54 a.out*
ahoover@video>
```

The executable has increased in size by 1,084 bytes. This increase in size is caused by the inclusion of the symbol table, and because the compiler was not allowed to optimize the code, so that its final output is not as efficient as it could be. Note that if you forget to compile for debugging, then the debugger will not be able to operate on your executable. Without the symbol table, or in the presence of optimizations, the debugger will be lost.

After compiling, we run the debugger gdb on the executable a.out that we just created. This does not immediately execute our program. It runs the debugger and loads our program into the debugger environment. This is emphasized by the fact that the prompt has changed. Instead of ahoover@video>, which is the shell prompt, we now see (gdb), which is the debugger prompt. One can think of a debugger as a wrapper around a program. Figure 1.6 shows a diagram. When the debugger is started, it uses the symbol table and original C code file to keep track of what the program is doing during execution.

Once the debugger is started, it has its own set of commands. One of these commands is run, which begins execution of the program. In our example, this results in the program running as it would from the shell, eventually producing the output sum=29 and then exiting. With the program finished, we are back at the debugger prompt (gdb). To exit the debugger, we issue the command quit that takes us back to the shell.

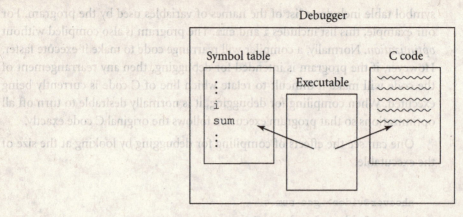

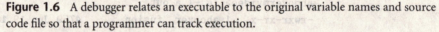

Figure 1.6 A debugger relates an executable to the original variable names and source code file so that a programmer can track execution.

Sometimes it is useful to execute a program all the way to completion within a debugger. However, more often it is useful to execute a program "halfway," or through only part of its complete code. This is accomplished by setting a *break-point*. It tells the debugger to execute the program until that point is reached, at which time execution is to be paused. The programmer is then able to give commands to the debugger while the program is paused. For example:

```
ahoover@video> gdb a.out
(gdb) break 13
Breakpoint 1 at 0x804837b: file sum.c, line 13.
(gdb) run
Starting program: /home/ahoover/a.out
Breakpoint 1, main () at sum.c:13
13          sum=sum+((i-3)/2+(i/3));
(gdb)
```

At this point, the program has reached line 13 in the file sum.c for the first time. This should happen when the variable i reaches a value of 5 in the loop. Execution of the program is paused while we decide what to do. For example, we can display the value of i:

```
(gdb) display i
1: i = 5
(gdb)
```

As expected, the value of i is 5. We can also ask the debugger to tell us where the program is paused in relation to the original source code:

```
(gdb) where
#0  main () at sum.c:13
#1  0x4004e507 in __libc_start_main (main=0x8048460 <main>,
    argc=1, ubp_av=0xbffffa34, init=0x80482e4 <_init>,
    fini=0x8048530 <_fini>, rtld_fini=0x4000dc14 <_dl_fini>,
    stack_end=0xbffffa2c)
    at ../sysdeps/generic/libc-start.c:129
(gdb)
```

As expected, the first line tells us that we are at line 13 in the file sum.c, which is where we set the breakpoint. For now, we can ignore the other strange-looking line. Chapter 6 discusses functions and variable scope.

When a program is paused, there are three different ways to start it executing again: step, next, and continue. The step command executes the next line of code and then pauses again. For example:

```
(gdb) step
9           for (i=0; i<10; i++)
(gdb)
```

We had paused the program prior to the execution of line 13 using a breakpoint. After the step command has finished, we have executed line 13 and moved to the next line, which in this case is back to the top of the for loop at line 9. The debugger has again paused the program, prior to executing this line, and is awaiting our command.

The next command does the same thing, but if the next line of code is a function call, then the debugger will execute all the lines of code in that function call and then pause after the function returns. In other words, it treats the entire execution of the function call as one line of code. The step command will go into the function call and pause inside it at the first line of its code. Successive step commands can then be used to go through the entire function.

Issuing step or next commands repeatedly allows a programmer to run a program one line at a time, pausing after each line. This is called *stepping through a program*. For example, picking up where we left off above:

```
(gdb) next
10          if (i < 5)
(gdb) next
Breakpoint 1, main () at sum.c:13
13          sum=sum+((i-3)/2+(i/3));
(gdb) next
9           for (i=0; i<10; i++)
```

```
(gdb) next
10          if (i < 5)
(gdb) next
Breakpoint 1, main () at sum.c:13
13          sum=sum+((i-3)/2+(i/3));
(gdb) next
```

Each time the command next is issued, one more line of code is executed. Note that if a breakpoint is reached, the debugger also informs us of that, although it would have paused anyway because the next line of code was finished executing. Depending on the situation, using next to step through a program is often preferred over using step. The step command may cause the debugger to go into system library function calls, such as printf() function calls, which is rarely useful. (We can—hopefully!—expect the system library code to be more bug-free than code we are currently writing.) It is also useful to know that pressing [ENTER] alone will cause the gdb debugger to issue the previous command, so that one does not need to type "next" over and over. Most debuggers have a similar shortcut or keystroke to simplify stepping through a program.

The third method of continuing program execution is enacted by the continue command. It restarts execution and allows it to continue until a breakpoint is reached, until the program exits normally, or until the program reaches a line of code doing something illegal. Illegal operations include things like trying to divide by zero, or trying to access a bad memory location.

There are two different ways to observe the value of a variable. The print command is a onetime request to see the value. The debugger displays the value once only and will not display it again until requested. The display command is a request for ongoing observation. The debugger will display the value of the variable each time the program is paused. For example:

```
ahoover@video> gdb a.out
(gdb) break 13
Breakpoint 1 at 0x8048490: file sum.c, line 13.
(gdb) run
Starting program: /home/ahoover/a.out
Breakpoint 1, main () at sum.c:13
13          sum=sum+((i-3)/2+(i/3));
(gdb) display i
1: i = 5
(gdb) continue
Continuing.
Breakpoint 1, main () at sum.c:13
13          sum=sum+((i-3)/2+(i/3));
```

```
1: i = 6
(gdb) continue
Continuing.
Breakpoint 1, main () at sum.c:13
13          sum=sum+((i-3)/2+(i/3));
1: i = 7
(gdb)
```

Notice that each time the program is paused, the value of i is displayed. The continue command is used to resume execution of the program each time, causing it to run until it again reaches the breakpoint. Each time this happens, the loop counter i has increased by 1.

Multiple breakpoints can be set. For example:

```
(gdb) break 13
Breakpoint 1 at 0x8048490: file sum.c, line 13.
(gdb) break 8
Breakpoint 2 at 0x8048467: file sum.c, line 8.
(gdb) run
Starting program: /home/ahoover/a.out
Breakpoint 2, main () at sum.c:8
8          sum=0;
(gdb) display i
1: i = 134518128
(gdb) continue
Continuing.
Breakpoint 1, main () at sum.c:13
13          sum=sum+((i-3)/2+(i/3));
1: i = 5
(gdb)
```

The order of the breakpoints does not matter. When any breakpoint is reached, the debugger pauses. In this example, we displayed the value of i at line 8, before it had been given any value in the program. The strange value 134518128 is essentially a random value that happens to be stored in i at the beginning of execution of the program; later when the program is inside the loop, we see the more normal looking value 5.

Breakpoints can be removed during debugging using the clear command. This can be useful during extended debugging sessions. Sometimes it is simpler for a programmer to quit and restart the debugging process from scratch, using new breakpoints. Sometimes when a program has done something unexpected, a programmer will want to start over in an effort to identify where the program misbehaved.

The gdb debugger (and many other debuggers as well) includes a large set of commands not discussed here. These commands include capabilities to pause execution based upon variables being read or written (called *watchpoints*), to pause execution based upon signals (called *catchpoints*), and others. While these commands are useful, they are not necessary for common debugging. The commands and concepts introduced in this section generally suffice for the vast majority of debugging problems. The reader is encouraged to get started with this set of concepts and to explore additional debugging capabilities as the need arises.

1.2.4 Integrated Development Environment (IDE)

As systems have evolved, so have system tools. The interdependence of the three tools outlined in the previous sections has been recognized for many years. This led to the establishment of an integrated development environment (IDE). An IDE combines the three tools, along with a compiler, into a single program or program interface. Rather than separately running a text editor, compiler, and debugger, they all can be run together from within a single IDE. This allows the tools to be even more tightly integrated. Usually an IDE supports graphics-based operations that tie the individual tools together in a manner that can further speed program development and management.

At the time of this writing, popular examples of IDEs include Microsoft's Visual Studio, Eclipse, Sun Microsystem's NetBeans, and the GNAT Programming Studio. Some IDEs are intended to support a single programming language, such as NetBeans (for Java). Other IDEs support multiplate languages, such as Visual Studio and Eclipse; the former is proprietary, while the latter is open source. The advantage of multiple language support is to be able to assist a team of programmers in large-scale software development, or in multiplatform development. The centralized control of program development within one environment is often one of the biggest advantages to using an IDE.

An IDE is a powerful tool and belongs in the repertoire of any serious system programmer. However, it is important to understand what comprises an IDE, and how it works, by understanding the individual tools within it. Students of system programming should be encouraged to use the basic tools to gain at least some proficiency. That basic proficiency should help in future transitions to other IDEs or systems.

1.3 • How to Debug

The previous section introduced the shell environment and the three most important tools for system programming: the shell, the text editor, and the debugger. In this section, we discuss methods to use the debugger. This includes deciding when and how to use the debugger to track down various problems.

In this discussion, we must make a distinction between fixing program logic and fixing program errors. Debugging is primarily inteded to help with the latter. Translating logical ideas into program code requires an understanding of how and when to use various programming constructs, such as a loop, a conditional, and an array. A debugger will not help a programmer determine whether a problem requires a pair of nested loops or whether a single loop will do the job. This is a logic concept, and should be approached through pseudocode writing, flowcharting, or other program development techniques. On the other hand, when a programmer is confident (or at least comfortable) with the logic being written into a program, then a debugger is an invaluable tool. It can assist the programmer in finding errors in the implementation or due to unanticipated details. For example, a debugger can help locate the use of an incorrect data type (e.g., using an `int` in place of a `float`), incorrect bounds on a loop, incorrect array indices, equation and logic errors, and typographical errors (some of the more devilish errors turn out to be nothing more than simple typos, such as a missing semicolon).

There are a handful of situations that are common to debugging problems. The following sections will describe each of these situations and go through an example debugging session. We will approach the debugging problem from the perspective of a programmer: we witness a symptom or some observed bad behavior on the part of a program. We then present a technique to locate the problem in the program code and, ultimately, to identify the cause of the program error.

1.3.1 Program Crashes

When a program stops executing in an unexpected manner, it is said to have *crashed*. Something went wrong, and the system was unable to continue running the program. For example, suppose the following code is contained in a file called `crash1.c`:

```c
#include <stdio.h>

main()
{
int     x,y;

y=54389;
```

```
for (x=10; x>=0; x--)
    y=y/x;
printf("%d\n",y);
}
```

At the shell, we compile[3] and execute the program, only to find that it crashes:

```
ahoover@video> gcc -o crash1 crash1.c
ahoover@video> crash1
Floating exception (core dumped)
ahoover@video>
```

The error message "Floating exception" gives only a limited idea of what went wrong, and almost no idea of where it went wrong. The system has created a *core dump* file to help the programmer. It contains a snapshot of the contents of memory and other information about the system right at the moment that the program crashed. However, core dump files are usually large, containing far more than is needed for common debugging. Typically, core dump files are used only in advanced system programming problems.

A naive programmer might open up the C code file and begin studying the code, looking for possible sources of error. In a program as small as our example, this might even work. However, using a debugger is far simpler and will save a great deal of time. The idea is to run the program in the debugger until it crashes, and at that point look at what happened:

```
ahoover@video> gcc -g -o crash1 crash1.c
ahoover@video> gdb crash1
(gdb) run
Starting program: /home/ahoover/crash1
Program received signal SIGFPE, Arithmetic exception.
0x0804848b in main () at crash1.c:10
10          y=y/x;
(gdb)
```

The debugger tells us that the program crashed at line 10, and shows us the line of code at line 10. Looking at that line, it is easy to see that not many things could have gone wrong. Something must be wrong with either the value of y or x. The most likely scenario is that the value of x is zero, and that the program is therefore attempting to divide by zero. We can test this by asking the debugger to display the value of x:

---

3. The option to the compiler -o crash1 tells it to name our executable crash1 instead of the default a.out. It is a good habit to give executables meaningful names instead of calling all of them a.out.

```
(gdb) display x
1: x = 0
(gdb)
```

As we suspected, x has a value of zero. Now we can review the code to determine whether this was intended or whether we have an implementation error. For example, we might not have intended the loop to run until x>=0, and instead intended it to run until x>0.

Dividing by zero is not the only thing that can cause a program to crash. Perhaps the most common error resulting in a crash occurs when using arrays or pointers. For example, suppose the following code is stored in a file called crash2.c:

```
#include <stdio.h>

main()
{
int     x,y,z[3];

y=54389;
for (x=10; x>=1; x--)
  z[y]=y/x;
printf("%d\n",z[0]);
}
```

When we compile and execute this code, the program crashes:

```
ahoover@video> gcc -o crash2 crash2.c
ahoover@video> crash2
Segmentation fault (core dumped)
ahoover@video>
```

Using the debugger, we run the program until it crashes to find out where the problem occurred:

```
ahoover@video> gcc -g -o crash2 crash2.c
ahoover@video> gdb crash2
(gdb) run
Starting program: /home/ahoover/crash2
Program received signal SIGSEGV, Segmentation fault.
0x080484a2 in main () at crash2.c:10
10            z[y]=y/x;
(gdb)
```

A "segmentation fault" is usually a bad memory access; in other words, the program has tried to access a memory location that does not belong to the program. For example, an array has a specified size. Trying to access a cell index outside the specified size is a bad memory access. Looking at the line of code where the program crashed, we can see an access to the array z[] at cell index y. We can ask the debugger for the value of y and compare it against the allowed range (z[] was defined as a three-element array, so the allowed range is 0 . . . 2):

```
(gdb) display y
1: y = 54389
(gdb)
```

As we suspected, the value for y is outside the allowed range for indices for the array z[]. Once again, we have quickly identified the point where the program has misbehaved and can now go about the process of determining if the program logic or implementation is at fault.

Using a debugger to discover where a program is crashing is probably the most popular use for a debugger. During program development, if a crash is observed, the first action should almost always be to run the program in a debugger to locate the problem.

1.3.2 Program Stuck in Infinite Loop

When a program runs for a long time without displaying anything new, or prompting the user for new input, then it is probably stuck in an infinite loop. This means that the code executing in the loop is never going to cause the conditional controlling the loop to fail, so that the loop runs over and over. Of course, a "long time" is a relative expression. Some programs may need 10 seconds, or a minute or longer, in order to complete a complex calculation. However, if you can go for a cup of coffee, check the baseball scores, come back and still see the program not responding, then it is probably stuck in an infinite loop. For example, suppose the following code is stored in the file infloop.c:

```c
#include <stdio.h>

main()
{
int     x,y;

for (x=0; x<10; x++)
  {
  y=y+x;
```

```
if (y > 10)
  x--;
}
}
```

When we compile and execute this code, the program seems to "run forever":

```
ahoover@video> gcc -o infloop infloop.c
ahoover@video> infloop
_
```

The "_" symbol indicates the cursor. The program is running but never ends, so we never see the shell prompt again. Eventually we press CTRL-C to force the program to stop executing.

We can perform the same operation using the debugger, but pressing CTRL-C in the debugger does not cause the program to quit. Instead, it tells the debugger to pause program execution at whatever line is currently being executed. We can then look at the surrounding code to determine which loop is executing infinitely:

```
ahoover@video> gcc -g -o infloop infloop.c
ahoover@video> gdb infloop
(gdb) run
Starting program: /home/ahoover/infloop
_                  [...user presses CTRL-C...]
Program received signal SIGINT, Interrupt.
0x08048444 in main () at infloop.c:8
8           for (x=0; x<10; x++)
(gdb)
```

In this simple example, there is only one loop, so it comes as no surprise that the program is currently executing a line of code somewhere in this loop. In order to determine why the program will not finish the loop, we can watch the loop counter through an iteration:

```
(gdb) display x
1: x = 0
(gdb) next
10          y=y+x;
1: x = 0
(gdb) next
11          if (y > 10)
1: x = 0
(gdb) next
12          x--;
```

```
1: x = 0
(gdb) next
8        for (x=0; x<10; x++)
1: x = -1
(gdb) next
10          y=y+x;
1: x = 0
(gdb)
```

After having watched a complete iteration of the loop, we find that the counter variable x has the same value (zero) at the beginning of every iteration. Since it never reaches 10, the loop never ends. Now we can go about the process of examining the code involving x within the loop to determine the problem.

This technique for debugging is particularly useful when there are many separate loops within a program. It is the fastest way to determine which loop is faulty, and a good way to determine why the loop is not terminating properly.

1.3.3   Program Working Partially

Sometimes a program is working correctly, up to a point, when it suddenly starts misbehaving. For example, a program may be processing a series of input commands from the user. For the first few commands, the program seems to work fine, but at some point it starts producing erroneous output. How can a debugger help find the problem? It can help by focusing time and effort on the code in question, skipping over all the code that is seemingly working correctly. For example, consider the following code:

```
#include <stdio.h>

main()
{
int     choice;
float   ppg,rpg;

ppg=rpg=0.0;
choice=0;
do
  {
  printf("(1) Enter points per game\n");
  printf("(2) Enter rebounds per game\n");
  printf("(3) Quit\n");
  scanf("%d",&choice);
  if (choice == 1  ||  choice == 2)
```

```
    {
    printf("Amount: ");
    if (choice = 1)
        scanf("%f",&ppg);
    else if (choice == 2)
        scanf("%f",&rpg);
    printf("Points=%f  Rebounds=%f\n",ppg,rpg);
    }
  }
while (choice != 3);
}
```

The program is supposed to keep track of two statistics, the points per game and the rebounds per game. The program is supposed to allow the user to update these statistics, running until the user decides to quit. When this code is compiled and executed, however, the following happens:

```
ahoover@video> gcc -o wrong wrong.c
ahoover@video> wrong
(1) Enter points per game
(2) Enter rebounds per game
(3) Quit
1
Amount: 14
Points=14.000000  Rebounds=0.000000
(1) Enter points per game
(2) Enter rebounds per game
(3) Quit
2
Amount: 5.3
Points=5.300000  Rebounds=0.000000
(1) Enter points per game
(2) Enter rebounds per game
(3) Quit
```

The first option seemed to work fine, placing the entered value 14 into the ppg variable. But the second option put the entered value 5.3 into the wrong variable. What went wrong?

Using the debugger, we can work to find the problem. We recompile the program for debugging and load it into the debugger:

```
ahoover@video> gcc -g -o wrong wrong.c
ahoover@video> gdb wrong
(gdb)
```

Now we have to decide where to pause execution of the program. It seems as if the display of the menu is working correctly and that the problem lies somewhere in the code where the values are input. A logical place to pause the debugger is therefore after the menu has been displayed but before any input has been received from the user. Using a text editor, we can see that the code if (choice == 1 || choice == 2) is at line 16. Therefore, we set a breakpoint at line 16 and run the program up to that point:

```
(gdb) break 16
Breakpoint 1 at 0x80484ec: file wrong.c, line 16.
(gdb) run
Starting program: /home/ahoover/wrong
(1) Enter points per game
(2) Enter rebounds per game
(3) Quit
2

Breakpoint 1, main () at wrong.c:16
16          if (choice == 1 || choice == 2)
(gdb)
```

At this point, the program is paused at line 16. Now we can step through the program, one line of code at a time, to see what happens:

```
(gdb) next
18          printf("Amount: ");
(gdb) next
19          if (choice = 1)
(gdb) next
20              scanf("%f",&ppg);
(gdb)
```

Up until that last step, things seemed to be working correctly. However, we entered 2 at the menu, and yet the program is proceeding to the code that asks the user for the ppg value. What went wrong? The only variable involved so far is choice, which decided what part of the code to execute next. We can display its value:

```
(gdb) display choice
1: choice = 1
(gdb)
```

For some reason, the program thinks we entered 1 when we know we entered 2. How could this have happened? Now that we are focused on the problem of finding an error involving the variable choice, we look backward over the last few lines of code and notice the problem. At line 19, the code reads if (choice = 1) instead of if (choice == 1). The wrong code actually changes the value of choice to 1 every time it executes.

This is a simple example because the program is short. However, the important idea is to use the debugger to pause execution near where a problem is occurring, and then to step through the code in question. As a program increases in length, this technique becomes increasingly useful.

1.3.4   Loop Behaving Incorrectly

The logic inside a loop can be complicated to the point that it is impossible to mentally outline every possible case through every iteration. If such a loop is behaving incorrectly, a debugger can be used to observe the loop, pausing to examine the variables controlling the logic at each iteration. This can be useful not only for finding errors but also in correcting any problems with the logic inside the loop. For example, consider the following code:

```
#include <stdio.h>

main()
{
char    word[80];
int     i,j;

printf("Enter any word: ");
scanf("%s",word);
i=0;
while (word[i] != '\0')
  {
  if (word[i] == word[i+1])
    {
    j=1;
    while (word[i] == word[i+j])
      j++;
    printf("%d consecutive %c\n",j,word[i]);
    }
  i++;
  }
}
```

This program is supposed to search the word given by the user for consecutive occurrences of any letter, and report them. Compiling and executing, it works correctly on the first test:

```
ahoover@video> gcc -o badloops badloops.c
ahoover@video> badloops
Enter any word: apple
2 consecutive p
ahoover@video>
```

However, on a test having three of the same letter in a row, the program outputs an additional erroneous line:

```
ahoover@video> badloops
Enter any word: appple
3 consecutive p
2 consecutive p
ahoover@video>
```

What caused the output of the extra line "2 consecutive p"? The debugger can be used to watch the iterations of the outer loop to see what happened. The first line in the outer loop is if (word[i] == word[i+1]), at line number 14. This line tests if two consecutive letters match, while the following code determines the total span of consecutive letters. Recompiling the code for debugging, the idea is to pause the program at the beginning of each iteration of this loop to see how it behaves on the problem test case.

```
ahoover@video> gcc -g -o badloops badloops.c
ahoover@video> gdb badloops
(gdb) break 14
Breakpoint 1 at 0x80484d4: file badloops.c, line 14.
(gdb) run
Starting program: /parl/ahoover/ece222/book/1/badloops
Enter any word: appple

Breakpoint 1, main () at badloops.c:14
14          if (word[i] == word[i+1])
(gdb)
```

The variable i controls the behavior of the loop. Therefore, it is prudent to watch the value of i through every iteration, before continuing execution of the program.

```
(gdb) display i
1: i = 0
(gdb) continue
Continuing.
```

```
Breakpoint 1, main () at badloops.c:14
14          if (word[i] == word[i+1])
1: i = 1
(gdb)
```

After the completion of the first iteration, we see that the program worked correctly. No output was displayed, because the first two letters of "appple" do not match. The next iteration should produce output.

```
(gdb) continue
Continuing.
3 consecutive p

Breakpoint 1, main () at badloops.c:14
14          if (word[i] == word[i+1])
1: i = 2
(gdb)
```

The expected output "3 consecutive p" was observed. However, at this point it is possible to see why there will be additional erroneous output. The value of i is 2, which means that the next iteration will begin by comparing the second "p" in "appple" to the third "p." The value of i should have jumped ahead to test the "l" against the "e." Looking at the code at the bottom of the loop, we now realize that i++ does not move ahead by enough characters in the case where multiple consecutive characters all match. The logic for this loop must be partially rewritten.

1.4 • Program Development

Program development concerns the writing of a program to solve a given problem. Knowledge of the syntax of a programming language is not enough. One must know how to use the language to approach programming problems. An analogy can be made to human conversation. Knowing the vocabulary and rules of grammar for a spoken language is not enough; one must be skilled in oratory in order to speak effectively. There is an art to using a programming language to develop and write programs to accomplish tasks, just as there is an art to using a human language to speak effectively.

One of the most important skills for program development is to be able to break a programming problem into a set of subproblems. Code can be written to solve each subproblem independently. That code can be tested before proceeding to the next subproblem. This is the ancient philosophy of divide and conquer. The subproblems may themselves be broken up repeatedly into subproblems until a reasonable amount of programming work can be undertaken in isolation. Almost all programming work benefits from following some variation of this approach.

In order to demonstrate, consider the following problem. Write a program that takes an integer as input and then determines whether or not the given number is a sum of two unique squares. For example, given the number 13, the program would find that $13 = 9 + 4$ is a sum of unique squares. Similarly, given 17, the program would find $16 + 1$; given 90, the program would find $81 + 9$.

How should this problem be approached? One possibility is to loop through all integers from 1 to X, where X is the largest integer whose square is less than the given number. Call this first integer i. For each of these numbers, a second loop could test all integers from 1 to i. Call this second integer j. Testing all possible pairs of i and j should find any sum of unique squares equal to the given number.

With a basic approach in mind, attention can be turned to writing code. Considering the above outline, the work can be broken into two parts. The first part is to prompt the user for a number, and loop through all possible integers whose square is less than the given number. For example:

```c
#include <stdio.h>

main()
{
int    i,number;

printf("Enter a number: ");
scanf("%d",&number);
i=1;
while (i*i < number)
    i=i+1;
printf("%d is the largest square within %d\n",i*i,number);
}
```

This code does not solve the whole problem; it tries only to identify the boundary on the range of the first loop. The output statement at the end will be used to debug this portion of the program. If this code is stored in a file named squares1.c, then compiling it and executing it produces results like the following:

```
ahoover@video> gcc -o squares1 squares1.c
ahoover@video> squares1
Enter a number: 5
9 is the largest square within 5
```

```
ahoover@video> squares1
Enter a number: 14
16 is the largest square within 14
ahoover@video>
```

After a few tests, it is possible to see that the code works correctly but that after the loop is finished the value of *i* is 1 too high. This can be corrected by subtracting 1 from *i* before printing it out. For example:

```
#include <stdio.h>

main()
{
int     i,number;

printf("Enter a number: ");
scanf("%d",&number);
i=1;
while (i*i < number)
  i=i+1;
i=i-1;
printf("%d is the largest square within %d\n",i*i,number);
}
```

If this code is stored in a file named squares2.c, then compiling it and executing it produces results like the following:

```
ahoover@video> gcc -o squares2 squares2.c
ahoover@video> squares2
Enter a number: 5
4 is the largest square within 5
ahoover@video> squares2
Enter a number: 14
9 is the largest square within 14
ahoover@video>
```

This shows that the first loop seems to be working correctly. However, an additional test shows another error:

```
ahoover@video> squares2
Enter a number: 4
1 is the largest square within 4
ahoover@video>
```

This error occurs when the given number is itself a perfect square. This can be fixed by changing the exit condition for the loop from < to <= as follows:

```
    .
    .
    .
while (i*i <= number)
    i=i+1;
    .
    .
    .
```

Further testing of this version of the program reveals that it is now working correctly.

After code has been written and debugged for the first part of the problem, it is easier to work on implementing code for the second part of the problem. For example:

```
#include <stdio.h>

main()
{
int     i,j,number;

printf("Enter a number: ");
scanf("%d",&number);
i=1;
while (i*i <= number)
  {
  j=1;
  while (j < i)
    {
    if (i*i + j*j == number)
      printf("Found: %d + %d\n",i*i,j*j);
    j++;
    }
  i=i+1;
  }
}
```

Code has been added for looping *j* through all values for the second integer. If this program is stored in a file named squares3.c, then compiling it and executing it produces results like the following:

```
ahoover@video> gcc -o squares3 squares3.c
ahoover@video> squares3
Enter a number: 90
Found: 81 + 9
ahoover@video> squares3
Enter a number: 14
ahoover@video> squares3
Enter a number: 101
Found: 100 + 1
ahoover@video>
```

The program works as expected.

Even for a problem as simple as this example, it is possible to see how a divide-and-conquer approach can benefit during program development. Two errors were uncovered while implementing code for the first part of the program design. Finding these kinds of errors is more difficult when the individual parts of a program are not tested prior to further development or code writing. As mentioned earlier, this approach can benefit almost any programming work and should be practiced whenever possible.

1.5 • Review of C

The following serves as a quick review of the basic data types, operations, and statements in the C programming language. The reader is directed to any one of a number of excellent books covering the syntax of C for a deeper coverage. The goal of this review is to remind the reader of a few key concepts. This section can also assist the reader who has not yet studied C but has studied an introduction to programming in a related language, such as C++ or Java. It is possible to learn the syntax of C while studying the concepts of system programming in this text, provided that the reader is willing to undertake the extra burden. Such a reader is strongly encouraged to acquire an additional textbook that covers the C programming language to use in conjunction with this text. Several excellent candidates include:

1. *The C Programming Language*, 2nd ed., B. Kernighan and D. Ritchie, Prentice Hall, 1988, ISBN 0131103628.

2. *Programming in C*, 3rd ed., S. Kochan, Sams, 2004, ISBN 0672326663.

3. *C Primer Plus*, 5th ed., S. Prata, Sams, 2004, ISBN 0672326965.

1.5.1   Basic Data Types

There are four basic data types in C: int, float, double, and char. The int data type is intended to store whole numbers. The float data type is intended to store real numbers. The double data type is also intended to store real numbers but has twice the precision so that it can store a larger range of numbers. The char data type is intended to store character symbols and controls used to display text. The following code demonstrates the differences between the types:

```
#include <stdio.h>

int main()
{
int     x,y;
char    a;
float   f,e;
double  d;

x=4;
y=7;
a='H';
f=-3.4;
d=54.123456789;
e=54.123456789;

printf("%d  %c  %f  %lf\n",x,a,e,d);
printf("%d  %c  %.9f  %.9lf\n",x,a,e,d);
}
```

Executing this code produces the following result:

```
4  H  54.123455  54.123457
4  H  54.123455048  54.123456789
```

In the first line of output, the float variable has seemingly been rounded downward in the last displayed digit, while the double variable has correctly been rounded upward in the last displayed digit. In fact, the float has simply run out of precision. This can be seen in the second line of output, where both variables are forced to print to nine decimal places. The double variable has the correct value, but the float has erroneous values in the latter digits.

The printf() and scanf() functions are the primary output and input functions in C. They are included in the C standard library, which is usually linked to an executable by default (in other words, a programmer can use these functions without worrying about where they come from). The syntax for them involves pairing up each variable in the list of arguments with a formatting symbol within the quoted string. For the details of this formatting, the reader is encouraged to consult a C programming book or the man page for either function.

1.5.2 Basic Arithmetic

The basic arithmetic operations supported in C include addition, subtraction, multiplication, division, and modulus (remainder). Within loops, it is common to increment (add 1 to) or decrement (subtract 1 from) a variable. The operators ++ and -- are provided for this reason. The following code demonstrates the basic arithmetic operations:

```c
#include <stdio.h>

int main()
{
int    x,y;
int    r1,r2,r3,r4,r5;

x=4;
y=7;
r1=x+y;
r2=x-y;
r3=x/y;
r4=x*y;
printf("%d  %d  %d  %d\n",r1,r2,r3,r4);

r3++;
r4--;
r5=r4%r1;
printf("%d  %d  %d\n",r3,r4,r5);
}
```

The output of executing this code is as follows:

```
11  -3  0  28
1  27  5
```

The modulus operator can be used only on integer variables. All the other arithmetic operators can be applied to all variables.

1.5.3 Loops

There are three basic types of loops in C: for, while, and do-while. The for loop is intended to be executed a fixed number of iterations, known before the loop is entered. Hence, it is given both a starting condition and an ending condition. The while loop is intended to be executed an unknown number of iterations. Hence, it is only given an ending condition. The do-while loop is also intended to be executed an unknown number of iterations but will be executed at least once. The while loop may be executed zero times if it fails the condition on the first attempt. The do-while loop does not test the condition until it has finished the loop, so it will execute the loop at least once. The following code demonstrates all three types of loops:

```c
#include <stdio.h>

int main()
{
int     i,x;

x=0;
for (i=0; i<4; i++)
  {
  x=x+i;
  printf("%d\n",x);
  }
while (i<7)
  {
  x=x+i;
  i++;
  printf("%d\n",x);
  }
do
  {
  x=x+i;
  i++;
  printf("%d\n",x);
  }
while (i<9);
}
```

The following is the output of executing this code:

```
0
1
3
6
10
15
21
28
36
```

The reader is encouraged to identify which lines of output came from which loop.

1.5.4 Conditionals and Blocks

The basic conditional in C is the if-else statement. It supports tests for equality (==), inequality (!=), and relative size (>, <, >=, and <=). Multiple conditions can be tested within a single statement using the logical AND (&&) and logical OR (||) operators to group the individual conditions. Statements (individual lines of code) are grouped using brackets ({}). In the absence of brackets, a conditional or loop statement applies only to the single following statement. The following code demonstrates conditionals and blocks:

```c
#include <stdio.h>

int main()
{
int     i,x;

x=0;
for (i=0; i<5; i++)
  {
  if (i%2 == 0  ||  i == 1)
    x=x+i;
  else
    x=x-i;
  printf("%d\n",x);
  }
}
```

The following is the output of executing this code:

```
0
1
3
0
4
```

The indentation in the code is for convenience only; it does not affect the grouping of statements. The topic of formatting code for easier management and understanding is addressed in Section 6.2.

1.5.5   Flow Control

Normally, loop iterations must be run to completion. When the bottom of a loop is reached, control is returned either to the top of the loop or to the statement immediately following the loop, depending on the result of evaluating the loop conditional. There are two flow control statements that change the way an interation through a loop is executed: continue and break. The continue statement returns control to the beginning of the loop, testing the loop conditional to start the next iteration. In effect, it skips the rest of the current iteration and starts the next one. The break statement terminates the loop and immediately proceeds to the next line of code following the loop. The following code demonstrates flow control:

```c
#include <stdio.h>

int main()
{
int     i,x;

x=0;
for (i=0; i<5; i++)
  {
  if (i%2 == 0)
    continue;
  x=x-i;
  if (i%4 == 0)
    break;
  printf("%d\n",x);
  }
}
```

Executing this code produces the following output:

```
-1
-4
```

Out of the five iterations in the loop, only two reach the printf() statement. The fourth iteration ends in the break statement, which terminates the loop, so that the fifth iteration never runs. Beginning students of C may be discouraged from using these flow control statements. The alternative is to use conditionals to control flow inside loops. The advantage to using control flow statements is that it simplifies (reduces) the number of program blocks, which usually simplifies the indentation that goes along with multiple program blocks.

There are also two control flow statements that are programwide: exit and goto. The exit statement immediately terminates the program. It is useful for handling unwanted situations, such as when a user inputs data outside an allowed range. The goto statement jumps program execution to the named line of code. In general, its use is discouraged. Unlike the other flow control statements, it can have complex consequences that can outweigh its benefits.

Questions and Exercises

1. System software on a Unix system performs the same basic services as system software on a Microsoft Windows system. However, there are some fundamental differences in how the system software is designed and developed. Describe at least two.

2. Briefly describe two operations that a debugger can perform (i.e., commands that you can give to a debugger).

3. Why must a program specifically be compiled for debugging to be able to execute that program in a debugger? What two things does the compiler do to assist a debugger?

4. Describe two ways a text editor can assist with writing program code (as opposed to writing generic text using a word processor).

5. A Unix system typically has many programs that can be run from its graphical user interface (menus). For the system you are using, pick five programs and identify the actual filename that is being executed. Use a shell to type the name of the program at the prompt to start the program instead of starting it from

the menu. Read the man page for the program and discover what options can be given to the program at startup.

6. For the text editor of your choice, identify what keystroke or menu option it provides in order to display the line number of the current cursor location. Also identify how to jump the cursor to a given line.

7. Debug the following code by compiling it for debugging and executing it within a debugger. At which line of code does the program crash? Why does it crash there?

```
              /* This code has a compile-time error, and at
              ** least one run-time error. */
    #include <stdio.h>
    #include <math.h>
    main(int argc,char *argv[])
    {
    int       n,i;
    int       d2,count,
    double    d1;


    while (1)
        {
        printf("Enter a number (0 to quit): ");
        scanf("%d",&n);
        if (n == 0)
            break;
        count=0;
        for (i=0; i<n; i++)
            {
            d1=(double)n/(double)i;
            d2=n/i;
            if (fabs(d1-(double)d2) < 0.00001)
                count++;
            }
        if (count == 2)
            printf("%d is prime\n",n);
        else
            printf("%d is not prime\n",n);
        }
    }
```

8. Write a program that prompts the user for a positive integer and then reports the closest integer having a whole number square root. For example, if the user enters 8, then the program reports 9. If the user enters 18, then the program reports 16. The program should work for any number having one to seven digits.

9. Write a program that prompts the user for a positive integer and then computes the sum of all the digits of the number. For example, if the user enters 2784, then the program reports 21. If the user enters 59, then the program reports 14. The program should work for any number having one to ten digits.

10. You are tasked with writing a program that manages contact information for a group of people. The program should save the first name, last name, and telephone number for up to 12 people. The program should have options to add a person, delete a person, update the information for a person, and display all information for all current entries. How could you go about breaking up the programming work into a set of subproblems that could be implemented separately? Describe the subproblems, the order in which you would work on them, and any testing you would do for each subproblem before proceeding to the next.

11. The following program compiles and executes but does not do what its designer intended. The program is supposed to allow a user to enter five integers, sorting the list from smallest to largest each time a new number is entered. However, when tested on a simple sequence, the program fails to sort correctly.

    Use a debugger to track down what is going wrong. Set a breakpoint at line 14 (w=n[i];). Use the display command to view the value for the variable n, which shows the current list of numbers, and the variables s and i, which show the indices of the two numbers about to be swapped. Use the continue command to pause the program at the same point (line 14) after one number has been entered, after two numbers have been entered, and after three numbers have been entered. By that point you should see the problem. Is it a bug or a program design flaw?

```
#include <stdio.h>
main()
{
int  n[5],s,i,j,w;

for (i=0; i<5; i++)
  {
  printf("Enter any integer: ");
  scanf("%d",&(n[i]));
```

```
s=0;              /* find index of smallest */
for (j=1; j<=i; j++)
    if (n[j] < n[s])
        s=j;
w=n[i];           /* swap smallest with current */
n[i]=n[s];
n[s]=w;
}
for (i=0; i<5; i++)
    printf("%d\n",n[i]);
}
```

2

Bits, Bytes, and Data Types

In theory, a variable is an abstract concept. It is a placeholder for a value used in some computation. In implementation, a variable occupies a fixed storage. It is important to understand how variables differ in storage because this affects how different variables can be used in different computations. It promotes efficiency in programming by utilizing the correct data types, and hence the correct amount of memory (using 64-bit variables to store whole numbers between 1 and 100 is a waste of space). It promotes correct coding of arithmetic operations (coding floating point computations on whole numbers is a waste of time). It leads to a better understanding of bitwise operations, which are critical for many computing algorithms, such as in graphics. Finally, a proper understanding of memory helps in program design and debugging, especially when more complex data types are used, such as arrays and pointers. This chapter, and the following two chapters, all develop an understanding of C data types based upon an understanding of the actual memory they occupy.

2.1 • Bit Models

In C, what is the difference between an int and a float? The simple answer is that one stores whole numbers, whereas the other stores real numbers. But how? Or, how about some tougher questions: How does a double store higher-precision numbers compared to a float? Does it double the numerical range of possible values, or double the precision, or something else? How do the qualifiers short or unsigned change the way a value is stored? In order to answer these questions, we have to understand the bit models that underlie the data types.

A bit, short for binary digit, is a binary valued variable. The two possible values are typically written as 1 and 0, or true and false. On a computing chip (processor, memory chip, etc.), they are represented by high and low voltages, where a high value is typically 1–5 V and a low value is typically 0.0–0.5 V. Everything in computing is based upon combinations of bits. Everything stored in a computing chip is based upon using a fixed number of bits to model (or represent) the thing of interest.

For our discussion, bits can be either 1 or 0. Since a single bit can only represent only two values, we must group bits together to represent a wider range of numbers. The most common grouping is a byte, which is 8 bits grouped in sequence. For example, the following is a byte:

0	0	0	1	0	0	1	1

When bits are grouped, there are a variety of methods for interpreting them collectively. Each method of interpretation is called a *bit model*. We will now examine several bit models for representing various types and ranges of numbers.

2.1.1   Magnitude-only Bit Model

The simplest bit model is for nonnegative whole numbers. In this case, each bit represents a nonnegative integer power of 2. The place values of the bits are as follows:

example bit value	0	0	0	1	0	0	1	1
place value	2^7	2^6	2^5	2^4	2^3	2^2	2^1	2^0
place value (base 10)	128	64	32	16	8	4	2	1

A bit value of 0 indicates a place value of 0; a bit value of 1 indicates a place value as given in the table. The total value of the number represented is found by adding up the place values of all the bits. In the example above, the value represented in the 8 bits (1 byte) is 19:

$$0 + 0 + 0 + 16 + 0 + 0 + 2 + 1 = 19$$

Given 8 bits, it is possible to store whole numbers in value up to

$$\sum_{i=0}^{7} 2^i = 2^8 - 1 = 255$$

or in the range 0 to 255.

The bits with the lowest powers of 2 (to the right in the above example) are called the *least significant bits*, or lowest-order bits, because they represent the smallest portions of the number. The bits with the highest powers of two (to the left in the above example) are called the *most significant bits*, or higher-order bits. The significance of bits can be thought of as which digits most change the number. It is common practice to list bits from highest to lowest, left to right, following the same convention used to write base 10 numbers.

Binary addition using this model is done similarly to base 10 addition. The easiest way to compute a sum by hand is to line up vertically the digits with similar powers. The digits in each power (column) are added, starting with the lowest power (rightmost column) and proceeding toward the highest power (leftmost column). If the sum in any single power exceeds the allowed range (9 in base 10, or 1 in base 2), then the sum is carried over to the next highest power. For example:

Base 10 (decimal)	Base 2 (binary)
7	00000111
+ 4	+ 00000100
11	00001011

In this example, there was a carry in base 10 from the one's digit to the ten's digit. There was also a carry in base 2 from the 2^2 digit to the 2^3 digit.

In general, storing numbers only within the range 0–255 is not terribly useful. Some things do use this range, such as graphical display pixel values, but obviously a wider range is needed for most computations. This is accomplished by grouping more bits together. For example, by grouping 4 bytes (32 bits) together, the magnitude-only bit model can represent whole numbers in value up to

$$\sum_{i=0}^{31} 2^i = 2^{32} - 1 = 4,294,967,295$$

or in the range 0–4,294,967,295. This number can be related to a size many personal computer enthusiasts are familiar with. At the time of this writing, most common personal computers and workstations can have a maximum of 4 GB of memory. Why? It is a result of the size of the memory bus, which can be thought of as the number of wires from the system to its memory. With 32 wires, a system can address 4,294,967,296 (which is about 4 billion, or 4 "giga") different memory locations. If each memory location is a byte (8 bits), then a "32-bit architecture" can have a maximum of 4 GB of memory.

In C, several data types use the magnitude-only bit model. An unsigned char is a 1-byte (8 bits) variable with a range of 0 to 255. On a 32-bit system, an unsigned int is a 4-byte (32 bits) variable with a range of 0 to 4,294,967,295, and an unsigned short int is a 2-byte (16 bits) variable with a range of 0 to 65,535. Technically, the C language does not define the size of an int. However, the 32-bit usage has become so predominant that we will treat it as the standard within this text. At the time of this writing, as 64-bit architectures are becoming more common, there is debate over whether to standardize the C int as 4 bytes or continue to allow it to vary depending on the system architecture. Regardless of size, the concepts taught in this text are valid, but it is easier to learn the concepts by solidifying the size of an int at a specific value.

2.1.2   Sign-magnitude Bit Model

In the case where signed whole numbers are desired, a common practice is to allocate the highest-order bit to be the *sign bit*. This is called the sign-magnitude model:

example bit value	1	0	0	1	0	0	1	1
place value	sign	2^6	2^5	2^4	2^3	2^2	2^1	2^0
place value (base 10)	+ or −	64	32	16	8	4	2	1

By common convention, a value of 0 in the sign bit indicates a positive number, while a value of 1 in the sign bit indicates a negative number. In this example, the decimal value represented using the 8 bits is −19. Using the sign-magnitude bit model, it is possible with 8 bits to represent whole numbers in the range −127 to +127.

The sign-magnitude model suffers from two drawbacks. First, notice that there are two possible bit values for zero: 00000000 can be interpreted as "positive zero," while 10000000 is interpreted as "negative zero." This does not make much sense. Even more important, using this bit model makes binary addition somewhat complicated. If we have zero or two negative numbers, we can perform addition exactly as outlined for the magnitude-only bit model. However, if we have one negative number and one positive number, we must instead perform a subtraction. While subtraction is not a terribly difficult task, it would be nice if we could use the same method for binary addition regardless of the signs of the two numbers.

Because of these two drawbacks, no data types in C use the sign-magnitude bit model. It is usually seen only in simple computing circuits, or in design problems where these drawbacks do not present any difficulty. The bit model discussed next was designed to overcome these drawbacks.

2.1.3 Two's Complement Bit Model

Using the two's complement bit model, positive integers (and zero) are represented exactly the same as they are in the magnitude-only bit model. Negative numbers are represented by applying the following sequence of steps:

1. Write the bits for the positive version of the number.

2. Invert (flip) all the bits.

3. Add 1.

For example, to represent −7, we proceed through the following steps:

positive value (+7)	0	0	0	0	0	1	1	1
invert all bits	1	1	1	1	1	0	0	0
add 1	1	1	1	1	1	0	0	1

The process of adding 1 is carried out exactly as described in the previous sections. Based on our example, we find that the two's complement bit representation for −7, using 8 bits, is 11111001.

When a two's complement number has a 1 in the highest bit, it indicates that the number is negative. To find the value, we perform the same steps:

unknown value (−?)	1	1	1	1	1	0	0	1
invert all bits	0	0	0	0	0	1	1	0
add 1	0	0	0	0	0	1	1	1

After performing these steps, the value provides the magnitude of the negative number. In this example, we get a magnitude of 7, so the original bit pattern 11111001 is known to be −7.

The two's complement bit model solves the double zero problem seen with the sign-magnitude model. The only bit pattern for zero is 00000000. Applying the steps that compute the negative value for the pattern yields the original pattern:

0 (base 10)	0	0	0	0	0	0	0	0
invert all bits	1	1	1	1	1	1	1	1
add 1	0	0	0	0	0	0	0	0

Since we only have 8 bits, the carry out of the highest-order bit is lost in this operation; it has no place to go. Therefore trying to compute "negative zero" results in the same bit pattern as "positive zero," thus there is only one bit pattern for zero.

Using the sign-magnitude model, the bit pattern 10000000 represented "negative zero." In the two's complement bit model, what does it represent? To find the value, we apply the usual operations for interpreting a two's complement number:

unknown value (−?)	1	0	0	0	0	0	0	0
invert all bits	0	1	1	1	1	1	1	1
add 1	1	0	0	0	0	0	0	0

Since the first bit is 1, we know the number must be negative. After inverting and adding 1, we obtain a magnitude of 128. Therefore, the bit pattern 10000000 using the two's complement bit model represents −128 (base 10). This is called the weird number. When following the two's complement conversion steps, it comes out the same as it started. However, at the beginning, we look only at the highest bit to determine that the number is negative. After converting, we see that the magnitude is 128, and so the complete value is −128. Thus, using the two's complement bit model, the range of integers that can be represented using 8 bits is −128 to +127.

Two's complement also makes addition and subtraction easier to implement because, regardless of the signs of the two numbers, they can always be added. For example, consider 7 + (−5):

	Base 10 (decimal)	Base 2 (binary)
carry bits		11111111
	7	00000111
	+ (−5)	+ 11111011
	2	00000010

The bit pattern for −5 was obtained through the two's complement conversion steps: +5 = 00000101; inverted it becomes 11111010; and after adding 1 it becomes 11111011. When performing the addition, there was a carry value of 1 in every bit place. The final carry bit at the end was again thrown away because it has no place to go. However, it must be checked. For the sum to be valid, the highest two carry bits must be either 11 or 00. In this example, the final two carry bits were 11, and so the sum is valid.

If the highest two carry bits are either 10 or 01, then the result is an *arithmetic overflow*. Arithmetic overflow is when the process of a calculation results in a number outside the range of values that can be represented by the available bits. For example:

	Base 10 (decimal)	Base 2 (binary)
carry bits		10000000
	(−127)	10000001
	+ (−126)	+ 10000001
	−253	00000011

The bit patterns for both −127 and −126 were computed normally (the reader is encouraged to work these out). Both of these values are fine; the two's complement bit model can represent them using 8 bits. However, the result of the addition is 00000011, which equates to 3 in base 10. This is of course wrong. What has happened is that an overflow has occurred. With 8 bits, we cannot represent −253 (it is outside of the allowed range of −128 to +127). We can see that an overflow has occurred by looking at the highest two carry bits, which in this example are 10.

Several data types in C use the two's complement bit model. A char uses 1 byte (8 bits) to represent numbers in the range −128 to +127. An int uses 4 bytes (32 bits) to represent numbers in the range −2,147,483,648 to +2,147,483,647. A short int uses 2 bytes (16 bits) to represent numbers in the range −32,768 to +32,767. The two's complement bit model is the most commonly seen bit model for representing signed whole numbers in computing systems.

2.1.4 Floating Point Bit Model

For storing real numbers, a method completely different from the previous bit models must be used. Some of the bits must be used to represent the fractional portion of the number. One possibility is to use bits to denote powers of 2 that are negative, and hence fractions. For example, we could use 1 byte (8 bits) as follows:

example bit value	1	0	0	1	0	0	1	1
place value	2^4	2^3	2^2	2^1	2^0	2^{-1}	2^{-2}	2^{-3}
place value (base 10)	16	8	4	2	1	0.5	0.25	0.125

This approach is called a *fixed point* bit model, because the position of the number of digits (in base 10) that can be represented in the fraction are fixed. In our example, the base 10 value that is represented by the 8 bits is 18.375. In this example, only three fractional digits of a base 10 number can be represented. This is generally considered a limitation, and a poor use of available bits.

It is possible to represent a wider range of fractions, using the same number of bits, using a *floating point* bit model. The general idea is to represent the number using scientific notation. For example, in base 10 notation:

$$123.456 = 1.23456 \times 10^2$$

In a computer we have only bits, so we must use base 2 scientific notation. For example, the bits representing 18.375 from above could be written as follows:

$$18.375 \text{ (base 10)} = 10010.011 \text{ (base 2)} = 1.0010011 \times 2^4$$

Since it is known that base 2 is used, we do not need to store the "2" each time; it is implied. Similarly, we can simplify the storage of a number by assuming that the leading mantissa (the value in front of the decimal point) is 1. Therefore the floating point bit model stores numbers in the following form:

$$\pm 1.f \times 2^e$$

The values that must be stored are the bits for the sign, the fraction f, and the exponent e. Obviously, only one bit is needed to store the sign. The remaining available bits can be divided between the fraction and the exponent. Given 32 bits (4 bytes), the standard[1] is to represent the fraction using 23 bits and the exponent using 8 bits:

Total bits	1	8	23
	sign	exponent (e)	fraction (f)
bit places	31	30 . . . 23	22 . . . 0

The bits in the fraction represent negative powers of 2, as described above. For example, bit 22 represents $2^{-1} = \frac{1}{2} = 0.5$; bit 21 represents $2^{-2} = \frac{1}{4} = 0.25$; bit 20 represents $2^{-3} = \frac{1}{8} = 0.125$; and so on. The 8 bits for the exponent are used to

---

1. The IEEE 754 floating point standard.

represent whole values in the range -127 to $+128$. The negative values support the representation of small fractions, and hence larger precision after the decimal point. Conversely, the positive values support the representation of large non-fractional numbers. Thus, there is a choice in how the available bits will be used. For example, it is possible to represent 0.123456 or 123.456 or 123,456.0, but it is not possible to represent 123,456.123456. The total precision available in base 10 is about eight digits using a 4-byte floating point bit model.

The following steps can be used to convert a number from base 10 to binary using the floating point bit model:

1. Write the sign bit.

2. Write the number in fixed point binary, without the sign.

3. Normalize, moving the radix (the decimal point) to just after the first "1" digit.

4. Take f as the values to the right of the radix, zero padded.

5. Take e as the given exponent, biased by adding $+127$.

The following example demonstrates these steps. The value -118.625 will be encoded:

(1) get sign bit	$s = 1$
(2) write # in fixed point binary	$118.625 = 1110110.101$
(3) normalize	$1110110.101 = 1.110110101 \times 2^6$
(4) get fraction from right of radix	$f = 110\ 1101\ 0100\ 0000\ 0000\ 0000$
(5) get exponent, biased $+127$	$e = 6+127 = 133 = 1000\ 0101$

The exponent is biased by adding 127 so that the exponent can be stored as a mangnitude-only, and yet still represent the range -127 to $+128$. For our example, the final 32-bit floating point representation is:

1 1000 0101 110 1101 0100 0000 0000 0000

Note that the spaces are for our convenience only; they are not represented in any way in the computing system. The following are some additional examples:

Real number	Bit pattern
4.125	0 1000 0001 000 0100 0000 0000 0000 0000
123456.123	0 1000 1111 111 0001 0010 0000 0001 0000
-6.429678	1 1000 0001 100 1101 1011 1111 1110 1100

In the C language, the `float` data type uses 4 bytes to store a real number, and the `double` data type uses 8 bytes to store a real number. The double still uses 1 bit for sign, but it uses 11 bits to store the exponent and 52 bits to store the fraction, so that it can represent a wider range of numbers.

2.1.5   ASCII and Unicode Bit Models

In order to represent nonnumeric data, another bit model must be used. The ASCII (American Standard Code for Information Interchange) bit model was developed to represent English text symbols, along with control characters necessary to print English text. A partial listing of the ASCII bit model is shown in Table 2.1 (a full listing is in Appendix A). There are 128 total ASCII bit patterns. Each bit pattern uses 7 bits. In order to fill a byte, an eighth bit is added to each pattern. Historically, this extra bit has been used for several purposes, such as parity (a form of error recovery) and extended ASCII sets (providing an additional 128 bit patterns). However, it is also common to leave the bit with a value of zero, in effect padding the 7-bit ASCII patterns with a preceding zero. Most of the bit patterns in ASCII represent printable symbols, such as the lowercase versions of letters in the English alphabet. The patterns for both the lower- and uppercase letters are stored in order, from 97 to 122 and from 65 to 90, respectively. The first 32 bit patterns (from 0000 0000 to 0000 1000) represent control characters, which do not correspond to printable symbols. Instead, these characters control some aspect of printing, such as a backspace, horizontal tab, or carriage return.

In C, both the `char` and `unsigned char` data types use the ASCII bit model. However, because of their 7-bit nature, the eighth bit allows for a second, different use of each data type. If we interpret each of the bit patterns as magnitude-only whole numbers, then we obtain the base 10 values listed in Table 2.1. The `unsigned char` data type can be interpreted in this manner, providing a range of values from 0 to 255. If we interpret each of the bit patterns using the two's complement bit model, then we obtain base 10 values in the range −128 to +127. The `char` data type can be interpreted in this manner. This dual interpretation of the bit patterns can be seen through the following C code:

```
char a;
unsigned char b;
a='A';
b='B';
printf("%c %c %d %d\n",a,b,a,b);
a=183;
b=255;
printf("%d %d\n",a,b);
```

Table 2.1 Partial listing of ASCII bit model.

Bit values	Base 10	Description
0000 0000	0	null character
0000 1000	8	backspace
0000 1001	9	horizontal tab
0000 1010	10	line feed
0000 1101	13	carriage return
0000 1000	27	escape
0010 0000	32	space (space bar)
0010 0001	33	! (exclamation point)
0011 0000	48	0 (numeric zero)
0011 0001	49	1 (numeric one)
0011 1001	57	9 (numeric nine)
0100 0001	65	A
0100 0010	66	B
0101 1010	90	Z
0110 0001	97	a
0110 0010	98	b
0111 1010	122	z

The output of executing this code is as follows:

```
A B 65 66
-73 255
```

Using the %c designator, the printf() function call will interpret the variable using the ASCII bit model. Using the %d (or %i) designator, the printf() function call will interpret the variable as a whole number. In this case, which bit model to use depends upon the data type. For the char data type, the printf() function interprets the variable using the two's complement bit model; whereas for the unsigned char data type, the printf() function interprets the variable using the magnitude-only bit model. The magnitude-only bit pattern for 183 is 1011 0111, which interpreted using the two's complement bit model is −73 in base 10. This is why the variable a appears to change in the second printf() output.

The ASCII bit model has a few problems. Many of the ASCII control characters are obsolete, relics of the earliest days of digital text transmission and printing. The eighth bit is open to interpretation, and has consequently been used in a variety of methods on different computing systems. Most important, the symbol range covers only the English language. In response to these problems, the Unicode bit model was developed. In its most straightforward implementation, it uses 16-bit patterns to represent 65,536 total symbols. These include the alphabets of many languages besides English. In C, a short int is commonly used to store a Unicode bit pattern. Because of the prevalence and continued use of the ASCII bit model, the first 128 bit patterns represent the same symbols in the Unicode bit model as they do in the ASCII bit model. The full details of Unicode can be found in the reference book *The Unicode Standard*, 5th ed., Unicode Consortium, Addison-Wesley, 2006.

2.1.6   Bit Model Summary

To summarize, what is 1100 0010 1110 1101 0100 0000 0000 0000 ?

The answer is that it depends on how the bits are grouped and interpreted. In other words, it depends upon the bit model. Here are some possible answers:

C variable(s)	Bit model	Value(s) or symbol(s)			
4 unsigned char	magnitude-only	194	237	64	0
4 char	two's complement	−62	9	64	0
4 char	ASCII	[x]	[x]	@	[NULL]
1 int	two's complement	−1,024,638,976			
1 unsigned int	magnitude-only	3,270,328,320			
1 float	floating point	−118.625			

The bits can be grouped together 8 at a time (1 byte at a time), or 32 at a time, or other possibilities not listed here. After grouping, different bit models can be applied to determine the value(s) or symbol(s) represented.

The important concept to understand is that bits alone do not provide data. They must be grouped and interpreted according to the appropriate bit model; otherwise they are meaningless. A common pitfall for naive computer operators is to open up any file within a text editor. However, not all bit patterns relate to printable symbols. Looking at the example above, 2 of the 4 bytes do not represent any regular ASCII symbols; 1 of the bytes represents a control value (the NULL character); and only 1 byte represents a printable symbol (the @ symbol). This is why using a text editor to view any random file will often display it as seemingly a bunch of garbage. A text editor interprets all the bits using the ASCII bit model, when the underlying data was not encoded that way.

A common pitfall for naive programmers is to use the wrong data type for the given data or computation. This amounts to using the wrong bit model, with consequences similar to opening a random file using a text editor. When seeing a value that looks very strange (i.e., garbage), one should look to make sure the correct data type is being used. The reason for *type casting* computations to use the same data type is to ensure that all the variables involved are using the same bit model. For example:

```
int    i=3;
double d=7.2;
float  f;
f=(float)i+(float)d;
```

In the last statement, the (float) in front of the variables i and d converts the bits used to represent the values to the float bit model so that the addition operation can be performed.

While programming, even when it is not necessary to understand how the individual bits are organized in variables, it is often important to understand how many bytes are used by variables. The sizeof() operator reports how many bytes a data type, or a variable, is using:

```
int    i;
char   c;
double d;
printf("%d %d %d %d\n",sizeof(i),sizeof(c),
        sizeof(d),sizeof(float));
```

The result of executing this code is:

```
4 1 8 4
```

This matches our expectations: a variable of type char is 1 byte in size; an int and float are 4 bytes each; and a double is 8 bytes. In Chapter 4, when we look at structures and pointers, we will revisit the sizeof() operator.

2.2 • Bitwise Operations

In some situations, a single bit can store all the information needed for a computation. For example, a file can be write-protected, or not. A user can be logged in, or not. A program can be currently running, or not. In many advanced algorithms, bits are frequently used in computations and data structures. For example, compression/decompression routines (codecs) commonly manipulate bit patterns to reduce the necessary storage size. Sorting methods commonly use trees and other binary structures during operation. Bitwise operations are also common in device drivers and graphics programming.

In the C language, the smallest data type available is the char, which is 1 byte (8 bits). How then can one store or manipulate a single bit? One possibility is to use an entire char to store the single bit. This is of course wasteful and, if used indiscriminately, would seriously raise the amount of memory necessary to operate a modern computing system. Another option is to figure out how to manipulate just 1 bit within a char, or within any other data type. In the C language, this is accomplished using bitwise operations.

In this section, we first describe the basic logic underlying bitwise operations. We then look at the C bit operators that are used to program bitwise operations. Finally, we look at bit masking, which is the most common type of coding problem involving bit manipulations. In later chapters in this text, we will again see bit coding problems when we look at file attributes (Chapter 5) and some graphics operations (Chapter 8).

2.2.1   Binary Logic Operations

Recall that a single bit can have a value of either 1 or 0, which can also represent true or false. The three most basic logic operations are AND, OR, and NOT. The operations work as follows:

AND	OR	NOT
0 AND 0 = 0	0 OR 0 = 0	NOT 0 = 1
0 AND 1 = 0	0 OR 1 = 1	NOT 1 = 0
1 AND 0 = 0	1 OR 0 = 1	
1 AND 1 = 1	1 OR 1 = 1	

The result of an AND operation is true only if both input values are true. The result of an OR operation is true if either input value is true. The result of a NOT operation is to reverse the bit value. Logic operations are independent of any particular programming language used to implement them. There are several other logic operations, for example NOR and NAND, which are commonly used in circuits. In this text, we are concerned only with the basic three operations and how to implement and use them in C programming.

2.2.2   Bit Operators

Bit operators are the symbols or syntax used in a programming language to affect individual bits within a variable. In the C programming language, there are six bit operators:

Operator	Symbol name	Action
~	tilde	bitwise NOT
&	ampersand	bitwise AND
|	vertical bar	bitwise OR
^	caret	bitwise XOR
>>	greater-than greater-than	right-shift
<<	less-than less-than	left-shift

The bit operators are intended to be used only on the whole number data types, char and int, and the related extensions (e.g., unsigned char). Although bits can be manipulated in any variable, it is rare to see bit operators applied to the real number data types.

The bitwise NOT operator inverts every bit in a variable. It is written using the tilde symbol (~). For example:

```
unsigned char a;
a=17;
a=~a;
printf("%d\n",a);
```

The result of executing this code is:

238

At the bit level, the result of the code is:

C code	Bits in variable a	Base 10 value
a=17;	0 0 0 1 0 0 0 1	17
a=~a;	1 1 1 0 1 1 1 0	238

The bitwise AND operator performs an AND between two variables, independently at every bit. It is written using the ampersand symbol (&). For example:

```
unsigned char a,b;
a=17;
b=22;
a=a & b;
printf("%d\n",a);
```

The result of executing this code is:

16

At the bit level, the result of the code is:

C code	Bits in variable a	Base 10 value
a=17;	0 0 0 1 0 0 0 1	17
b=22;	0 0 0 1 0 1 1 0	22
a=a & b;	0 0 0 1 0 0 0 0	16

Prior to the bitwise AND, only one bit position had a value of 1 in both variables a and b. Therefore, after the bitwise AND, this is the only bit position with a value of 1.

The bitwise OR operator performs an OR between two variables, independently at every bit. It is written using the vertical bar symbol (|). For example:

```
unsigned char a,b;
a=17;
b=22;
a=a | b;
printf("%d\n",a);
```

The result of executing this code is:

23

At the bit level, the result of the code is:

C code	Bits in variable a	Base 10 value
a=17;	0 0 0 1 0 0 0 1	17
b=22;	0 0 0 1 0 1 1 0	22
a=a	b;	0 0 0 1 0 1 1 1	23

After the bitwise OR, the variable a has a value of 1 in any bit position in which either of the two input variables a or b had a value of 1.

Like the arithmetic or logic operators in C, the bit operators can be applied to either variables or constants. For example:

```
char x,y;
x=7;
y=6;
x=x&y;
y=x|16;
printf("%d %d\n",x,y);
```

The result of executing this code is:

6 22

At the bit level, the result of the code is:

C code	Bits in variable a	Base 10 value
x=7;	0 0 0 0 0 1 1 1	7
y=6;	0 0 0 0 0 1 1 0	6
x=x & y;	0 0 0 0 0 1 1 0	6
y=x	16;	0 0 0 1 0 1 1 0	22

The left-shift and right-shift bit operators move bits into higher-order and lower-order bit positions, respectively. When a bit pattern is written out horizontally, this is equivalent to moving the bits toward the left, or toward the right, respectively. A left-shift is written in C using two consecutive less-than symbols (<<) and a right-shift is written using two consecutive greater-than symbols (>>). The value following the shift operator indicates how many bit positions to move. For example:

```
unsigned char a,b;
a=17;
a=a << 2;
b=64;
b=b >> 3;
printf("%d %d\n",a,b);
```

The result of executing this code is:

68 8

At the bit level, the result of the code is:

C code	Bits in variable a	Base 10 value
a=17;	0 0 0 1 0 0 0 1	17
a=a << 2;	0 1 0 0 0 1 0 0	68
b=64;	0 1 0 0 0 0 0 0	64
b=b >> 3;	0 0 0 0 1 0 0 0	8

After the left-shift, every bit value in the variable a has moved to the left (to a higher-order bit) by two bit positions. After the right-shift, every bit value in the variable b has moved to the right (to a lower-order bit) by three bit positions. Any bits that move beyond the highest or lowest available bit are discarded. For example:

Original bits	Shifting	Discarded bits	Result
01101111	left 3	011	01111 000
01101111	right 3	111	000 01101

The new bit values that take up residence in the now vacated bit positions are given values that depend upon the bit model used by the variable. For a magnitude-only bit model, the new bit values are always zero, as shown above. For a two's complement bit model, the new bit values are zero for left-shifts, and copies of the original highest-order bit for right-shifts. The latter maintains the original sign of the value, while shifting the negative number in a manner synonymous with positive numbers. For example:

```
char a,b;
a=17;
a=a >> 2;
b=-65;
b=b >> 2;
printf("%d %d\n",a,b);
```

The result of executing this code is:

```
4 -17
```

At the bit level, the result of the code is:

C code	Bits in variable a	Base 10 value
a=17;	0 0 0 1 0 0 0 1	17
a=a >> 2;	0 0 0 0 0 1 0 0	4
b= -65;	1 0 1 1 1 1 1 1	−65
b=b >> 2;	1 1 1 0 1 1 1 1	−17

2.2.3   Bitmask Operations

Bitmasking is perhaps the most common type of bitwise operation. It involves using a *bitmask* to change or query one or more designated bits within a variable. The bitmask indicates which bits are to be affected by the operation. The idea is to operate on a variable, changing or affecting only the bits indicated by the bitmask:

variable → bitmask (bit N) → variable (only bit N changed)

The bitmask indicated that bit N should be changed (N is the bit position, which is also the power of 2 of the bit). The following are examples of bitmasks for an 8-bit variable (e.g., unsigned char):

Bitmask	Base 10 value	Indicated bits to work on
0 0 0 0 0 0 0 1	1	bit 0
0 0 0 1 0 0 0 0	16	bit 4
1 0 1 0 1 1 0 0	172	bits 2, 3, 5, and 7

A bitmask can indicate that any number of bits are to be affected. The three most common bitmask operations work on a single bit: set the bit, clear the bit, or query the value of the bit. Each of these operations can be accomplished through the following logic:

Operation	Logic
set Nth bit	$x = x$ OR 2^N
clear Nth bit	$x = x$ AND NOT(2^N)
read Nth bit	$= x$ AND 2^N

The act of setting a bit gives the bit a value of 1, regardless of its initial value. At the same time, it leaves all the other bits unchanged. The act of clearing a bit gives the bit a value of 0, regardless of its initial value, and similarly leaves all the other bits unchanged. The act of querying a bit determines the current value of a bit, leaving all bit values unchanged. Each of these operations can be implemented in C as follows:

Operation	C code
set Nth bit	x = x | (1<<N);
clear Nth bit	x = x & (~(1<<N));
read Nth bit	(x & (1<<N)) >>N

When reading the Nth bit, the final right-shift operation results in a value of 1 or 0 regardless of which bit is being read. Without that final right-shift, the read value will be equal to the value of the bit position (the power of 2 of the bit place).

The following code demonstrates setting, clearing, and reading bits:

```
char a;
int i;
a=17;
a=a | (1 << 3);     /* set 3rd bit */
printf("%d\n",a);
a=a & (~(1<<4));    /* clear 4th bit */
printf("%d\n",a);
for (i=7; i>=0; i--)
  printf("%d ",(a&(1<<i)) >> i);  /* read i'th bit */
printf("\n");
```

The result of executing this code is:

```
25
9
0 0 0 0 1 0 0 1
```

At the bit level, the result of the code is:

C code	Operation	Bits in variable a	Base 10 value
a=17;		0 0 0 1 0 0 0 1	17
a=a | (1 << 3);	set bit 3	0 0 0 1 1 0 0 1	25
a=a & (~(1 << 4));	clear bit 4	0 0 0 0 1 0 0 1	9

2.3 • Memory Map

In this section, we introduce the *memory map* concept. A memory map is a table, listing all the variables in a piece of code. The table includes the variable names, values, and memory addresses. The addresses indicate the sizes of the variables, in bytes. Each address is assumed to represent 1 byte. For example, consider the following code:

```
char a,b,c;
a=7;
b=-13;
c=0;
```

The memory map for this code could be written as follows:

Label	Address	Value
a	400	7
b	401	–13
c	402	0

The starting address is not important; 400 was picked so that the range of values in the addresses differs significantly from the values in the variables, so that they are easier to read. The important thing to note in the address column is that each variable occupies only 1 byte. This is because a char variable is only 1 byte in size.

If variables of different types are used, then the address column should reflect their relative sizes. For example, consider the following code:

```
char a;
int b;
float c;
double d;
a=7;
b=-13;
c=0.1;
d=42.5;
```

The memory map for this code could be written as follows:

Label	Address	Value
a	400	7
b	401–404	-13
c	405–408	0.1
d	409–416	42.5

In this example, we see the appropriate sizes of the different data types reflected in the address column. A char is 1 byte, an int and a float are both 4 bytes, and a double is 8 bytes in size.

It is important to remember that what resides in memory are bit patterns. In order to be interpreted as a value (or symbol), the appropriate bit model must be applied. Which model is determined by the data types. For example, consider the following code:

```
char a;
short int b;
char c;
a=6;
b=13;
c='6';
```

The memory map for this code could be written as follows:

Label	Address	Bits	Value/symbol
a	400	0000 0110	6
b	401–402	0000 0000 0000 1101	13
c	403	0011 0110	'6'

This example emphasizes the difference between the symbol '6' and the integer value 6, which have different bit patterns. In most cases, it is not necessary to include the bit patterns in a memory map. One can differentiate between symbols and values using appropriate notation, such as enclosing symbols within single quotes (as in C coding).

A memory map can be used in a dynamic manner, keeping track of variable values as a piece of code executes. As a tool, it lets a programmer work through a piece of code to determine its result. For example, consider the following code:

```
int i,n;
n=0;
for (i=1; i<=4; i++)
    n=n+i;
```

The memory map for this code could be written as follows:

Label	Address	Value
i	400–403	1 2 3 4 5
n	404–407	0 1 3 6 10

Note that the final value of i in the memory map is 5, which is 1 beyond the loop bounds. This is because the loop is not terminated until the tested condition i<=4 is false, which is when i=5. This is a common programming mistake (recognizing the value of a loop counter after the loop terminates) that can be caught by working through code using a memory map.

The memory map can point out another common programming mistake. Consider the following code, which is intended to compute the sum of the first five even integers:

```
int i,sum;
for (i=1; i<=10; i++)
    if (i%2 == 0)
        sum=sum+i;
```

Have you spotted the coding error? Through a partial execution of the program, the memory map could be written as follows:

Label	Address	Value
i	400–403	1 2
sum	404–407	?

In the first iteration, i=1, i%2 is equal to 1, and so the if statement fails. In the second iteration, i=2, i%2 is equal to 0, and so the if statement is true. The program now comes to the line that adds i to sum. However, sum has not previously been given a value. What is its current value? The answer is that the value is unknown. Every variable always has a value. There is no such thing as a "blank" variable; the wires storing the bits for the variable must have either high or low voltages, corresponding to 1's and 0's. However, because the program did not previously give this variable a value, the current value is unknown. It could be zero, or it could be anything. We can change the code to see this effect:

```
int i,sum;
printf("%d\n",sum);
for (i=1; i<=10; i++)
if (i%2 == 0)
   sum=sum+i;
printf("%d\n",sum);
```

Executing this code yields (results will vary from machine to machine, and even moment to moment):

3457056
3457086

Executing the program again yields:

14852128
14852158

Additional executions of the program yield similarly strange numbers, always having a difference of 30. That difference is due to the desired calculation, while the rest of it is due to the original unknown value in the variable when the program started each time.

The examples shown in this section are relatively simple. The true power of a memory map becomes apparent when it is used to work with pointers, arrays, and structures. In Chapters 3 and 4, the memory map will be used repeatedly to look at these constructs.

Questions and Exercises

1. Show the total number of bits used, and all the bit values, for the following variables:

```
char c=35;
char d='G';
int x=-42;
float f=17.25;
int i=1099563008;
double a=17.25;
```

2. Convert each of the following bit patterns into whole numbers. Assume the values are stored using the two's complement bit model.

   ```
   00101101
   01011010
   10010001
   11100011
   0010100010110110
   0110111100101011
   1100101111001000
   1000000010100011
   ```

3. Assume a real value is stored using a 4-byte floating point bit model, with 8 bits for the mantissa representing values of −127 to 128. Approximately what is the largest value that can be represented? Approximately what is the smallest fraction that can be represented?

4. Convert each of the following bit patterns into real numbers. Assume the values are stored using the floating point bit model.

   ```
   00111111100000000000000000000000
   01000100100010101110001110001110
   11000001000101101011100001010010
   11000111100010100010011101000000
   ```

5. Use the following lines of code to start a program:

   ```
   #include <stdio.h>
   main()
   {
   char n[10];
   int x;
   printf("Enter a three-digit nonnegative number: ");
   scanf("%s",n);
   .
   .
   .
   printf("The number is %d\n",x);
   }
   ```

   Write code that performs the conversion from the ASCII bit model for the variable n to the magnitude-only bit model for the variable x. You may assume that the user enters exactly three digits for the input. (Hint: what are the magnitude only values for the bit patterns that represent the ASCII numeric symbols?)

6. What does 10011001 represent?

7. Suppose that account identification numbers are written using nine digits, for example, 972-54-5990. What C variable type should be used to store these? Why?

8. Money in the United States is valued according to dollars and cents, where dollars can have any nonnegative whole value and cents can have a whole value from 0 to 99. What C variable type should be used to store monetary values? Why?

9. What is the output of the following code?

```
unsigned char x,y,z;
x=15;
y=35;
z=133;
x=x|64;
y=y&3;
z=~z;
printf("%d %d %d\n",x,y,z);
```

10. What is the output of the following code?

```
int x=7;
x=(x|16)<<1;
printf("%d\n",x);
```

11. What is the output of the following code?

```
char i;
double d;
int t;
t=0;
for (i='z'; i>='w'; i--)
  for (d=1.0; d<=1.5; d+=0.1)
    if (d-1.3 > 0)
      t++;
printf("%d\n",t);
```

12. What is the output of the following code?

```
int i,j;
j=0;
for (i=1; i<100; i=i<<1)
  {
  if (i % 5 > 1)
    j=j | i;
  printf("%d %d\n",i,j);
  }
```

13. What is the output of the following code?

```
int i,j,k;
j=0;
k=32;
for (i=100; i>0; i-=10)
    {
    if (k/4 > 0)
        j=j | k;
    if (i <= 70  &&  i >= 40)
        k=k<<1;
    else
        k=k>>1;
    printf("%d %d %d\n",i,j,k);
    }
```

14. Using the sign-magnitude bit model, shifting to the left is the same as what simple mathematical operation? How about shifting to the right? (Hint: write out a few examples by hand, and look at both the binary and base 10 values.)

15. Write a program that lets a user manipulate bits individually in a 4-byte variable. The program should begin with all bits having a value of zero. The program should enter a loop where it prints out the current bit values as a single integer using the two's complement bit model. It should then prompt the user to either set a bit, clear a bit, or exit. If the user desires to set a bit or clear a bit, then the program should prompt the user for which bit, change the appropriate value, and then cycle back to the beginning of the loop. Setting a bit changes its value to 1 regardless of its current value; clearing a bit changes its value to 0 regardless of its current value.

16. Write a program that allows the user to perform simple arithmetic in binary. Upon starting, the program should tell the user that it is a binary math program, along with brief instructions on how to use the program. The program should then enter a loop, where it gives a prompt, such as "input:". Upon receiving input from the user, the program should process it, report the output result (or error), and loop back to the prompt. This should continue until the user gives the keyphrase to exit the program (the keyphrase is of your choosing; good choices are "quit", "end", "exit", etc.).

Input from the user should be of the form BSB, where B represents a binary number and S represents a mathematical symbol. There should be no spaces between the three parts (the two B's and the S). A binary number should consist of seven 0's and 1's, for example, 1101100. The bits represent sign-magnitude, not two's complement. The mathematical symbol should be from the set $+ - /$ * %. These symbols correspond to their natural use in the C language: addition, subtraction, division, multiplication, and modulus.

If the user inputs a binary number with more than seven digits, the program should report an error (and the error message should be meaningful). If the user inputs a mathematical symbol outside the expected set, the program should report an error. If the input provided by the user is not of the form BSB (e.g., if it is only SB, or only B), then the program should report an error. All error messages should be meaningful in their context, telling the user what was wrong with the input.

If a grammatically correct input is received, the program should convert the two binary numbers to base 10 and perform the given operation. The program should then convert the result back to binary and report it to the user. For example:

```
Input: 0000101+0001100
0010001
```

If the mathematical operation given by the user results in an answer requiring more than 7 bits to represent, the program should report an error message of bit overflow. If the mathematical operation given by the user is invalid (e.g., a divide by zero), the program should report a relevant error message.

17. Write a memory map for the following code. Show all values at the end of execution of the program.

```
#include <stdio.h>
main()
{
int i;
double d;
char s[10];
s[0]='f'; s[1]='r'; s[2]='o'; s[3]='g';
d=0.0;
for (i=0; i<4; i++)
  d=d+(double)(s[i]-'a');
}
```

3

Arrays and Strings

Beyond the four basic data types (char, int, float, double), the C language supports some advanced data constructs. These include arrays, strings, pointers and structures. Like the basic data types, each of these advanced data constructs is intended to store something different:

Data construct	Intended to store:
array	list of same-type values
string	text
pointer	address of another variable
structure	group of mixed-type values

An array is intended to group together a list of values, all of the same type, under one variable name. It is much easier to code computations on an array than on a list of independently named variables:

```
for (i=0; i<100; i++)      /* array coding */
    sum=sum+qty[i];


sum=qty1+qty2+qty3+...     /* without an array */
```

A structure is intended to group together an assortment of values of different types under a single variable name. Like an array, it makes it easier to code computations. A string is intended to group together a series of character symbols under one variable name. It is closely related to an array, but because it is intended only for text data, a number of functions have been crafted to perform text-specific operations on strings. A pointer is intended to hold the address of another variable, to provide a "gateway" or path of *indirect access* to the other variable. It is used most often in passing values between pieces of code (functions). This chapter examines arrays and strings; pointers and structures are discussed in the next chapter.

It is assumed that the reader is familiar with the basic syntax and use of arrays and strings (although this will be briefly reviewed). The first purpose of this chapter is to describe *how* arrays and strings work, by examining how they are constructed in memory. To accomplish this, we will use the memory map. An understanding of how each data construct resides in memory is useful for program design, and especially debugging. The second purpose of this chapter is to describe the functions provided by the C standard library that operate on string data. Once familiar with the concepts of strings, a programmer saves time and effort by using this system resource.

3.1 • Arrays

An array is a construct used to store a set of values using only one variable name. Each of the values occupies a *cell*. Every cell in the array is the same size, meaning it occupies the same amount of memory. The size of each cell is dictated by the data type (char, int, float, double) given in the variable declaration. The number of cells is also given in the variable declaration. Here are some examples:

```
int a[2];      /* 2 cells, each cell 4 bytes (32 bits) */
float b[3];    /* 3 cells, each cell 4 bytes (32 bits) */
double c[4];   /* 4 cells, each cell 8 bytes (64 bits) */
char d[5];     /* 5 cells, each cell 1 bytes (8 bits) */
```

Cells are accessed using *indices*, with syntax similar to that used in the variable declarations. For example:

```
a[0]=5;
b[1]=4.0;
c[2]=14.7;
d[4]='a';
```

The memory map for these code segments could be written as:

Label	Address	Value
a[0]	400–403	5
a[1]	404–407	
b[0]	408–411	
b[1]	412–415	4.0
b[2]	416–419	
c[0]	420–427	
c[1]	428–435	
c[2]	436–443	14.7
c[3]	444–451	
d[0]	452	
d[1]	453	
d[2]	454	
d[3]	455	
d[4]	456	'a'

Most of the cells in the arrays were not given values in this code example. Therefore their values are unknown. It is convenient to leave these entries blank in the memory map table. This does not mean that they do not have a value, just that their values are unknown (see Chapter 2).

When accessing an array, the index used should be from zero to one less than the total number of cells in the array. These are called the *array bounds*. However, the C language does not check to make sure that program code stays within the array bounds. It is possible to compile and execute code that goes outside the array bounds. For example, if we add the following code to that from above:

```
b[4]=15.9;
printf("%lf\n",b[4]);
```

Even though index 4 is past the array bounds for the variable b, the output of this code still produces the expected output:

```
15.900000
```

Why did it work? Looking at the memory map, one can see what happens. The four bytes after b[2] can be accessed using the name b[3]:

Out-of-bounds access	Label	Address	Value
	a[0]	400–403	5
	a[1]	404–407	
	b[0]	408–411	
	b[1]	412–415	4.0
	b[2]	416–419	
b[3] ? b[4] ?	c[0]	420–427	
b[5] ? b[6] ?	c[1]	428–435	
	c[2]	436–443	14.7
	c[3]	444–451	
	d[0]	452	
	d[1]	453	
	d[2]	454	
	d[3]	455	
	d[4]	456	'a'

In the memory map, these bytes occupy addresses 420–423 and are used by the variable c[0]. However, the C compiler allows a programmer to access them by "going off the end" of the b array. Past the array bounds, accesses simply move ahead the appropriate number of bytes. The next four bytes, at memory addresses 424–427, can be accessed using the name b[4]. These operations "work" because although they are accessing memory outside the array bounds, they are still accessing memory used by this program. Therefore, the program compiles and executes with seemingly correct output.

Of course, it is possible for an access outside the array bounds to *clobber* a variable. This happens when the out-of-bounds array access overwrites a value in another variable. In our example above, half the variable c[0] is clobbered by writing to b[3], and the other half of c[0] is clobbered by writing to b[4]. Encountering this error, a programmer will observe a variable to suddenly change value. Seemingly, no line of code in the program changes that variable's value, yet when displayed it has changed. This mistake often frustrates novice programmers. With some practice, one will recognize that it is likely the result of an out-of-bounds array access that has clobbered another variable.

It is also possible for an out-of-bounds array access to cause a program to crash. For example, consider adding the following code fragment to those from above:

```
b[33333]=15.9;
printf("%lf\n",b[33333]);
```

This code still compiles, but when executed produces a segmentation fault. This is because the out-of-bounds array access went far beyond the memory used by this program, and perhaps tried to access memory used by another program (or that was otherwise restricted). The operating system will recognize the problem and terminate the program, reporting a segmentation fault.

Faulty addressing can lead to another type of crash called a *bus error*. A bus error occurs when a program tries to access a memory address that is physically impossible (or nonexistant). A bus error can also occur on some systems when a program tries to address an "unaligned" address. This means that the program attempts to read multiple bytes that are not aligned with the width of the data bus (for example, on a 32-bit system the data bus is 4 bytes wide). If an error of this type happens, the operating system will recognize the problem and terminate the program, reporting a bus error.

Why does the C compiler allow out-of-bounds array accesses? The question is actually more complicated than it seems. Not all arrays have a fixed, known size. Sometimes a programmer needs to decide on the size of an array after a program has been compiled and is executing. Sometimes a programmer needs an array to change size while a program is executing. These needs make it impossible for the C compiler to know, in all cases, if an array access is out-of-bounds. The answer may not be known until the program is running and reaches the code that accesses the array.

3.1.1 Multidimensional Arrays

Arrays in C can have more than one dimension. But computer memory is all arranged in one-dimensional order, as though it were one long street of bytes. How then are multidimensional arrays stored in computer memory? Does a computing system have some other strange, multidimensional space for use only by these arrays? Of course not. The answer is that the cells in the multidimensional array are listed out, one at a time, in one-dimensional order. For example, consider the following code:

```
int a[3][2];
a[0][1]=7;
a[1][0]=13;
```

The memory map for this code could be written as:

Label	Address	Value
a[0][0]	400–403	
a[0][1]	404–407	7
a[1][0]	408–411	13
a[1][1]	412–415	
a[2][0]	416–419	
a[2][1]	420–423	

There are a total of six cells in this array. They are listed in order by cycling through the range on the rightmost index, incrementing the next index to the left when done. The same procedure works for any number of dimensions. For example, consider the following code for a three-dimensional array:

```
int b[2][3][4];
b[0][2][0]=7;
b[1][0][2]=13;
```

There are 24 cells in this array, occupying a total of 96 bytes. The memory map for this code could be written as:

Label	Address	Value	Label	Address	Value
b[0][0][0]	400–403		b[1][0][0]	448–451	
b[0][0][1]	404–407		b[1][0][1]	452–455	
b[0][0][2]	408–411		b[1][0][2]	456–459	13
b[0][0][3]	412–415		b[1][0][3]	460–463	
b[0][1][0]	416–419		b[1][1][0]	464–467	
b[0][1][1]	420–423		b[1][1][1]	468–471	
b[0][1][2]	424–427		b[1][1][2]	472–475	
b[0][1][3]	428–431		b[1][1][3]	476–479	
b[0][2][0]	432–435	7	b[1][2][0]	480–483	
b[0][2][1]	436–439		b[1][2][1]	484–487	
b[0][2][2]	440–443		b[1][2][2]	488–491	
b[0][2][3]	444–447		b[1][2][3]	492–495	

The order of incrementing dimension indices is similar to how base 10 numbers are counted, cycling through the one's digit before incrementing the ten's digit, then cycling through the ten's digit before incrementing the hundred's digit, and so on.

Everything stored in computer memory is somehow stretched out in one-dimensional order. Things not typically viewed as one-dimensional, such as images, video, databases, maps, and three-dimensional models are all actually stored by listing out the data in one-dimensional order. We will revisit this principle in Section 5.4 when we look at files.

3.2 • Strings

A string is a specific type of array: it is an array of char, containing a sequence of values where a value of '\0' signifies the end of the string. Although the array could be of any size, it is assumed that the valid data in the array starts at the first cell, and ends with the first cell having a value of '\0'. For example:

```
char d[8];
d[0]='H'; d[1]='e'; d[2]='l'; d[3]='l'; d[4]='o';
d[5]='\0';  /* '\0' indicates the end of string */
```

The memory map for this code could be written as:

Label	Address	Value
d[0]	400	'H'
d[1]	401	'e'
d[2]	402	'l'
d[3]	403	'l'
d[4]	404	'o'
d[5]	405	'\0'
d[6]	406	
d[7]	407	

Although the array has eight cells, only the first six are used. The cell containing the '\0' character is not seen during either printing or the scanning of input. It is a *nonprintable* character[1] used to control how text data is processed. Any code working on a string is supposed to stop processing the array when the '\0'

---

1. The slash-symbol pair within the single quotes is called an *escape sequence* or *control sequence* and is used to represent the nonprintable character because there is no single visible symbol to represent the action.

character is reached. It is assumed that the values in the remaining cells (two in this case) are not used.

The value of the '\0' character is zero. '\0' is simply another way of saying zero. It is used to specify a specific "type" of zero. For example, it is informative to use a different zero for a whole number (0) than for a real number (0.0) to show that they are representing slightly different information. '\0' is a way to say zero for a char representing an ASCII symbol that means end of string. Zero has another alias called NULL. NULL is usually used to indicate a value of zero for an address (discussed further in Chapter 4), but it is sometimes used for the end of string character. Any of these aliases can be used; they all result in the same bit pattern being placed in the cell, which is all zeros. For example, all of the following lines of code are equally valid and do the exact same thing:

```
d[5]='\0';        /* ASCII zero */
d[5]=0;           /* integer zero */
d[5]=(char)NULL; /* address zero */
```

The basic functions for reading string input from the keyboard and for writing string output to the screen are scanf() and printf(), respectively. Just as each basic data type has its own % identifier (char uses %c, int uses %i or %d, float uses %f, double uses %lf), a string uses %s. The %s identifier makes it simpler for a programmer to print out a string. How does it work? Consider the following code to print out the example from above:

```
printf("%c%c%c%c%c\n",d[0],d[1],d[2],d[3],d[4]);
```

This brute force approach is tedious; code must be written to specifically print out each character, and we must know exactly how many are to be printed. The %s identifier tells printf() to assume the variable is an array of char, ending with a value of zero, and to print each byte using the ASCII bit model. Using this identifier, we can rewrite the printf() as follows:

```
printf("%s\n",d);
```

Notice that there are no indices given for the variable d in the printf() when using the %s identifier. The printf() is given the variable name d, not d[0] through d[4]. We can explain this using the memory map:

Address label	Label	Address	Value
d	d[0]	400	'H'
	d[1]	401	'e'
	d[2]	402	'l'
	d[3]	403	'l'

Label	Address	Value
d[4]	404	'o'
d[5]	405	0
d[6]	406	
d[7]	407	

The variable name d is a label for an address rather than for a value. It identifies address 400. Given that address, the printf() function will print out bytes until it encounters a value of zero. Thus, it will print out the bytes at addresses 400–404, and upon seeing a value of zero at address 405, it stops. What if we were to code the following?

```
printf("%s\n",d[0]);  /* what does this do? */
```

This code does not make any sense. It seemingly asks printf() to print character symbols, starting with the value 'H'. But which 'H'? How is printf() supposed to know that the programmer intended printing to start with the specific 'H' at address 400? In fact, this code will crash. It asks printf() to start printing bytes at "address 'H'", which causes a segmentation fault.

When reading input using the scanf() function, the & symbol is required in front of the variable name for the basic data types (char, int, float, and double). However, it is not required for a string. For example:

```
int x;
float f;
char s[6];
scanf("%d",&x);
scanf("%f",&f);
scanf("%s",s);
```

This can be explained by looking at the memory map:

Address label(s)	Label	Address	Value
&x	x	400–403	
&f	f	404–407	
&(s[0]) s	s[0]	408	
	s[1]	409	
	s[2]	410	
	s[3]	411	
	s[4]	412	
	s[5]	413	

The variable names x and f each refer to the values stored for those variables. Similarly, s[0] through s[7] refer to values. The syntax &x is used to identify the address of x, which is 400. The syntax &f identifies the address of f, which is 404, and &(s[0]) identifies the address of s[0], which is 408. The variable name s is simply a shorthand for writing &(s[0]). The nature of the operation involving the %s identifier in scanf() is to store a series of characters, ending it with a value of zero. This is why it must be given an address, where the storing of characters is to start.

3.2.1   Multidimensional Strings

One of the common uses for multidimensional arrays is to store a list of strings. Since each string is a one-dimensional array, a list of strings requires a two-dimensional array. For example:

```
char n[2][4];
n[0][0]='T'; n[0][1]='o'; n[0][2]='m'; n[0][3]=0;
n[1][0]='S'; n[1][1]='u'; n[1][2]='e'; n[1][3]=0;
```

The memory map for this code can be written as:

Address label(s)			Label	Address	Value
&(n[0][0])	n[0]	n	n[0][0]	400	'T'
			n[0][1]	401	'o'
			n[0][2]	402	'm'
			n[0][3]	403	0
&(n[1][0])	n[1]		n[1][0]	404	'S'
			n[1][1]	405	'u'
			n[1][2]	406	'e'
			n[1][3]	407	0

Each string in the two-dimensional array can be referenced using the address label for the one-dimensional array that stores it. For example, the following code prints out the two strings:

```
printf("%s %s\n",n[0],n[1]);
```

Both n[0] and n[1] identify addresses (400 and 404, respectively). In the case of a multidimensional array, the variable name by itself provides a third alias for the starting address of the entire array. In this example, &(n[0][0]), n[0], and n all refer to the same thing, the address 400.

3.3 • String Library Functions

There are a handful of calculations that are common to a large number of text processing problems. These calculations include finding the length of a string and comparing the contents of two strings. Because they are so common, the C standard library has evolved to include functions to perform these calculations. In Chapter 8 (Section 8.3) we take a deeper look at the C standard library, which contains functions for a variety of purposes; in this section, we are concerned only with the portion of the library involved in text processing. Even that portion of the library includes dozens of functions.[2] However, there are five functions that cover the most common calcuations and operations:

Function	What it does
strlen()	count the total characters in the string
strcmp()	compare two strings, determine if identical
strcpy()	copy one string into another string variable
strcat()	append one string to another string
sprintf()	print formatted output into a string variable

The following sections examine each of these functions from the perspective of memory. Studying the operations at the memory level is a good way to approach many text processing problems and is particularly helpful when tackling problems outside the scope of the string library functions.

3.3.1 String Length: strlen()

Suppose we wish to count the number of characters in a string. For example:

String	Length
"Hello"	5
"H.i;"	4
"h e y"	5

We can calculate the length of a string using the following code:

---

2. For a complete listing, consult a reference such as *C: A Reference Manual*, 5th ed., S. P. Harbison and G. L. Steele, Prentice Hall, 2002.

```
int length;
char s[6];
s[0]='S'; s[1]='u'; s[2]='e'; s[3]='\0';
length=0;
while (s[length] != '\0')
    length++;
```

The memory map during execution of this code may be written as:

Label	Address	Value
length	400–403	Ø 1 2 3
s[0]	404	'S'
s[1]	405	'u'
s[2]	406	'e'
s[3]	407	'\0'
s[4]	408	
s[5]	409	

Notice how the '\0' value is used to control the calculation. Upon reaching it, the calculation ends. This type of value is sometimes called a *sentinel* or a *flag*. The value of a sentinel is not intended to be used in a computation; rather, it is intended to terminate the processing of a list of data. Sentinels are used in many computational problems besides text processing.

The same calculation can be performed by calling the strlen() function:

```
length=strlen(s);
```

It does not save us a lot of code for this one calculation (1 line versus 3 lines of code). However, after having written code for the same calculation a few hundred (or thousand) times, the savings add up. In addition, calling the same function prevents accidentally inserting an error into the calculation. Even experienced programmers can make mistakes, and the benefit of using proven code can save the time it takes to track down bugs.

3.3.2   String Compare: strcmp()

Suppose we wish to compare two strings to determine if they are the same. Further, if they are different, we desire to know which string first reaches an index having a value less then the same index in the other string. For example:

Strings	Comparison (meaning)
"Hello" vs. "Hello"	0 (same)
"Hello" vs. "Hellp"	−1 (first string smaller)
"Hey" vs. "Hallo"	1 (second sting smaller)
"Hillo" vs. "Hi"	1 (second sting smaller)

We can compare two strings using the following code:

```
int i,a;
char s[4],t[4];
s[0]='S'; s[1]='u'; s[2]='e'; s[3]='\0';
t[0]='S'; t[1]='u'; t[2]='n'; t[3]='\0';


i=0; a=0;
while (a == 0)
  {
  if (s[i] < t[i]) a=-1;
  if (s[i] > t[i]) a=1;
  if (s[i] == '\0'  ||  t[i] == '\0')
    break;
  i++;
  }
```

The memory map during execution of this code may be written as:

Label	Address	Value
i	400–403	Ø *1* *2* 3
a	404–407	Ø −1
s[0]	408	'S'
s[1]	409	'u'
s[2]	410	'e'
s[3]	411	'\0'
t[0]	412	'S'
t[1]	413	'u'
t[2]	414	'n'
t[3]	415	'\0'

The loop compares the values in the cells at the same indices of the two strings (s[0] to t[0], s[1] to t[1], etc.) until it finds an index where the values are different, or until it reaches the end of one of the strings. The comparison result is stored in a. If the strings are the same, the comparison result is 0. If the first string is less than the second, the result is −1; if the first string is greater than the second, the result is 1. This provides an alphabetical comparison, so long as the case of the letters is equivalent. For our example, since "Sue" is less than "Sun," the comparison result is −1.

The same calculation can be performed by calling the strcmp() function:

```
a=strcmp(s,t);
```

This saves us slightly more code than the strlen() function, but like strlen(), its real value lies in repeated use.

3.3.3 String Copy: strcpy()

Suppose we wish to copy the contents of a string to a second string variable. The following code accomplishes this task:

```
int i;
char s[4],t[4];
s[0]='S'; s[1]='u'; s[2]='e'; s[3]='\0';
i=0;
while (s[i] != '\0')
    {
    t[i]=s[i];
    i++;
    }
t[i]='\0';
```

The memory map during execution of this code may be written as:

Label	Address	Value
i	400-403	Ø 1 2 3
s[0]	404	'S'
s[1]	405	'u'
s[2]	406	'e'
s[3]	407	'\0'
t[0]	408	'S'
t[1]	409	'u'

t[2]	410	'e'
t[3]	411	'\0'

Notice that the loop will not copy the '\0' character. It must be added to the new string separately after the loop is completed. This is a common programming mistake. Without the '\0' character, any processing of the new string will be erroneous. Any code or function processing that string will continue until it finds a zero byte somewhere in memory (which could cause a crash or other problem).

The same calculation can be performed by calling the strcpy() function:

```
strcpy(t,s);
```

The source string comes second in the argument list; the destination string comes first.

3.3.4   String Concatenate: strcat()

Suppose we wish to append a string (the addendum) to the end of another string (the original). For example:

Original	Addendum	Result
"Hi"	" there"	"Hi there"
"Sun"	"ny"	"Sunny"
"a"	".out"	"a.out"

We can concatenate two strings using the following code:

```
int i,j;
char s[8],t[4];
s[0]='S'; s[1]='u'; s[2]='\0';
t[0]='s'; t[1]='a'; t[2]='n'; t[3]='\0';
i=strlen(s);
j=0;
while (t[j] != '\0')
{
s[i+j]=t[j];
j++;
}
s[i+j]='\0';
```

The memory map during execution of this code may be written as:

Label	Address	Value
i	400–403	2
j	404–407	0 1 2 3
s[0]	408	'S'
s[1]	409	'u'
s[2]	410	0 's'
s[3]	411	'a'
s[4]	412	'n'
s[5]	413	0
s[6]	414	
s[7]	415	
t[0]	416	's'
t[1]	417	'a'
t[2]	418	'n'
t[3]	419	0

In this example, we make use of another string library function (`strlen()`) to accomplish the task. It is common to see library functions that make use of other functions (or even other libraries). We will look at this principle in Chapter 8 when we examine libraries in general. In this example, we also had to explicitly add the `'\0'` character at the end of the result so that the string remains valid for further processing.

The same calculation can be performed by calling the `strcat()` function:

```
strcat(s,t);
```

The original string comes first in the argument list; the addendum string comes second. The result is placed in the original string variable.

3.3.5 String Print: sprintf()

The `sprintf()` function works just like the `printf()` function, except that the output "prints" into a string variable. This can be useful for converting numeric data types into ASCII text, or for creating long strings from multiple components. For example:

```
char a[24];
float f;
int i;
```

```
f=3.72;
i=9;
sprintf(a,"Price %f, qty %d",f,i);
printf("%s\n",a);
```

The output of this code is:

```
Price 3.720000, qty 9
```

The memory map for this code is revealing; it highlights the difference between text-storage and value-storage of numbers:

Label	Address	Value	Label	Address	Value
a[0]	400	'P'	a[13]	413	'0'
a[1]	401	'r'	a[14]	414	','
a[2]	402	'i'	a[15]	415	' '
a[3]	403	'c'	a[16]	416	'q'
a[4]	404	'e'	a[17]	417	't'
a[5]	405	' '	a[18]	418	'y'
a[6]	406	'3'	a[19]	419	' '
a[7]	407	'.'	a[20]	420	'9'
a[8]	408	'7'	a[21]	421	0
a[9]	409	'2'	a[22]	422	
a[10]	410	'0'	a[23]	423	
a[11]	411	'0'	f	424–427	3.72
a[12]	412	'0'	i	428–431	9

How many bytes does it take to store each of the numbers as a numeric value (float or int) versus as text?

3.3.6 String Functions Example

The following code demonstrates several of the string functions just covered, together in a complete program:

```
#include <stdio.h>     /* for printf(), scanf() */
#include <string.h>    /* for strlen(), strcmp() */
main()
{
char    look[80],test[80];
```

```
printf("Look for: ");
scanf("%s",look);
while (1)
  {
  printf("Enter a string (0 to quit): ");
  scanf("%s",test);
  if (strcmp(test,"0") == 0)
    break;
  if (strlen(test) < strlen(look))
    printf("%s is too short for %s\n",test,look);
  else if (strcmp(test,look) == 0)
    printf("Found one!\n");
  else if (strncmp(test,look,3) == 0)
    printf("Started the same...\n");
  else
    printf("Not what we're looking for\n");
  }
}
```

Compiling and executing the code, we obtain the following (the text given at each input was selected to demonstrate the various functions):

```
Look for: sun
Enter a string (0 to quit): s
s is too short for sun
Enter a string (0 to quit): sun
Found one!
Enter a string (0 to quit): sunny
Started the same...
Enter a string (0 to quit): sleet
Not what we're looking for
Enter a string (0 to quit): 0
```

The last function call, strncmp(), is a variant on strcmp(). It takes a third argument indicating how many characters (three in this example) are to be compared. If no difference is found between the two strings after that many characters have been compared, then the function returns zero. Otherwise, the strncmp() function works exactly the same as the original strcmp() function. There are similar variants on the strcpy() and strcat() functions, called strncpy() and strncat().

3.3.7 Nonlibrary Problems

A naive programmer can become too reliant upon the string library functions. Not every text processing problem is easily solved through use of the library functions. For many problems, individual character processing of string data must be coded. This section demonstrates an example.

Suppose we want to remove all occurrences of the letter 'a' from a string, compressing characters to fill any created gaps. For example:

Original	Result
"Saturday"	"Sturdy"
"a ball"	" bll"

There is no single function within the C standard library that will accomplish this task. Instead, we must write code to process the string at the character level. The following code accomplishes 'a'-removal:

```
int i,j;
char s[6];
s[0]='a'; s[1]='b'; s[2]='a'; s[3]='c'; s[4]=0;
i=0; j=0;
while (s[i] != 0)
    {
    if (s[i] != 'a')
        {
        s[j]=s[i];
        j++;
        }
    i++;
    }
s[j]=0;
```

The memory map during execution of this code may be written as:

Label	Address	Value
i	400–403	0̸ 1 2 3 4
j	404–407	0̸ 1 2
s[0]	408	'a̸' 'b'
s[1]	409	'b̸' 'c'	(continued)

Label	Address	Value
s[2]	410	'a' 0
s[3]	411	'c'
s[4]	412	0
s[5]	413	

A serious programmer should be well-versed in the common string processing functions of the C standard library and should use them when appropriate. However, any serious programmer must also be able to process strings at the character level, in order to accomplish the given task. Studying the problem at the memory level is often a good approach. Writing out one or two examples in memory, especially those involving the trickiest cases, will often facilitate code design and debugging.

3.4 • Command Line Arguments

As discussed in Chapter 1, a command line argument is anything typed at the shell prompt after the name of the program to execute. Command line arguments are typically used to provide information about how the user wishes to run a program. For example:

```
ahoover@video> ls -l -t
drwxr-xr-x  26 ahoover  fusion    4096 Jul 20 16:03 ece222/
drwxr-xr-x   7 ahoover  325       4096 Jul 19 17:01 public_html/
drwx------   2 ahoover  fusion    4096 Feb  7 14:33 mail/
drwxr-xr-x   3 ahoover  fusion    4096 Dec 14  2005 ece854/
drwxr-xr-x   3 ahoover  fusion    4096 Dec 14  2005 ece429/
drwxr-xr-x   2 ahoover  fusion    4096 Mar 19  2005 ece893/
drwxr-xr-x   3 ahoover  fusion    4096 Mar 19  2005 ece468/
drwxr-xr-x  15 ahoover  fusion    4096 Dec 14  2005 Projects/
ahoover@video>
```

The command line argument -l tells the program ls to provide a long listing in its output. The command line argument -t causes the output to be sorted according to time last modified. This example shows two command line arguments; it is possible to have any number. They must be separated from each other by one or more spaces.

How is a program made aware of its command line arguments? When executed, into what variables are the values for the command line arguments placed? The answer lies in the full function declaration for main():

```
int main(int argc, char *argv[])
```

The variable argc stores the number of command line arguments, including the name of the program. For the example ls -l -t, this equals 3. The variable argv stores a list of strings, one string per command line argument. Although the declaration for argv looks strange, including a pointer symbol and an empty pair of array brackets, it can be accessed just like a two-dimensional array. For example, the following code prints out all the command line arguments, one character at a time:

```
int i,j;
for (i=0; i<argc; i++)
  {
  j=0;
  while (argv[i][j] != '\0')
    {
    printf("%c",argv[i][j]);
    j++;
    }
  printf("\n");
  }
```

The partial memory map for argc and argv, based on our example, may be written as follows:

Address label(s)		Label	Address	Value
&(argc)		argc	400–403	3
&(argv[0][0])	argv[0]	argv[0][0]	404	'l'
&(argv[0][1])		argv[0][1]	405	's'
&(argv[0][2])		argv[0][2]	406	'\0'
&(argv[1][0])	argv[1]	argv[1][0]	407	'-'
&(argv[1][1])		argv[1][1]	408	'l'
&(argv[1][2])		argv[1][2]	409	'\0'
&(argv[2][0])	argv[2]	argv[2][0]	410	'-'
&(argv[2][1])		argv[2][1]	411	't'
&(argv[2][2])		argv[2][2]	412	'\0'

Each string can be accessed through its own address label, so that the code example just given can be simplified as follows:

```
for (i=0; i<argc; i++)
  printf("%s\n",argv[i]);
```

Although the variable argv can be accessed as though it were a two-dimensional array, it actually occupies memory a little differently. Using pointers, what we have been calling the "address labels" in this chapter are given their own storage locations. This is a primary subject of the next chapter.

Questions and Exercises

1. Write a memory map for the following code. Show all values at the end of execution of the program.

```
#include <stdio.h>
main()
{
int i,j,k,swap;
char c[8];

c[0]='f'; c[1]='r'; c[2]='o'; c[3]='g'; c[4]=0;
for (i=0; i<4; i++)
  {
  k=i;
  for (j=i+1; j<4; j++)
    if (c[j]-c[k] < 10)
      k=j;
  swap=c[i];
  c[i]=c[k];
  c[k]=swap;
  }
}
```

2. Write a memory map for the following code. Show all values at the end of execution of the program.

```
#include <stdio.h>
main()
{
```

```
int a[4],i;
float b[3];
char c[3];
double d[4];

b[2]=6.7;
for (a[0]=2; a[0]>0; a[0]--)
  b[a[0]-1]=b[a[0]]+2.3;
c[1]='N';
d[0]=12.6;
for (i=1; i<3; i++)
  d[i]=d[0]+(double)b[i];
}
```

3. Consider the following variable declarations. Assume each variable stores the values in a matrix. Write code that multiplies the matrix a by the matrix b and stores the result in the matrix c.

```
float  a[2][3],b[3][2],c[2][2];
```

4. Write a memory map for the following code. Show all values at the end of execution of the program.

```
#include <stdio.h>
main()
{
int  x[2][3][2];
int i,j,k;

for (i=0; i<3; i++)
  for (j=0; j<2; j++)
    x[0][i][j]=i*3+j;
for (k=0; k<2; k++)
  for (j=0; j<2; j++)
    x[1][k][j]=x[0][j][k]-1;
}
```

5. Consider the following code:

```
int i,j,t;
char name[50];
printf("What is your name? ");
scanf("%s",name);
t=0;
```

```
for (i=0; i<strlen(name); i++)
   for (j='a'; j<=name[i]; j++)
      t++;
printf("%d\n",t);
```

If the user types "dad" (not including the quotes—just the three letters dad followed by the [ENTER] key) at the prompt, what is the output?

6. Consider the following program:

```
#include <stdio.h>
main()
{
char s[10],t[10];
int i,j;

strcpy(s,"frog");
for (i=0; i<strlen(s); i++)
   t[i]=s[i];
j=0;
for (i=0; i<strlen(t); i++)
   j=j+(int)t[i];
printf("%d\n",j);
```

The expected output of the program is 430, but it often produces a different result. The result seems to change depending on when the program is run, or on which computer it is run. Why?

7. Write code to split an input string (variable "name") into two output strings (variables "first" and "last"). Assume that the user provides input containing only the characters a through z and A through Z. Assume there are exactly two capital letters in the input, one at the beginning of the first name, and one at the beginning of the last name. For example, given the input "JoeSmith", your code should split it into "Joe" and "Smith". Your code should use the following lines:

```
char name[50],first[25],last[25];
printf("What is your name? ");
scanf("%s",name);
```

8. Write a complete program that prompts the user for an input string, sorts its characters, and prints out the sorted output. Assume the string contains no spaces and is at most 30 characters. Sort the characters according to byte values, irrespective of the symbols those values represent, from smallest to largest. The

output should be one contiguous string, printed on one line. Example: "Input: apple" should print "aelpp".

9. What is the output of the following code?

```
double d[4][3];
int i,j;

for (i=0; i<4; i++)
  for (j=0; j<3; j++)
    if (j == 0)
      d[i][j]=(double)i /10.0;
    else
      d[i][j]=d[i][j-1]+(double)i*2.0;
printf("%lf\n",d[3][2]);
```

10. Write code to "de-vowel" an input string. Assume that the user provides input containing only the characters a through z (and all lowercase). Your code should create an output string that deletes all vowels from the input string, pushing the letters together to fill any gaps. For example, given the input "theturtleandthe-hare" your code should print out "thtrtlndthhr".

Your program should create an output string from the input string, before presenting its output, and should include the following lines:

```
char input[80],output[80];
printf("Enter a string: ");
scanf("%s",input);
```

11. Write out the memory map for the following code, providing all values at the end of execution. Assume the user enters 8654115 at the prompt. How many total bytes does this code declare for variables?

```
main()
{
char    x[3][8];
int     j,length;
float   number;
double  avg;

for (j=0; j<3; j++)
  if (j == 0)
  {
    printf("Enter input string: ");
    scanf("%s",x[0]);
```

```
        length=strlen(x[0]);
        }
    else if (j == 1)
        {
        x[0][0]='9'; x[1][0]='7'; x[2][0]='5';
        number=(float)(x[0][0]+x[2][0]);
        }
    else
        avg=(double)(x[0][0]+x[1][0])/2.0;
    }
```

12. Write a complete program that prompts a user for a filename and then prints out only the suffix of the filename. Assume the filename will take the form of "filename.suffix"—where both the filename and the suffix will contain one or more characters each, and the period will always be present to demarcate the boundary.

13. Write a program that looks at all the command line arguments and reports if any of the arguments are the same (i.e., they match exactly). The program should print out the matching argument and the positions it occupies in the list of arguments.

14. Write a program that accepts up to six arguments at the command line prompt. The program should print the first character of any odd-numbered arguments (numbers 0, 2, and 4), and the second character of any even-numbered arguments (numbers 1, 3, and 5). The characters printed should be separated by spaces. The program should inform the user of the correct program usage if fewer than two or more than six arguments are provided. Assume each argument contains at least two characters. For example:

```
ahoover@video> myprog arg1 200 list all arg5
m r 2 i a r
ahoover@video>
```

15. Write a program that allows the user to perform pseudo arithmetic on a string. Upon starting, the program should tell the user that it is a string math program, along with brief instructions on how to use the program. The program should then enter a loop, where it gives a prompt, such as "input:". Upon receiving input from the user, the program should process it, report the output result (or error), and loop back to the prompt. This should continue until the user gives the keyphrase to exit the program (the keyphrase is of your choosing, good choices are "quit", "end", "exit", etc.).

Input from the user should be of the form SOS, where S represents a string and O represents a mathematical symbol. There should be no spaces between the three parts (the two S's and the O). A string should consist of from one to nine lowercase letters. The mathematical symbol should be from the set + - / *. These symbols correspond to their natural use in the C language: addition, subtraction, division, and multiplication.

If the user inputs a string containing symbols outside the lowercase letters, or if the string has more than nine characters, the program should report an error. If the user inputs a mathematical symbol outside the expected set, the program should report an error. If the input provided by the user is not of the form SOS—for example, if it is only SO, or only S—then the program should report an error. The error messages can be generic; they do not have to describe specifically what the user did wrong.

If a grammatically correct input is entered, the program should convert the two strings to integer arrays and perform the given operation on each cell independently. The resulting array should then be converted back to a string, and displayed to the user. For example:

```
Input> abc+aab
abc + aab => bce
```

The output must be exactly in that format, showing the two strings and mathematical symbol separated by spaces, to demonstrate that the program has correctly subdivided the input into its three parts.

The mathematical operations should work as follows. Each character should be converted to an integer in the range 1–26 (a is 1, b is 2, c is 3, . . . , z is 26). The operation should then be performed using integer math. If the result is inside the range 1–26, then the output character should be the corresponding lowercase letter. If the result is outside the range 1–26, then the output character should be the uppercase version of the input character from the first string. For example:

```
Input> wxy+bbb
wxy + bbb => yzY
```

If the two input strings are not the same length, then each output character beyond the length of the shorter string should be a copy of the character from the longer string. For example:

```
Input> xyz+a
xyz + a => yyz
```

Finally, here are some additional examples to clarify all expected operations. These do not necessarily encompass all checks for errors, or all the cases that need to be tested.

Example input	Correct output
abc-aa	Aac
dog*cat	loG
turtle/frog	caable
Frog+turtle	bad input
bird/tiger	BabDr
emu+zebra	Erwra

This lab should be done entirely without string functions. Avoid any usage of strlen(), strcpy(), strcmp(), and the related functions.

16. Write a program that allows the user to spell check an ASCII text file. The program should read in a dictionary of words from the plain ASCII file linux.words (usually found in /usr/share/dict, depending on your system's installation of ispell) and store it in a suitable array. The program should then read words, one at a time, from the user-given input file. Each word should be compared to the dictionary. If an exact match is found, the program should continue to the next word. If no exact match is found, then the program should begin searching for suitable suggestions for replacement.

The search for replacement words should work as follows. Let N be the length of the original input word, minus 1. Starting with that value of N, the program should search for any exact matches of the first N characters of the input word with any words in the dictionary, and add them to a suggestion list. Following that, the program should search for any exact matches of an N substring anywhere inside the input word, as compared to anywhere inside a dictionary word. Decrease the value of N by 1, and repeat. This process should stop when 10 words have been suggested, or when N reaches 0.

The program should provide the list of suggestions to the user through a simple text menu. One option in that menu should be to keep the original word.

Either upon verifying that the original word is found in the dictionary, or upon the user selecting a replacement, the program should write the appropriate word to an output file. The program should discover the names of both the input file and the output file from command line arguments. The program should check to make sure that the appropriate number of command line arguments is given by the user and, if not, report an error along with the proper usage of the program.

The program does not have to be concerned with spacing or arrangement between words. Words can be output one per line, for example, even though that does not match how they were arranged in the input file. The program does not need to handle punctuation characters and can disregard them while checking spelling.

is given by the user, and if not, report an error along with the proper usage of the program.

The program does not have to be concerned with spacing or arrangement between words. Words can be output one per line, for example, even though that does not match how they were arranged in the input file. The program does not need to handle punctuation characters and can disregard them while checking spelling.

4

Pointers and Structures

In the last chapter, we used the memory map to study how arrays and strings work. Writing out a memory map is often useful during program design. During debugging, it can be invaluable. In this chapter, we extend these ideas to pointers and structures. All variables have an address in memory, much the same way that all houses and businesses have a street address in the real world. However, the organization of buildings and streets becomes clearer by looking at a map. It tends to be easier to explore an unknown city or to reach a destination using a map. In much the same way, it tends to be easier to design code for a problem involving pointers or to debug the code using a memory map. Pointers (and to some degree, structures) can be the most difficult tool to master in the C programming language. The goal of this chapter is to increase the proficiency of the reader with these tools through a deeper understanding of how they work.

4.1 • Pointers

A pointer is a construct used to store an address of a variable. We declare a variable to be a pointer-type variable by preceding its name with the asterisk symbol (*). For example:

```
char c,*cp;
int i,*ip;
float f,*fp;
double d,*dp;
```

The variables c, i, f, and d are normal variables, each holding a different type of value. The variables cp, ip, fp, and dp are all pointers, each holding an address.

How big is each of these variables? From previous chapters, we know that a char is 1 byte, an int and a float are 4 bytes each (although they use the bits differently), and a double is 8 bytes. How many bytes does a pointer use?

To answer that question, consider what a pointer holds: an address. A pointer needs enough bits to store all the possible addresses on the computing system. How many addresses are there? At the time of this writing, a common computing system can have a maximum of 4 GB of memory. It takes 32 bits to store roughly 4 billion different addresses, one for each byte of memory. In fact, this is precisely why such a computing system is limited to 4 GB of memory; it is because it has a 32-bit address bus connecting the CPU to memory. Throughout this book,[1] we have been assuming a 32-bit architecture to explain memory concepts.

Knowing how many bytes a pointer variable requires, we can now draw a memory map for our example above:

Label	Address	Value
c	400	
cp	401–404	
i	405–408	
ip	409–412	
f	413–416	
fp	417–420	
d	421–428	
dp	429–432	

An address is an address, regardless of what resides at that address. All addresses require 4 bytes. Therefore all pointers, regardless of the type of variable "pointed to," require 4 bytes.

The use of pointer variables involves two symbols: & and *. The ampersand symbol (&) indicates the "address of" a variable, and the asterisk symbol (*) indicates "at the address given by" a variable. For example:

```
cp=&c;
ip=&i;
*ip=42;
```

The memory map for this code can be filled in as follows:

Label	Address	Value
c	400	
cp	401–404	400
i	405–408	42
ip	409–412	405
f	413–416	
fp	417–420	
d	421–428	
dp	429–432	

The first two lines store the addresses of the variables c and i into the pointer variables cp and ip. The last line looks at the address stored in ip, which is 405, and places the value 42 at that address. Address 405 is where the variable i resides, so in effect i is the variable with a new value.

A pointer can hold the address of any variable, including a cell in an array. For example:

```
char ca[3],*cp;
ca[1]=3;
cp=&(ca[1]);
*cp=7;
```

The memory map for this code may be written as:

Label	Address	Value
ca[0]	400	
ca[1]	401	3̶ 7
ca[2]	402	
cp	403–406	401

When writing code using multiple symbols, it is a good practice to use parentheses to emphasize the order of operations. Although it is possible to write &ca[1], and it means the same thing as &(ca[1]), the latter is preferable because of its clarity. This becomes increasingly true as variables are used in greater complexity. An advanced programmer may not need to be reminded of the order of operations, but including the parentheses never hurts.

An address can be printed out using the printf() function in a few different ways. Since it is a 4-byte whole number, it can be printed as an int (using %i or %d), but this interprets the highest bit as a sign bit, so that the value may be negative. It is easier to read if it is printed as an unsigned int (using %u) so that the number is always positive. The printf() function also provides the %p identifier for pointers, to display the address in hexadecimal. For example:

```
char a,*b;
a=7; b=&a;
printf("%d %u %p  value=%d\n",b,b,b,*b);
```

The output of this code is as follows:

```
-1073764873 3221202423 0xbfffa5f7  value=7
```

The unsigned base 10 display of an address is often the easiest to read, but the hexadecimal display of an address is sometimes preferred because it is the easiest to translate to binary (each hexadecimal digit converts to four binary digits). Notice that the address, in unsigned base 10, is a much larger number than the range we have been using (the 400's). For purposes of code design, it is convenient to use small numbers for addresses when writing a memory map, but during debugging, it may be necessary to work with large actual address values like these.

4.1.1   Pointer Arithmetic

There are two different uses for the * symbol,[2] one during variable *declaration*, and one during variable *usage*. This can lead to some confusion. The distinction is that in the first case, the * symbol is indicating the variable type (pointer), while in the second case, the * symbol is using the pointer to place a value at another address. It is natural to ask why we use the complicated notation

```
char *cp;
```

to declare a variable, instead of something simple like

```
pointer cp;
```

After all, if we have keywords to define the four basic data types, why not a keyword to define this "fifth data type" that stores an address? The answer is pointer arithmetic. When adding or subtracting amounts from an address, pointer arithmetic acts in quantities of bytes equal to the size of the thing referenced. For example, consider the following code:

---

2. Of course, the * symbol is also used for multiplication; here we are strictly talking about pointers.

```
char ca[3],*cp;
int ia[3],*ip;
cp=&(ca[0]);
ip=&(ia[0]);
```

The memory map for this code may be written as:

Label	Address	Value
ca[0]	400	
ca[1]	401	
ca[2]	402	
cp	403–406	400
ia[0]	407–410	
ia[1]	411–414	
ia[2]	415–418	
ip	419–422	407

Now consider the following lines of code involving pointer arithmetic:

```
*(cp+2)=8;     /* cp + 2 what? */
*(ip+2)=33;    /* ip + 2 what? */
```

In each line of code, the * symbol indicates that a value is to be placed at the given address. But at what address? In the first line, we have the value of "cp+2" as the address. The value of cp is 400. Adding 2 gives an address of 402. Looking at the memory map, the variable ca[2] resides at that address, so this seems to make sense. Now consider the second line, where we have the value of "ip+2" as the address. The value of ip is 407. Adding 2 gives an address of 409, which is the midpoint of the variable ia[0]. This does not make sense.

Pointer arithmetic uses the units of the type of variable "pointed to." Those units are set during the variable declaration. Since cp is a pointer to char, its units are 1-byte increments. Since ip is a pointer to int, its units are 4-byte increments. Using the correct units, we can determine that:

```
cp+2 = cp+2 (1 byte units) = 400+2 = 402
ip+2 = ip+2 (4 byte units) = 407+8 = 415
```

The resulting memory map may be written as follows:

Label	Address	Value
ca[0]	400	
ca[1]	401	
ca[2]	402	8
cp	403–406	400
ia[0]	407–410	
ia[1]	411–414	
ia[2]	415–418	33
ip	419–422	407

Notice that using pointer arithmetic, the offsets match the indices of the arrays. This is the whole point. Pointers and arrays can be used interchangeably; in fact, they are often the same thing. This concept is discussed more in the next section.

4.2 • Using Pointers

Pointers are a difficult tool to master. They are the source of many coding errors and bugs, leading to a number of flaws and security problems. Why then do we use them? This section discusses some of the most common reasons for using pointers.

4.2.1   Passing Values Back from a Function

The most common reason for using pointers is to pass values back from a function. Consider the following program:

```
#include <stdio.h>

int division(int numerator, int denominator,
             int *dividend, int *remainder)
{
printf("address stored in dividend: %u\n",dividend);
printf("address stored in remainder: %u\n",remainder);
if (denominator == 0)
  return(0);
*dividend=numerator/denominator;
*remainder=numerator%denominator;
```

```
   return(1);
}

main()
{
int     x,y,d,r;
x=9;
y=2;
printf("address of d: %u\n",&d);
printf("address of r: %u\n",&r);
division(x,y,&d,&r);
printf("%d/%d = %d with %d remainder\n",x,y,d,r);
printf("x=%d\n",x);
}
```

First, we look at the label and address (the size of each variable) columns of the memory map. This may be written as follows:

Label	Address	Value
numerator	400–403	
denominator	404–407	
dividend	408–411	
remainder	412–415	
x	700–703	
y	704–707	
d	708–711	
r	712–715	

The parameters of the division() function are variables, so they must be included in the memory map. They should be treated just like variables declared inside a function. The addresses used for the main() function (700's) have been somewhat separated from those used for the division() function (400's), simply to help organization. In reality, they might be right next to each other in memory, or far apart, or anywhere in between. The size of every variable is 4 bytes, because they are all either int or pointer variables.

When the code executes, the values 9 and 2 go into x and y, and then the function call happens. What does that do? It makes a copy of all the parameters, and places them in the local memory locations for the function. At this point, the memory map may be written as:

Label	Address	Value
numerator	400–403	9
denominator	404–407	2
dividend	408–411	708
remainder	412–415	712
x	700–703	9
y	704–707	2
d	708–711	
r	712–715	

Notice that the values of x and y are copied to numerator and denominator, but that it is the addresses of d and r that are copied to dividend and remainder. After this, the function code is executed. Using the pointer to dereference the address, the results are placed in the memory locations for d and r. At this point, the memory map may be written as:

Label	Address	Value
numerator	400–403	9
denominator	404–407	2
dividend	408–411	708
remainder	412–415	712
x	700–703	9
y	704–707	2
d	708–711	4
r	712–715	1

Notice that those results are never in any local memory location for the division() function, they are stored only in the original main() function variables. This is why pointers are necessary. It allows a function to be called to do some work, putting the results in variables residing in the original function. Variables like x and y are known as "call by value" parameters, while those like d and r are known as "call by reference" parameters. These phrases refer to how a variable value is passed to a function.

Suppose we added the following line of code to the end of the division() function:

```
numerator=7;
```

Looking at the memory map, we can see why this will have no effect upon the variable x in the main() function. Changing the value at address 400, where numerator resides, has no effect upon the value at address 700, where the variable x resides. This shows why we *must* use a pointer to pass a result back from a function call.

4.2.2 Pointers and Arrays

The second most common use of a pointer is when an array is used. Arrays are pointers, insofar as they are both addresses. We saw in the last chapter that an array name is a label for the starting address of the array. We saw in the last section that pointer arithmetic works similarly to array indexing. We will now put these ideas together and show how array and pointer syntax are interchangeable. Consider the following program:

```
#include <stdio.h>

main()
{
double  array[5];
double  *d_ptr;
double  value;
int     i,offset;

for (i=0; i<5; i++)
   array[i]=(double)i+10.0;    /* fill array with #'s */

d_ptr=&(array[0]);             /* set up pointer */

while (1)
   {
printf("Address(hex)\tAddress(base10)\tValue\n");
for (i=0; i<5; i++)
   printf("%p\t%u\t%lf\n",&(array[i]),&(array[i]),array[i]);
printf("Enter offset value (0 0 to quit): ");
scanf("%d %lf",&offset,&value);
if (offset == 0  &&  value == 0.0)
   break;                      /* break out of loop */
if (offset < 0  ||  offset > 4)
   {
   printf("Offset out of bounds\n");
```

```
            continue;              /* go back to start of loop */
        }
        /* three ways to do the same thing: */
        array[offset]=value;       /* using array syntax */
        *(d_ptr+offset)=value;     /* using pointer syntax */
        *(array+offset)=value;     /* using mixed syntax */
    }
}
```

This program sets up an array of five doubles, and then enters a loop. The user can select an array index and new value, which the program then places into the given index. The program also checks for valid array indices (within the bounds 0 to 4), and uses the index/value pair 0/0 to quit.

The last three lines of code are the most interesting. They show how we can access the same memory using array indexing, pointer arithmetic, or even a mix of both. All three of those lines of code do the exact same thing. We can see this by looking at the memory map:

Address label(s)	Label	Address	Value
array &(array[0])	array[0]	400–407	10.0
	array[1]	408–415	11.0
	array[2]	416–423	12.0
	array[3]	424–431	13.0
	array[4]	432–439	14.0
	d_ptr	440–443	400
	value	444–451	
	i	452–455	0 1 2 3 4 5
	offset	456–459	

The value at address 400 can be accessed through its original name array[0], or through the pointer value of d_ptr, or through mixed notation using a pointer to the original address label array. It can even be accessed using another mixed notation based on the other original address label &(array[0]):

```
*(&(array[0])+offset)=value;
```

There is one important difference between using an address label, such as array, and a pointer variable, such as d_ptr. The former has a fixed value that cannot be changed. It refers to the address 400, and that cannot be changed. However, the value stored in the pointer variable can be changed at any time. This is sometimes used as an argument to support the idea that pointers and arrays are different. However, looking at the memory underneath, we can see that both can be used to access an ordered block of memory. This is why they can be interchanged and are often considered the same thing.

4.2.3 Dynamic Memory Allocation

Variables are normally given space through static memory allocation. This means that the size (in bytes) of each of the variables is known before the program runs. Upon starting execution of the program, the operating system (O/S) finds a place in memory for all the global variables in the program (in an area called the data segment). As each function is entered, including main(), space for its variables and parameter values are found (in an area called the stack). Without going into the details of the implementation of these memory areas, it is important to note that the entire time that the program is running, the size of a statically allocated variable does not change.

Sometimes a program does not know how much memory it needs prior to execution. For example, in reading a line of text from a file, the program might not know how big a string is needed to store all the words before the particular file has been selected, and read. In this case, a programmer might decide to declare a string of sufficient size to store any possible line of text. This is wasteful and perhaps, in some cases, impossible. The maximum size of something to be read might not be known beforehand. The alternative is to use dynamic memory allocation.

Dynamic memory allocation uses a pointer variable to request memory from the O/S while the program is running. The basic function call for dynamic memory allocation is `malloc()`, and works as follows:

```
#include <stdlib.h>  /* header file for malloc() */
double  *a;          /* pointer variable */
a = (double *) malloc (40);
/*     ^^^^^^^^^ ^^^^^^ ^^           */
/*    typecast  request how many bytes? */
/*             to O/S                */
```

The typecast identifies the type of pointer arithmetic expected for the address returned from malloc() (see Section 4.2.2 on pointer arithmetic). The malloc() function call is the request to the O/S for memory. It takes one parameter, which is the number of bytes needed. In this example, we request 40 bytes, which is 5 doubles (8 bytes per double).

How does it work? One of the primary jobs of the O/S is to manage memory. A malloc() call asks the O/S for a chunk of memory of the given size. The chunk of memory is obtained from an area of memory called the heap. Compared to the other memory areas (e.g., the stack or the data segment), the heap can normally support larger variables. In general, a program can dynamically acquire much larger chunks of memory than can be obtained using static variable declarations. The address of that chunk of memory, if available, is returned. The memory map for this code may be written as follows:

Label	Address	Value
a	400–403	10000
[DM]	10000–10039	

Dynamically allocated memory does not have an existing label, so we use [DM] to temporarily provide it a name. In order to give it a name that our program can use, we must use either pointer or array syntax based upon the variable a. Either syntax can be used to address, or label, different parts of the 40 bytes requested. For example, we can write the following code:

```
a[0]=8;
*(a+2)=3;
a[3]=9;
```

The memory map for this code may be written as:

Label(s)		Address	Value
a		400–403	10000
*(a+0)	a[0]	10000–10007	8
*(a+1)	a[1]	10008–10015	
*(a+2)	a[2]	10016–10023	3
*(a+3)	a[3]	10024–10031	9
*(a+4)	a[4]	10032–10039	

Every cell of memory in the chunk of bytes has both a pointer-based label and an array-based label and can be accessed using either syntax. It is quite common to see a pointer variable used for dynamic memory allocation and then accessed using array syntax.

Every time a function ends, its statically declared memory is released from the stack and returned to the O/S. This includes the ending of the main function, which is the end of the program. Dynamic memory allocation is different. Because the allocation can be made at any point in a program, the program must also be responsible for releasing the memory and returning it to the O/S. This is done by calling the free() function:

```
free(a);
```

Failure to call the free() function appropriately may result in a program losing track of the memory it uses. Sometimes this is referred to as a memory leak. For example, consider the following code:

```
double *a;
a=(double *)malloc(70);
a=(double *)malloc(300);  /* memory leak */
```

The program requests 70 bytes from the O/S, and then 300 bytes, each time storing the address of the bytes in a. But the second request overwrites the address of the first request. What happens to those 70 bytes? They are still reserved for use by the program, but the program has lost any record of the address where they reside! This is a common programming mistake and can lead to a program crashing.

There are several variants on the malloc() function that request bytes in slightly different ways. A common variant is calloc(), which in addition to requesting the bytes also initializes the value of every byte to zero. For example:

```
double *a;
a=(double *)calloc(70,sizeof(double));
```

The calloc() function takes two arguments; the first is the number of cells of memory, and the second is the size of each cell. The sizeof() operator is a convenient tool for denoting the number of bytes in a data type. It is evaluated by the compiler at compile time to find the size of a variable or variable type. It is often used with structures and complex data type combinations, which we will see more of in the next section. For this example, the sizeof() operator returns 8, which is the size of a double, so the total number of bytes requested is 560.

4.2.4   Double Pointers

In the last section, we saw how a chunk of dynamically allocated memory can be accessed as an array. In effect, this is like creating a variable-length, one-dimensional array, where the length is determined while the program is running. This concept can be extended to multidimensional arrays by using multiple pointers. For example, we can use a double pointer to act like a two-dimensional array. Consider the following code, which declares a double pointer:

```
double  **ptr;
```

It may be understood by rewriting it, emphasizing the order of applying each of the * operators:

```
double  *(*ptr);
```

We know that *ptr is an address of a double. The * symbol means "at the address given by;" therefore, *(*ptr) must mean "the double at the address given by the address given by." How big, in bytes, is a double pointer? It's still just an address, so it is 4 bytes. All addresses are 4 bytes, even an address of an address.

The following code demonstrates using a double pointer like a two-dimensional array:

```
double **m;
m=(double **)calloc(2,sizeof(double *));
m[0]=(double *)calloc(3,sizeof(double));
m[1]=(double *)calloc(2,sizeof(double));
m[0][1]=6.3;
m[1][0]=-2.8;
```

The first calloc() function call asks for enough bytes to store two pointers (addresses), or 8 bytes total. Each of these pointers is then used to store the address of a number of doubles (3 doubles in the second calloc(), and 2 doubles in the third calloc()). Once all the memory is allocated, it may be accessed as though it were a two-dimensional array. The memory map for this code may be written as:

Label(s)		Address	Value
m		400–403	10000
*(m+0)	m[0]	10000–10003	10008
*(m+1)	m[1]	10004–10007	10032
((m+0)+0)	m[0][0]	10008–10015	
((m+0)+1)	m[0][1]	10016–10023	6.3
((m+0)+2)	m[0][2]	10024–10031	
((m+1)+0)	m[1][0]	10032–10039	-2.8
((m+1)+1)	m[1][1]	10040–10047	

The variable m holds a double pointer, or the address of a list of addresses (10000). The list of addresses is m[0] and m[1], each of which holds an address of a list of doubles (10008 and 10032).

Another common use of double pointers is the passing of a pointer variable to a function. This is necessary when a function needs to dynamically allocate memory and then pass that memory back to the calling function. The following code demonstrates this use of a double pointer:

```c
#include <stdio.h>
#include <stdlib.h>

int integers(int listsize,int **list)
{
int    i;
*list=(int *)malloc(listsize*sizeof(int));
if (*list == NULL)
    return(0);
for (i=0; i<listsize; i++)
   (*list)[i]=10+i;  /* mixed array/pointer syntax */
return(1);
}

int main(int argc, char *argv[])
{
int    *numbers;
int    i;
i=integers(3,&numbers);
for (i=0; i<3; i++)
printf("%d\n",numbers[i]);
}
```

The integers() function dynamically allocates space for a list of ints and then puts values in each cell. One of its parameters indicates how large a list to create. At the completion of execution of the program, the memory map may be written as:

Label(s)	Address	Value
listsize	400–403	3
list	404–407	708
i	408–411	0̸ 1̸ 2̸ 3
argc	700–703	

(continued)

Label(s)		Address	Value
argv		704–707	
numbers		708–711	10000
i		712–715	0 1 2 3
(*list)[0]	numbers[0]	10000–10003	10
(*list)[1]	numbers[1]	10004–10007	11
(*list)[2]	numbers[2]	10008–10011	12

This memory map brings up a few interesting points. First, it includes argc and argv, which are variables local to the main() function. The latter (argv) is a double pointer and in memory looks like the examples just shown. Second, it includes two variables named i. Each of these is local to a different function, which is why the same name can be used twice. Third, the syntax (*list)[0] shows a mixed pointer/array reference to the double pointer. In most cases, it is easier to read code that sticks to a pure pointer or pure array syntax. For example, the line

```
*(list)[i]=10+i;
```

may be rewritten as

```
*((*list)+i)=10+i;
```

4.3 • Structures

A structure is a construct used to group a set of variables together under one name. The first step in using a structure is to declare its organization. For example:

```
struct person {      /* "person" is name for structure type */
char    first[32];   /* first field is array of char */
char    last[32];    /* second field is array of char */
int     year;        /* third field is int */
double  ppg;         /* fourth field is double */
};                   /* ending ; to end definition */
```

This code does not create a variable. There are no bytes of storage named yet. Instead, this code creates a *template* for a new variable type called struct person. One can think of a struct person as being a similar construct to an int or double. It is a name for a data type, not a name for a variable. In this example, the struct person consists of two arrays of 32 char, an int, and a double, for a total of 76 bytes.

We can use this definition of a struct person to declare a variable as follows:

```
struct person    teacher;
```

We now have a variable named teacher that provides 76 bytes of storage. Each part of the variable is called a field and is accessed using the period (.) symbol. For example:

```
teacher.year=2006;
teacher.ppg=10.4;
strcpy(teacher.first,"Adam");
strcpy(teacher.last,"Hoover");
```

The memory map for this code may be written as:

Address label(s)	Label(s)	Address	Value
teacher.first	teacher teacher.first[0]	400	'A'
	teacher.first[1]	401	'd'
	teacher.first[2]	402	'a'
	teacher.first[3]	403	'm'
	teacher.first[4]	404	'\0'
	teacher.first[5]-[31]	405–431	
teacher.last	teacher.last[0]	432	'H'
	teacher.last[1]	433	'o'
	teacher.last[2]	434	'o'
	teacher.last[3]	435	'v'
	teacher.last[4]	436	'e'
	teacher.last[5]	437	'r'
	teacher.last[6]	438	'\0'
	teacher.last[7]-[31]	439–463	
	teacher.year	464–467	2005
	teacher.ppg	468–475	10.4

There are two labels for the data at address 400, teacher.first[0] and teacher. The former refers to the char (1 byte) at that address, while the latter refers to the struct person (76 bytes) at that address. Of course, the latter includes the former as its first byte. It should come as no surprise that a label can refer to multiple bytes starting at a given address. For example, teacher.ppg refers to the double (8 bytes) starting at address 468, not just byte 468. The number of bytes is known by the data type of the label. In the case of `teacher`, the data type is a `struct person`, and so the label refers to 76 bytes.

Having a label that refers to the entire structure is convenient for two purposes. First, it allows assignment statements between structure variables. For example, continuing the code from above:

```
struct person   mailman,teacher;
mailman=teacher;     /* copy entire contents of struct */
```

Assigning a structure to another copies every byte. Of course, the structures must be of the same type. The second convenience is in passing a structure as a parameter to a function. For example:

```
DisplayStats(struct person   Input)
{
printf("%s, %s:  %lf PPG in %d\n",Input.last,Input.first,
                         Input.ppg,Input.year);
}

main()
{
struct person   teacher;
/* .... */
DisplayStats(teacher);
}
```

When the function call to DisplayStats() is made, all 76 bytes in the variable `teacher` are copied to `Input`. These examples demonstrate the whole point of using a structure. It is convenient to group a number of variables (hence, a large number of bytes) under a single variable name.

Looking back at the memory map for `teacher`, from above, we had the following line:

Address label(s)	Label(s)		Address	Value
teacher.first	teacher	teacher.first[0]	400	'A'

Unlike an array variable name, a structure variable name is a label for the values in the given bytes, not for the address. In this manner, a structure variable name acts like a regular (char, int, float, double) variable name. In the example, we see that the label `teacher.first` is a name for address 400, which is the beginning address of an array of char. The label `teacher` is a name for the values of the 76 bytes starting at address 400; it is not another label for address 400. However, we can use the & symbol prior to either regular label to turn it into an address label (for example, &teacher or &(teacher.first[0])).

4.4 • Using Structures

Structure variables can in many cases be treated exactly like regular variables. For example, they can be used in assignment statements and passed as function parameters, and a field of a structure variable can be used in regular calculations. However, structures can be combined with arrays, pointers, and other structures, making the syntax and usage complicated. A good approach to unraveling a strange combination, in order to design, debug, or understand code, is to examine it at the memory level. The following sections demonstrate this approach.

4.4.1   Arrays and Structures

It is possible to create an array of structs, just like it is possible to have an array of any data type. The template for the structure definition remains unchanged; it still must be declared first. Using our definition of a struct person from above, we may write the following code:

```
struct person    class[54];     /* array of "struct person" */


class[0].year=2006;   /* notice where array subscript goes */
class[0].ppg=5.2;
strcpy(class[0].first,"Jane");
strcpy(class[0].last,"Doe");
class[1].first[0]='B'; /* array field in a struct array */
class[1].first[1]='o';
class[1].first[2]='b';
class[1].first[3]=0;
```

The memory map for this code may be written as:

Address label(s)	Label(s)	Address	Value
class class[0].first	class[0] class[0].first[0]	400	'J'
	class[0].first[1]	401	'a'
	class[0].first[2]	402	'n'
	class[0].first[3]	403	'e'
	class[0].first[4]	404	'\0'

(continued)

Address label(s)	Label(s)	Address	Value
	class[0].first[5]-[31]	405–431	
class[0].last	class[0].last[0]	432	'D'
	class[0].last[1]	433	'o'
	class[0].last[2]	434	'e'
	class[0].last[3]	435	'\0'
	class[0].last[4]-[31]	436–463	
	class[0].year	464–467	2006
	class[0].ppg	468–475	5.2
class[1].first	class[1] class[1].first[0]	476	'B'
	class[1].first[1]	477	'o'
	class[1].first[2]	478	'b'
	class[1].first[3]	479	'\0'
	class[1].first[4]-[31]	480–507	
class[1].last	class[1].last[0]-[31]	508–539	
	class[1].year	540-543	
	class[1].ppg	544–551	
	class[2]	552–627	
	class[3]	628–703	
	class[4]--[53]	704–4503	

Back in Chapter 3, we learned that an array name by itself is an address label. This is true regardless of the type of array. Thus, class, which is the name for an array of struct person, is an address label. So is class[0].first, which is the name for an array of char. Both of these refer to address 400. On the other hand, class[0] is not the name of an array; it is the name of a cell within the array. Therefore it is not an address label; it is a regular label. So is class[0].first[0]. The labels class[0] and class[0].first[0] do differ in how many bytes are labeled. The former labels 76 bytes as a group, while the latter labels only 1 byte.

4.4.2 Definitions and Scope

Structure variables can be global or local to a function, just like any other variable. Structure definitions can also be global or local. In addition, when making a definition, a variable using that definition can be declared at the same time. Consider the following code:

```
                        struct fraction {    /* structure definition */
                                  int     x,y;
                                  } global; /* variable using this definition */
                                  /* variable outside a function is global */
            main()
            {
                  /* "throw away" structure template (used only once) */
            struct {     /* notice there is no name for structure def. */
                  char     title[20];
                  float    cost;
                  } paperback;  /* variable using this definition */
            int     n;
            struct fraction local;

            n=3;
            paperback.cost=4.50;
            strcpy(paperback.title,"C");
            }

            some_function()
            {
            struct fraction x;  /* var. names are independent of fields */

            global.x=1;
            x.x=2;                    /* so "x" can be a var. and field name */
            }
```

At the end of a structure definition, one or more variables can be declared that use that definition. Thus, `global` and `paperback` are both variables. The former is a `struct fraction` type variable, while the latter . . . has no name for its type! It is possible to define a structure template but never give that template a name and use it only to define a variable at the end of its definition. This makes it impossible to declare a variable using that particular structure definition at a later time. This sort of thing is rarely done and in general is not recommended. However, a programmer should be able to understand these sorts of tricks, which are best examined using a memory map:

Address label(s)	Label(s)	Address	Value
	global global.x	100–103	1
	global.y	104–107	
paperback.title	paperback.title[0]	400	'C'
	paperback.title[1]	401	'\0'

(continued)

Address label(s)	Label(s)	Address	Value
	paperback.title[2]-[19]	402–419	
	paperback.cost	420–423	4.5
	n	424–427	3
	local local.x	428–431	
	local.y	432–435	
	x x.x	700–703	2
	x.y	704–707	

Writing out the memory map enforces an understanding of which things are variables: fraction is a structure definition, not a variable name. It does not belong in the memory map. This memory map also shows how a label can be used for both a structure variable (x) and a field within that structure (x.x). Although they label bytes starting at the same address (700), x refers to a struct fraction (8 bytes), while x.x refers to an int (4 bytes).

4.4.3   Nested Structures

Structures can be nested, so that a field within a structure is itself another structure. For example:

```
struct name {
        char    first[32];
        char    last[32];
        };

struct person {
        int        age;
        float      ppg;
        struct name    title;       /* nested structure */
        };                          /* "name" must be defined above */
```

```
struct person    boss;
boss.age=80;
boss.ppg=0.1;
strcpy(boss.title.first,"Dean");
strcpy(boss.title.last,"Smith");
```

The memory map for this code may be written as:

Address label(s)	Label(s)	Address	Value
	boss boss.age	400–403	80
	boss.ppg	404–407	0.1
boss.title.first	boss.title boss.title.first[0]	408	'D'
	boss.title.first[1]	409	'e'
	boss.title.first[2]	410	'a'
	boss.title.first[3]	411	'n'
	boss.title.first[4]	412	'\0'
	boss.title.first[5]-[31]	413–439	
boss.title.last	boss.title.last[0]	440	'S'
	boss.title.last[1]	441	'm'
	boss.title.last[2]	442	'i'
	boss.title.last[3]	443	't'
	boss.title.last[4]	444	'h'
	boss.title.last[5]	445	'\0'
	boss.title.last[6]-[31]	446–471	

The label boss is a name for a struct person (72 bytes), while the label boss.title is a name for a struct name (64 bytes). The other nested structure names, boss.title.first and boss.title.last, are address labels for arrays of char, referring to addresses 408 and 440, respectively.

4.4.4 Pointers and Structures

The address of a structure variable can be stored in a pointer variable, just like the address of any other type of variable. For example:

```
struct fraction {
            int     x;
            int     y;
            }

struct fraction   f[3],*g;
f[0].x=3;
f[0].y=7;
g=&(f[0]);
g++;
```

The memory map for this code may be written as:

Address label(s)	Label(s)		Address	Value
f	f[0] f[0].x		400–403	3
	f[0].y		404–407	7
	f[1] f[1].x		408–411	
	f[1].y		412–415	
	f[2] f[2].x		416–419	
	f[2].y		420–423	
	g		424–427	~~400~~ 408

The variable g holds an address of a struct fraction. Using pointer arithmetic, this means that the units of addition for g are 8 bytes. Therefore, g++ adds 8 to the current value of g.

Continuing from this code example, we can access the bytes of the structure through the pointer variable. There are two different syntaxes available to do this. The following demonstrates each syntax:

```
(*g).x=5;
g->y=11;
```

The first line uses the same syntax as all other types of pointers. The value of g is 408; the * symbol says to go to that address; then the .x says to go to that field at the given address. The C language provides a second syntax that accomplishes the same steps. The -> syntax (hyphen followed by greater-than symbol) means "in the field at the given address." The memory map for this code may be updated as follows:

Address label(s)	Label(s)		Address	Value
f	f[0] f[0].x		400–403	3
	f[0].y		404–407	7
	f[1] f[1].x		408–411	5
	f[1].y		412–415	11
	f[2] f[2].x		416–419	
	f[2].y		420–423	
	g		424–427	~~400~~ 408

A pointer variable for a structure can also be used to dynamically allocate memory. For example:

```
g=(struct fraction *)malloc(sizeof(struct fraction));
```

A struct fraction is 8 bytes in size; the sizeof() operator is a convenient method to determine the number of bytes needed.[3] By default, the malloc() function returns a void pointer (void *), which means that the returned value is an address but that the type or size of variable at that address could be anything. This lets the malloc() function be used to allocate space for any type of pointer. It is common practice to typecast the return value from the malloc() function call to make the code easier to read by showing how the pointer is dereferenced. As noted above, the variable g holds a pointer to struct fraction, which increments in units of 8 bytes. The memory map after this allocation may be updated as:

Address label(s)	Label(s)	Address	Value
f	f[0] f[0].x	400–403	3
	f[0].y	404–407	7
	f[1] f[1].x	408–411	5
	f[1].y	412–415	11
	f[2] f[2].x	416–419	
	f[2].y	420–423	
	g	424–427	~~400~~ ~~408~~ 10000
	g.x	10000–10003	
	g.y	10004–10007	

Questions and Exercises

1. Write out the memory map for the following code, providing all values at the end of execution. How many total bytes does this code declare for variables?

```
#include <stdio.h>
main()
{
char a,*b,c[3];
int i,*j,k[3];
```

---

3. It is especially convenient because a struct may not always contain a number of bytes equal to the size of its members. The compiler may pad odd-sized fields, for example, placing an unused byte at the end of an array of 3 char, in order to align fields on data bus boundaries.

```
a='N';
b=&(c[2]);
j=&(k[0]);
for (i=0; i<3; i++)
    {
    *b=a-(char)i;
    b--;
    *j=i+5;
    j++;
    }
}
```

2. Write out the memory map for the following code, providing all values at the end of execution. How many total bytes does this code declare for variables?

```
double d[3],*e;
int i,*j;
char a,*b,c[3];

i=3;
j=&i;
d[0]=4.2;
e=&(d[1]);
*(e-1)=1.5;
e[1]=2.3;
for (i=0; i<5; i++)
  c[i%3]=(char)(*j+i);
b=&a;
*b=c[2];
```

3. When is it necessary to use dynamic memory allocation? Give two reasons.

4. In the following code, the first printf() reached produces the output "14," but the second printf() can cause a bus error or a segmentation fault. Why?

```
main()
{ int *p;
funct(p);
printf("%d\n",*p);
}
funct(int *p2)
{
p2=(int *)malloc(4);
*p2=14;
printf("%d\n",*p2);
}
```

5. Consider the following variable declarations. Write code that uses these variables to perform a matrix multiplication. The program should prompt the user for the sizes of the two matrices to be multiplied (from these, it can calculate the size of the result matrix). It should then dynamically allocate memory for the matrices and prompt the user for values for all entries in the matrix. Finally, the program should perform the matrix multiplication and report the result.

```
double  **m1,**m2,**mr;
int     m1_rows,m1_cols,m2_rows,m2_cols,mr_rows,mr_cols;
```

Example: if the first matrix is 1×3 with values [1 7 4] and the second matrix is 3×2 with values [1 3], [1 9] and [6 2] in each row, then the result matrix should be 1×2 with values [32 74].

6. A phonebook typically lists the name, address, and telephone number of everyone living in an area. Write code defining a structure template that could be used to store this data. Assume that a name and address will be no more than 30 characters each, and that a telephone number has exactly seven digits.

7. What is the exact output of the following code?

```
struct comp {
            char address[80];
            char phone[11];
            } tc;
struct inv  {
            char barcode[12];
            float price;
            struct comp *manuf;
            };

main()
{
struct inv s;
sprintf(tc.address,"313 Main St.");
strcpy(tc.phone,"3035552479");
s.price=6.42;
strcpy(s.barcode,"1961354128");
s.manuf=&tc;
printf("%c %s\n",s.manuf->address[5],&(tc.phone[6]));
}
```

8. Use the following code to describe a rectangle. Assume the rectangle sides are parallel to the x and y axes (no rotation), and that the corners of the rectangle are located properly according to their compass designations in the structure.

```
struct point {
        int x,y;
        };
struct rect  {
        struct point ne,se,sw,nw;
        };
```

Write a function called RectArea() that returns an integer value equal to the area of the given rectangle. The rectangle should be passed in as an argument.

9. Use the same code to describe a rectangle as given in the previous problem. Write a function called RotateRect() that takes in a rectangle and rotates it 90 degrees clockwise. The function should have one parameter that passes the rectangle in and out. The function should have no return value.

10. Write out the memory map for the following code, providing all values at the end of execution. How many total bytes does this code declare for variables?

```
double testd;
int testi;
struct frog {
        double *x,y;
        };
struct frog turtle,*apple,tv[3];

testi=2;
apple=&turtle;
apple->x=&testd;
*(turtle.x)=7.3;
(*apple).y=3.6;
turtle.y=1.5;
for (testi=0; testi<3; testi++)
  tv[testi].x=&(tv[(testi+1)%3].y);
*(tv[1].x)=6.4;
```

11. Write out the memory map for the following code, providing all values at the end of execution. How many total bytes does this code declare for variables?

```
struct ID {
        int     number;
        float   cost;
        double  *barcode;
        };
```

```
            struct ID list[3],*item;
            float *f;
            double *d,d2;

            d2=888;
            list[2].number=12;
            list[2].cost=44.11;
            list[2].barcode=&d2;
            item=&(list[2]);
            f=&(item->cost);
            d=item->barcode;
            *d=(*d)+1;
```

12. Write out the memory map for the following code, providing all values at the end of execution. How many total bytes does this code declare for variables?

```
        struct passport {
                    char        last[10];
                    int         number;
                    float       fees;
                    double      *country_code;
                    };
        struct passport list[3],*passenger;
        char who[7],a,*b;
        double *d,d2;
        int i,*j;

        d2=888;
        i=12;
        j=&i;
        strcpy(who,"person");
        strcpy(list[1].last,"jones");
        list[1].number=129783;
        list[1].fees=105.37;
        list[1].country_code=&d2;
        passenger=&(list[1]);
        b=&(passenger->last[0]);
        d=passenger->country_code;
        *b='t';
        passenger->last[4]='y';
        for (i=0; i<5; i++)
          who[i%3]=(char)(*j+i);
```

13. Consider the lines of code below. Indicate which are invalid, meaning either that they would not compile or that they may produce a memory fault. Consider each line independently of all others.

```
struct passport {
                char    last[10];
                int     number;
                float   fees;
                double  *country_code;
                };
struct passport list[3],*passenger;
char who[7],a,*b;
double *d,d2;

b="Hello";
list->country_code=277;
list[0].country_code=d;
list[2].country_code=&d2;
*(list[3].country_code)=277;
passport.country_code=463;
passenger=&passport;
who[6]='a';
a=5;
b=&(list[0].last[5]);
passenger=&list;
passenger =&(list[0]); list[2]=(* passenger);
list[0].fees="world";
list[0].fees='p'+0.65;
*(passenger->country_code)=*d=(double)(list[0].last[12]);
```

14. Write a program that allows the user to manipulate the entries in a vector, or in a matrix. The program should keep track of one vector of variable length, and of one matrix of exactly 4 × 4 size. The program should enter a loop, displaying a set of options (given below). Once the user selects an option, the program should display the vector (or matrix, as appropriate) before and after the operation chosen by the user. For example, if the user selects "reverse vector" and the current vector is [-3 0 2 5], then the program should display:

```
-3 0 2 5
reversed
5 2 0 -3
```

The program should run until the user selects an option to quit. The program must use the following structure definitions:

```
struct vector {
    float  *data;
    int    size;
    };
struct matrix {
    struct vector  rows[4];
    };
```

Two of the options of the program should be to enter data into the vector, and to enter data into the matrix. For the vector, numbers should be read until the user enters -1, indicating the end of the vector (that number should not be included in the vector). The maximum number of values in the vector should be eight; if the user enters eight values then the program should stop prompting for more. For the matrix, the program should simply prompt the user for the 16 numbers, in row order (all of row 1 first, then row 2, etc.). All numbers should be real numbers.

Each option that manipulates the vector or matrix must be implemented inside a different function. The options are:

- Sum the vector. This function should take in one argument, a vector, and sum its entries. It should return the sum as a float.
- Reverse the vector. This function should take in one argument, a vector, and reverse its entries. It should have no return value.
- Distribution of vector. This function should take in three arguments: a vector and two counters. Upon completion, the counters should hold the total numbers of positive and negative values in the vector. The function should have no return value.
- Mirror the vector. This function should take in one argument, a vector. It should return a second (new) vector that is a copy of the first, followed by a reverse copy of the first. If the input vector is more than four values in length, the operation should use only the first four entries. The input vector should not be changed.
- Sum the matrix. This function should take in one argument, a matrix, and sum its entries. It should return the sum as a float.
- Reverse the matrix. This function should take in one argument, a matrix, and reverse the order of entries in each column. It should have no return value.
- Distribution of matrix. This function should take in three arguments: a matrix and two counters. Upon completion, the counters should hold the total

numbers of positive and negative values in the matrix. The function should return the number of values equal to zero.

- Matrix kazaam. This function should take in one argument, a matrix. It should return a second (new) matrix that is a copy of the first, but with all positive entries multiplied by 2, and all negative entries multiplied by −3. It should return the number of original values that were negative. The input matrix should not be changed.

15. Write a program that provides a simple spreadsheet. The program should allow the user to enter numeric values, text, or formulas into any cell. As new data is entered, the spreadsheet should be updated and redisplayed. The program should run until the user quits.

The maximum size of the spreadsheet should be 9 x 9 cells. Rows should be labeled with numbers, starting from 1, and columns should be labeled with letters, starting from A. Cells should be referenced by a letter number pair, with no space or symbol between; for example, E9. Lowercase and uppercase letters to reference cells are allowed and must be recognized.

The program cannot prompt what type of entry is being made into a cell. It should prompt only for an input. If the user types data consisting only of numeric values, for example 4.53, then the program must recognize that input as a number. All numbers should be considered real numbers. If the user types input describing a formula (discussed below), then the program must recognize that input as a formula. Everything else defaults to text.

The display of the spreadsheet should be aligned in an easy-to-read 9 x 9 grid. If text entries or other displayed content go beyond the given display size, the display should be truncated. When entering a new input for a cell, the program must display the old (previous) input.

Optional: include formulas in the program. Formulas are of the form =AVERAGE(A2,A5). This formula would return the average value from the four cells A2, A3, A4, and A5. Three formulas are required: AVERAGE, SUM, and RANGE. RANGE should return the difference between the largest and smallest value in the input. SUM should return the cumulative total. The input must be a horizontal or vertical 1D range of cells, described by the end points. The formula should compute a result using only values within the given range of cells; it should ignore empty cells and those containing text or another formula. If there are no values within the given range of cells, the result should default to zero.

5

Input/Output

In order to do something interesting, most programs have to get input from somewhere and send output to somewhere. This is commonly called input/output, or I/O for short. There are several different situations in which I/O occurs. User I/O involves interactions between a program and a user, typically through a keyboard and display. File I/O involves interactions between a program and the file storage system. Device I/O involves interactions between a program and a piece of hardware, such as a sensor or peripheral component. Regardless of the particular situation, all these I/O transactions make use of a similar set of concepts. These concepts include streams, buffers, pipes, file attributes and functions, and device drivers. The goal of this chapter is to introduce the reader to these concepts.

It is assumed that the reader is familiar with basic user I/O, such as reading input from a keyboard and printing text to a terminal display. The reader is likely also familiar with basic file I/O, such as reading and writing text to a file. It is common for a student to first learn text-based I/O; unfortunately, this can bias the student toward thinking of all I/O as text-based. The goal of this chapter is to provide a broader picture into the aspects of generic I/O. It is important to remember that text is only one type of data. When considering generic I/O, we should remember to think of the data as raw bytes. It is up to the sender or receiver of the data to interpret the bytes.

5.1 • Streams

An I/O transaction occurs when a program receives bytes from a source or sends bytes to a destination. Example sources that send bytes to a program include a keyboard, mouse, file, and sensor. Example destinations to which a program sends bytes include a display, file, printer, and actuator. Programs can also send bytes to other programs, acting as sources or destinations.

Most modern operating systems, including Unix, use the stream model to control I/O. In this model, any input or output transaction can be viewed as a flow of bytes from a source to a destination. The flow of bytes is commonly referred to as a stream. The operating system creates and manages streams based upon the function calls made by the program. The program has some control over how the stream is operated, but in general it is managed by the operating system.

An I/O connection can be established using the fopen() function. For example, consider the following code:

```
FILE *fpt;
fpt=fopen("output.txt","w");
fprintf(fpt,"This is a test.");
fclose(fpt);
```

Figure 5.1 shows a step-by-step diagram of the process. When fopen() is called, a stream connection is established between the program and the file. When fprintf() is called, bytes are passed along the stream from the program to the file. When fclose() is called, the stream connection is broken. As we will see in Section 5.5, all I/O transactions use streams in the same manner.

5.1.1 Transporting Bytes on Streams

There are several functions that can be used to transport bytes on streams. These include the familiar fprintf() and fscanf() functions. For example:

```
#include <stdio.h>
main()
{
FILE *fpt;
fpt=fopen("data.txt","w");
fprintf(fpt,"Fortytwo 42 bytes of data on the wall...");
fclose(fpt);
}
```

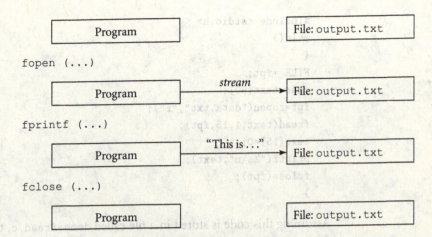

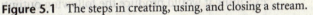

Figure 5.1 The steps in creating, using, and closing a stream.

In this example, bytes are being sent down a stream using the fprintf() function. For the rest of the examples in this section, we will assume that this code has been successfully executed, so that the file data.txt exists and is available for access. For example, consider the following code:

```
#include <stdio.h>
main()
{
FILE *fpt;
char text[80];
fpt=fopen("data.txt","r");
fscanf(fpt,"%s",text);
printf("%s\n",text);
fclose(fpt);
}
```

In this example, bytes are being transported on a stream using the fscanf() function. Assuming this code is stored in a file called demo-fscanf.c, then compiling and executing it would produce the following output:

```
ahoover@video> gcc -o demo-fscanf demo-fscanf.c
ahoover@video> demo-fscanf
Fortytwo
ahoover@video>
```

The generic functions for transporting bytes on streams are fread() and fwrite(). The fread() function reads bytes from a source into the program. For example:

```
#include <stdio.h>
main()
{
FILE *fpt;
char text[80];
fpt=fopen("data.txt","r");
fread(text,1,15,fpt);
text[15]=0;
printf("%s\n",text);
fclose(fpt);
}
```

Assuming this code is stored in a file called demo-fread.c, then compiling and executing it would produce the following output:

```
ahoover@video> gcc -o demo-fread demo-fread.c
ahoover@video> demo-fread
Fortytwo 42 byt
ahoover@video>
```

The first parameter to the fread() function provides the address at which the received bytes are to be stored. In the above example, the program is storing bytes in the variable text, which is an array of 80 char. The second and third parameters in the fread() function indicate how many bytes are to be received. The parameters adopt the style of an array, indicating the number of cells (the third parameter) and the size in bytes of each cell (the second parameter). In the above example, the program is receiving 15 cells of data, where each cell is 1 byte in size. The fourth parameter in the fread() function is the file pointer to the stream on which bytes are being received.

The fread() function reads bytes from the source regardless of what the bytes represent. Note that in the above example, the value of text[15] had to be set to zero so that the bytes in the array could be interpreted as a string (all strings must end with a NULL byte). The fread() and fwrite() functions do not assume that the bytes being moved represent text. Since they do not perform cleanup or modifying operations to the bytes, they are sometimes referred to as "raw" byte movers. However, this gives an unfortunate connotation as it implies that these functions are doing something sinisterly different from the more familiar fscanf() and fprintf() functions. It is in fact the opposite that is true. The fprintf() and fscanf() functions are actually specialized functions intended to work only with ASCII formatted text data. They manipulate the bytes according to a set of rules for formatting text, before either sending or receiving the bytes on the stream. For example, consider the following code:

```
FILE *fpt;
char text[30];
int x;
fpt=fopen("data.txt","r");
fscanf(fpt,"%s",text);
fscanf(fpt,"%d",&x);
fclose(fpt);
```

We will look at the byte transfers done in each fscanf() separately. A memory map of the result of the first fscanf() can be written as follows:

File			Memory		
Byte	**Value**		**Label**	**Address**	**Value**
0	'F' (70)		text[0]	400	'F' (70)
1	'o' (111)		text[1]	401	'o' (111)
2	'r' (114)		text[2]	402	'r' (114)
3	't' (116)	⇒	text[3]	403	't' (116)
4	'y' (121)		text[4]	404	'y' (121)
5	't' (116)		text[5]	405	't' (116)
6	'w' (119)		text[6]	406	'w' (119)
7	'o' (111)		text[7]	407	'o' (111)
8	' ' (32)		text[8]	408	'\0' (0)

Values for the bytes are shown as ASCII symbols and as two's complement integers in parentheses. The first fscanf() results in 8 bytes being transferred from the file to the variable text. In the file, the next byte has a value of 32 (the space character), but this byte is not transfered. Instead, the next byte in the text array is given a value of 0 (the NULL character). A memory map of the result of the second fscanf() reveals more byte manipulations during the transfer:

File			Memory		
Byte	**Value**		**Label**	**Address**	**Value**
9	'4' (52)	⇒	x	430-433	42
10	'2' (50)				
11	' ' (32)				

The second fscanf() results in 2 bytes being transferred from the file to the variable x. However, the 2 bytes are also converted into a 4-byte (int variable size), two's complement representation of an integer. From these examples, we can see that the fscanf() and fprintf() functions are doing extra operations besides the byte transfers. At the heart of both functions are calls to fread() and fwrite() to actually move the bytes after the desired byte manipulations have been completed.

The fwrite() function moves bytes from the program to a destination. For example:

```
#include <stdio.h>
main()
{
FILE *fpt;
char text[80];
sprintf(text,"Fortytwo 42 bytes of data on the wall...");
fpt=fopen("data2.txt","w");
fwrite(text,1,strlen(text),fpt);
fclose(fpt);
}
```

Executing this code will produce a file data2.txt that is identical to the file data.txt from our original example. The parameters of the fwrite() function are identical to those in the fread() function. Note that this example uses the strlen() function to determine the number of cells in the array to send on the stream, which in this case is 40.

Using the fwrite() and fread() functions affords another advantage: it allows the programmer a simple way to check when the end of a file has been reached. The return value of both functions is an indicator of the number of bytes actually moved along the stream. For example:

```
#include <stdio.h>
main()
{
FILE *fpt;
char text[80];
int bytes_read;
fpt=fopen("data.txt","r");
bytes_read=fread(text,1,70,fpt);
printf("%d\n",bytes_read);
fclose(fpt);
}
```

Assuming this code is stored in a file called demo2-fread.c, then compiling and executing it would produce the following output:

```
ahoover@video> gcc -o demo2-fread demo2-fread.c
ahoover@video> demo2-fread
40
ahoover@video>
```

Since the file data.txt contains only 40 bytes, the fread() function is not capable of reading the requested 70 cells × 1 byte/cell = 70 bytes of data. Once the end of the file has been reached, the fread() terminates. The return value for the fread() function is the number of cells of data moved along the stream. If each cell is 1 byte, then this is equivalent to the number of bytes moved; otherwise, to realize the number of bytes moved, the return value must be multiplied by the size of each cell requested (the second parameter of the fread() function).

There are a number of other functions that can be used to move bytes on streams, such as fgetc(), fputc(), gets(), and puts(). All of these functions are similar to fscanf() and fprintf() in that they manipulate the byte values in some manner before placing them on the stream, or after retrieving them from the stream. Although these functions can simplify programming involving text data, they should be used with care. It is common for a novice programmer to fall into traps using these functions by not understanding the precise manipulations made upon the bytes by these functions. It is more prudent to use the generic fread() and fwrite() functions to move bytes on streams, custom coding any desired byte manipulations. In this manner, a programmer can be more certain of what is happening on a stream transaction.

5.1.2 System I/O Functions

There is another set of functions that can be used for I/O. These functions include open(), close(), read(), and write(). They look very similar to the fopen(), fclose(), fread(), and fwrite() functions just discussed. How then are the non-f-versions of the I/O functions different from the f-versions?

The non-f I/O functions are system calls. Depending on which operating system they are called from, they may behave differently. The f-versions of the I/O functions are standardized in the C library. A programmer can expect them to behave similarly regardless of the underlying system. Unless otherwise motivated, a programmer is encouraged to always use the f-versions of the I/O functions.

A general rule of thumb is that the f-versions of the I/O functions are buffered, while the non-f-versions are not (buffers will be discussed shortly). This is not always true, as some system implementations of I/O functions may include buffering. However, in practice a programmer can expect to frequently encounter this distinction. This issue is discussed further in Chapter 7 on system calls.

5.1.3 Standard Streams

Most programs get user input from a keyboard and display text output to a screen. It is somewhat monotonous to write code to create these streams for every program. Therefore, every time a program[1] is started, the O/S automatically creates three streams. The first stream is called the "standard in" stream and is abbreviated stdin. It connects the keyboard to the program. The second stream is called the "standard out" stream and is abbreviated stdout. It connects the program to the display. The third stream is called the "standard error" stream and is abbreviated stderr. It connects the program to a secondary display that is intended only for the display of errors.

The standard streams are most commonly used by calling the scanf() and printf() functions. The scanf() function is actually a specialized version of the more generic fscanf() function. While the fscanf() function can receive bytes from any stream, the scanf() function is "hardwired" to the stdin stream. In the following example, the scanf() and fscanf() function calls perform the exact same operation:

```
char s[80];
scanf("%s",s);
fscanf(stdin,"%s",s);
```

The same is true with regards to printf() and fprintf(). While the fprintf() function can send bytes along any stream, the printf() function is hardwired to the stdout stream. In the following example, the printf() and fprintf() function calls perform the exact same operation:

```
int x=42;
printf("%d is a nice number\n",x);
fprintf(stdout,"%d is a nice number\n",x);
```

The definitions for the standard streams can be found in the include file stdio.h (most often found in /usr/include). Searching that file will uncover code similar to the following:

```
/* Standard streams.  */
extern FILE *stdin;    /* Standard input stream.  */
extern FILE *stdout;   /* Standard output stream.  */
extern FILE *stderr;   /* Standard error output stream.  */
```

---

1. In this context, we are discussing terminal-based programs. On some systems, GUI-based programs do not automatically get connected to the three standard streams.

The stderr stream is intended as a backup output stream for programs. It is commonly used to report errors or warnings. It is often connected to the same terminal display as the stdout stream but can be connected to a different display. For example, if a program is left running in the background, the program may be disconnected from its stdout stream but still have its stderr stream connected to a main terminal display.

5.2 • Buffers

A buffer is a temporary storage between the sender and receiver of bytes on a stream. When a stream is created, one can think of it as having an address from which bytes are sent and an address at which bytes are received. Each address is at a memory location controlled by the operating system. The buffer is an additional piece of memory that is used to moderate the flow of bytes from the source to the destination.

A buffer is useful in a variety of situations. For example, what if the sender puts bytes into the stream faster than the receiver can handle? Or what if a program is in the middle of a calculation and is not prepared to receive any bytes? The buffer can store up the bytes until the program is able to handle them, receiving them either at the reduced rate or when it is ready for them.

There are three basic types of buffering: block buffering, line buffering, and unbuffered. They differ in how the temporary storage is *flushed*. Flushing is the act of emptying out the temporary storage, sending all the bytes in the buffer on down the stream to the receiver. Each type of buffering differs as to how it flushes. In a block buffer, a fixed-size chunk of memory is filled before being passed on to the receiver. A block can be any size, although byte sizes that are powers of 2 are typical (e.g., 1 KB, 16 KB, etc.). In a line buffer, any bytes inside the buffer are sent to the receiver once a newline character (byte value of 13) is received. The newline character is also sent to the receiver. Finally, if the stream is unbuffered, then each byte is sent to the receiver as soon as it is placed in the buffer. The buffer operates as though it is transparent.

Block buffering is commonly used for large data transfers, such as file I/O. It makes the transfer more efficient by saving up a large number of bytes before actually transporting them. If a program is doing a lot of large data transfers, block buffering will speed it up. Line buffering is typically used for text-based I/O, such as when interacting with a user. It allows bytes to be modified before actually committing them to the stream transport. For example, a delete or backspace key can be used to modify the bytes in the line buffer, while the enter key can be used to initiate the flush. Finally, buffering may be completely turned off when responsiveness is critical. For example, a program may want to take action after any keypress provided by the user, without having to wait for flushing. In this case, the input stream would likely be unbuffered.

The effect of buffering can be seen through the following C code:

```
#include <stdio.h>
main()
{
int i;
for (i=0; i<5; i++)
    {
    printf("i=%d ",i);
    sleep(1);
    }
}
```

Executing this code, no output is seen until the program ends, which is 5 seconds after it started. This means that the stdout stream is buffered, either block or line. The type of buffering can be determined by modifying the printf(), adding a newline at the end, as follows:

```
    printf("i=%d\n",i);    /* add newline */
```

Executing the code with this modification, a new line of output is seen once per second. This indicates that the stream is line buffered. The buffer can also be forced to flush using the fflush() function call, as follows:

```
    printf("i=%d ",i);
    fflush(stdout);        /* force flushing of the buffer */
```

By calling fflush(), the program does not have to print a newline character each time the buffer is to be flushed. Note that fflush() can be used on any stream, not just the stdout stream, and it can be used to flush streams that are either block or line buffered.

A program typically does not need to know many of the details of how a stream or buffer is operating. Some of these details are hidden inside the FILE struct definition, and others can be accessed via system calls. For example, a program does not generally need to know the memory location of the temporary buffer storage or its size. It is, however, sometimes important to control the type of buffering on the stream. The `setvbuf()` function can be used to change the type of buffering on an existing stream.

The topic of buffering is revisited in Section 8.4.1 in the context of graphics and interfaces, along with the related topics of echoing and blocking. Controlling buffering is often more important for graphical interfaces than for text streams.

5.3 • Pipes

The term *pipe* is used in several contexts in I/O. Sometimes, the word "pipe" is used interchangeably with "stream" to refer to a flow of bytes between a source and destination. More often, it is used in contexts where streams are reconnected to alternate sources or destinations. An analogy to plumbing can be made as follows: imagine a water pipe that is disconnected at its source but left connected at its other end. The disconnected end is then reconnected to an alternate source. By modeling a stream on this concept, one can think of the connections at stream ends as pipe fittings. The process of connecting and reconnecting streams is referred to as *piping*, or *pipelining*. The analogy also extends to replacing a single pipe-to-pipe fitting with a three-way fitting, connecting one source to two destinations. One can imagine reconnecting the standard out stream so that it simultaneously sends the same bytes to a file and a display. This is another example of piping.

Section 5.1 discussed how streams can be created and terminated using file I/O functions. There is another set of functions, including `pipe()` and `dup()`, that can be used to manipulate stream connections. These functions are system calls and are discussed in more detail in Chapter 7. In this section, we focus on manipulating stream connections at the shell level.

Recall that the O/S automatically creates three streams for every running program. Most shells provide the ability to redirect those streams at startup. Table 5.1 lists the three most common options. In order to demonstrate their functionality, we will make use of the following code:

```
#include <stdio.h>
main()
{
int x,s;
s=0;
```

```
while (1)
{
printf("#? ");
scanf("%d",&x);
if (x == 0)
  break;
s=s+x;
printf(" sum=%d\n",s);
}
}
```

This code prompts the user for integers, reporting the sum as each new number is entered. It exits when a value of zero is entered. If the code is stored in a file called summer.c, then compiling and executing the code with the input shown produces the following output:

```
ahoover@video> gcc -o summer summer.c
ahoover@video> summer
#? 4
  sum=4
#? 1
  sum=5
#? 7
  sum=12
#? 0
ahoover@video>
```

Now suppose we create a file named input1.txt that contains the following:

```
4
1
7
0
```

Table 5.1 Common shell symbols for pipelining standard streams.

Symbol	Stream reconnection
<	standard in comes from the given file
>	standard out goes to the given file
|	standard out from the first program goes to standard in for the second program

This is the exact same sequence of bytes that was input through the keyboard to the program. The < symbol allows the user to redirect the stdin stream to a file instead of the keyboard. For example:

```
ahoover@video> summer < input1.txt
#?   sum=4
#?   sum=5
#?   sum=12
#? ahoover@video>
```

Running the program in this manner, the user provides input to the program from the file input1.txt instead of from the keyboard. In fact, the program is disconnected from the keyboard. Nothing the user types would be sent to the program; instead, it would be buffered until the program ended, and then sent to the shell. Note also that the bytes being sent to the program from the file are not being displayed. This is because they are not coming from the keyboard, which automatically echoes (copies) its bytes to the stdout stream.[2]

The stdout stream can be treated similarly. The > symbol allows the user to redirect the stdout stream to a file instead of to the display. For example:

```
ahoover@video> summer > output1.txt
4
1
7
0
ahoover@video>
```

Running the program in this manner, the program provides output to the file output1.txt instead of to the terminal display. In this case, we can see the input bytes being typed at the keyboard, but we see none of the output. In order to verify the output, we can execute the following command:

```
ahoover@video> more output1.txt
#?   sum=4
#?   sum=5
#?   sum=12
#?
ahoover@video>
```

All the output that we had previously seen in the terminal is now stored in the file output1.txt instead.

---

2. The topic of echoing is discussed in detail in Section 8.4.1.

Finally, we can connect the stdout stream of one program to the stdin stream of a second program. In order to demonstrate, we will make use of the following additional code:

```
#include <stdio.h>
main()
{
char s[80];
while (1)
{
scanf("%s",s);
if (strcmp(s,"sum=5") == 0)
    printf("Bingo!\n");
else if (strcmp(s,"sum=12") == 0)
    break;
}
}
```

This program looks for the line sum=5 and displays Bingo! if it sees it; otherwise, it looks for the line sum=12 to exit. Assuming this code is stored in a file named bingo.c, then compiling it and executing it as follows will produce the following output:

```
ahoover@video> gcc -o bingo bingo.c
ahoover@video> summer | bingo
4
1
7
0
Bingo!
ahoover@video>
```

The input to the program summer is being provided from the keyboard. However, note that no output from summer is being sent to the terminal display. Instead, it is being sent to the second program bingo on its stdin stream. In other words, the first program is acting like a user on a keyboard inputting data to the second program.

Most shells provide additional stream redirections. For example, it is often possible to redirect the stderr stream to a file. It is also often possible to redirect the stdout stream to concatenate its flow of bytes to an existing file. However, different shells use different symbols to implement these additional stream redirections. The three redirections shown in this section are universal; for others, the interested reader is encouraged to look at the documentation for a specific shell.

5.3.1 Pipeline Chaining

Multiple piping redirections can be done simultaneously. For example, using the programs and files from the previous section, the following can be executed:

```
ahoover@video> summer < input1.txt | bingo > output2.txt
ahoover@video> more output2.txt
Bingo!
ahoover@video>
```

In this example, both the stdin and stdout streams of the program summer are being redirected, the latter to the second program bingo, which also has its stdout stream redirected to a file.

Pipelining the output of one program to the input of another program can be done repeatedly. This allows us to write programs that perform single, simple operations, and to link them together into complex chains in order to accomplish tasks. For example:

```
ahoover@video> ls /usr/lib | grep libcu | sort -r
libcurses.so@
libcurses.a@
libcurl.so.3.0.0
libcurl.so.3@
libcups.so.2
libcupsimage.so.2
ahoover@video>
```

In this example, the program ls is retrieving a full file listing of the directory /usr/lib. This output is being sent as input to the program grep, which is searching for any occurrences of "libcu." This output is being sent as input to the program sort, which is alphabetically sorting the data into reverse order.

A set of standard programs has been built up over the years, following this methodology. Table 5.2 provides a list of some of the most common; Appendix C provides a longer list. Most Unix systems come with these programs installed as well as hundreds of others. There are a few of which all system users should be aware; more will become known and useful as one becomes more invested in system programming. Note that even these simple programs have lots of options, controlled by command line arguments, to affect how they operate.

Table 5.2 A sample of system programs designed for pipeline chaining.

Program	What it does
grep	search for the given string
sort	sorting
wc	count lines, words, bytes (chars)
more	interactive program to pause lengthy display
diff	compare two files

5.3.2 Program Testing

Pipelining techniques can be useful for testing programs. As already discussed, a set of inputs to a program can be stored in a file and then piped to the program via the stdin stream. Running a program in this manner, the user does not have to manually type input at each prompt. This can save a great deal of time while a program is being developed. During development, it is common for the program to be altered slightly, recompiled, and then executed. This cycle may happen dozens of times. Each time, the input can be piped from a file instead of being manually keyed.

This type of file can be considered a test pattern, or test input. When considering the content of a test file, there are usually two considerations. First, it is desirable for the test file to contain a variety of inputs for which the desired output is known. For example, if a program is designed to compute the square root of a number, then a test file for that program should contain a variety of positive whole numbers. Second, it is desirable for the test file to contain input sequences that are improper or that could lead to errors. For example, for a square root calculator, the test file should contain one or more negative numbers, nonnumber sequences, and other potential errors.

We will use the following code to demonstrate the usefulness of pipelining techniques for program development and debugging:

```c
#include <stdio.h>
#include <stdlib.h>
#include <string.h>

int main (int argc, char *argv[])
{
char  in[80],out[80];
int  i,j;
```

```
while (1)
  {
  scanf("%s",in);
  if (strcmp(in,".") == 0)
    break;
  strcpy(out,in);
  for (i=0; i<strlen(out); i++)
    if (out[i] == '.'  ||  out[i] == ','  ||
        out[i] == '"'  ||  out[i] == ';'  ||
        out[i] == '!'  ||  out[i] == '?'  ||
        out[i] == '('  ||  out[i] == ')'  ||
        out[i] == ':')
      {
      for (j=i; j<strlen(out)-1; j++)
        out[j]=out[j+1];
      out[j]='\0';
      }
  printf("%s\n",out);
  }
}
```

This program removes punctuation (nine specific symbols) from any given input.
It outputs one word from the input per line with the punctuation removed. The
program ends when a single period (.) is given as input. If this code is stored in
a file named depunct.c, then compiling and executing it produces the following
output:

```
ahoover@video> gcc -o depunct depunct.c
ahoover@video> depunct
Turtles, frogs hello! .
Turtles
frogs
hello
ahoover@video>
```

In this example, the first and third words have had punctuation marks removed,
while the second word remains unchanged.

Now we consider the task of creating a test file:

```
This is a big test; how can I check the output?
I want to make sure it's "perfect".
Here are some test cases:
```

```
        railroad.
        don't
        .railroad
        "Happy days" are here again!
        stra?nge
        This is (a) clue.
Have I covered enough te-st 000 cases?
```

Note that this test data includes words containing each of the punctuation marks that the program is supposed to remove. It also contains other punctuation marks. It contains punctuation marks at the beginning, middle, and end of various words. Some words have multiple punctuation marks. If this test data is stored in a file named input3.txt, then piping it to stdin produces the following output:

```
ahoover@video> depunct < input3.txt
This
is
a
big
test
[... long output abbreviated ...]
000
cases
ahoover@video>
```

Instead of having to retype each of these cases every time the program is modified, this test file can be used repeatedly during development.

Pipelining can also be used to verify the correctness of output. This can be seen using the preceding example. While it is possible to manually peruse the long output and check each word carefully for errors, the manual checking is itself prone to errors. Instead, a second test file can be created as follows:

```
This
is
a
[... each word manually processed ...]
000
cases
```

If this data is stored in a file named expected3.txt, then it can be used to verify the correctness of the program as follows:

```
ahoover@video> depunct < input3.txt > output3.txt
ahoover@video> diff output3.txt expected3.txt
18c18
< perfect.
---
> perfect
ahoover@video>
```

This shows that for one of the words, the output did not match the expected output. What went wrong in the program? Finding the error is left as an exercise for the reader at the end of the chapter. The point is that finding this sort of problem with a program is made easier through the use of test files and pipelining techniques.

5.4 • Files

Every computer user is familiar with files, but what exactly is a file? A file is a one-dimensional array of bytes. Regardless of what sort of data is inside the file, it is always stored as a one-dimensional array of bytes. This may seem counterintuitive for a file that contains an image, or a movie, or a database. Chapter 3 discussed how multidimensional arrays can be stored in one-dimensional memory by writing out all the array cells in a long list. The same principle applies to file storage. An image, movie, or database can be stored as a one-dimensional array of bytes by writing all the elements out in a long list. Furthermore, it does not matter what sort of data is inside the file. If the file contains text, an image, a song, or an executable program, it is still a one-dimensional array of bytes. The difference is only in which bit model was used to group and encode the bytes. Therefore, when we think of reading from or writing to a file, we can always consider the process as being similar to accessing a one-dimensional array of bytes.

One of the jobs of an operating system is to manage file storage. A system typically provides a set of function calls, for use by programs, to interact with files. These include the operations already examined, such as the ability to read and write data, plus additional operations. We will explore these additional operations and related functions as we discuss each associated topic.

5.4.1 File Pointer

A file pointer is a marker used to keep track of the location for reading or writing on a stream. When a file is opened, the file pointer points to the first byte in the file. Each time a byte is read, the file pointer is automatically advanced to the next byte. If multiple bytes are read, then the file pointer is advanced beyond all the bytes that have been read. For example, consider the following data in a file:

```
abcdef
```

Assuming that these bytes are stored in a file named data.txt, the following code will be used to access the file and demonstrate the motion of the file pointer:

```c
#include <stdio.h>
main()
{
char byte;
FILE *fpt;
fpt=fopen("data.txt","r");
fread(&byte,1,1,fpt);
fclose(fpt);
}
```

When the file is first opened, the file pointer has a value of 0, indicating that it points to the first byte in the file:

```
abcdef
```

After the first byte is read, the file pointer is advanced to point to the second byte in the file:

```
abcdef
```

The process can also be explained using a memory map of the file:

File

Byte	Value
0	'a' (97)
1	'b' (98)
2	'c' (99)
3	'd' (100)
4	'e' (101)
5	'f' (102)

When the file is opened, the file pointer has a value of 0, indicating the point of next access in the file. After the first byte is read from the file, the file pointer takes a new value of 1.

The value of the file pointer, and hence its location, can be manipulated by the fseek() function. The fseek() function moves the file pointer to a new value without reading or writing any data on the stream. The current value of the file pointer can be obtained using the ftell() function. The following code demonstrates the use of both these functions:

```
#include <stdio.h>
int main(int argc,char *argv[])
{
FILE       *fpt;
char       byte;
long int   where,move;

if (argc != 2)
   {
   printf("Usage:  fileseek filename\n");
   exit(0);
   }
if ((fpt=fopen(argv[1],"r")) == NULL)
   {
   printf("Unable to open %s for reading\n",argv[1]);
   exit(0);
   }

while (1)
   {
   where=ftell(fpt);          /* where is file pointer? */
   fread(&byte,1,1,fpt);      /* moves fpt ahead one byte */
   fseek(fpt,-1,SEEK_CUR);    /* back up one byte */
   printf("Byte %d: %d (%c)\n",where,byte,byte);
   printf("Enter #bytes (+ or -) to move, or 0 to quit: ");
   scanf("%d",&move);
   if (move == 0)
      break;
   fseek(fpt,move,SEEK_CUR);  /* move to desired byte */
   }
fclose(fpt);
}
```

This program opens a file and allows the user to move the file pointer. It reads 1 byte and displays the byte value using both the ASCII and two's complement bit models, as well as the file pointer value for that byte. It then prompts the user as to how to move the file pointer. This is repeated until the user enters 0 to quit.

Assuming this code is stored in a file named `fileseek.c`, then compiling it and executing it on the `data.txt` file from above produces the following output:

```
ahoover@video> gcc -o fileseek fileseek.c
ahoover@video> fileseek data.txt
Byte 0: 97 (a)
Enter #bytes (+ or -) to move, or 0 to quit: 2
Byte 2: 99 (c)
Enter #bytes (+ or -) to move, or 0 to quit: 3
Byte 5: 102 (f)
Enter #bytes (+ or -) to move, or 0 to quit: -4
Byte 1: 98 (b)
Enter #bytes (+ or -) to move, or 0 to quit: 0
ahoover@video>
```

The ftell() function takes only one argument, the stream, and returns its current file pointer byte value. The fseek() function takes three arguments. The first argument is the stream, the second and third arguments indicate where to move the file pointer. The third argument is the base value, which can indicate the beginning of the file (SEEK_SET), the end of the file (SEEK_END), or the current file pointer position (SEEK_CUR). The second argument gives an offset from the base value. These options provide some flexibility in manipulating the file pointer.

5.4.2   File Attributes

If a file is only a one-dimensional array of bytes, where is all the other stuff that is associated with a file? How does a system know when a file was last modified, or if the file is an executable program, or if the file is write protected? How does a system know the size of a file (the number of bytes)? A file listing produces a great deal of information about a file. For example:

```
ahoover@video> ls -l
total 40
-rw-r--r-- ahoover fusion     808 Jul  5 16:58 fileseek.c
-rwxr-xr-x ahoover fusion   14196 May 28 16:18 ls1
-rw-r--r-- ahoover fusion     468 May 28 20:21 ls1.c
-rw-r--r-- ahoover fusion     803 Jul  5 16:58 statfile1.c
-rw------- ahoover fusion     758 Jul  5 16:58 statfile2.c
-rw-r--r-- ahoover fusion       7 Jul  5 16:58 testme.txt
ahoover@video>
```

In this list, each row provides information about a file. The filename itself is in the rightmost column. The first column provides the *permissions* of the file, which indicate who is allowed to access the file, and what types of access are allowed. The letters "r," "w," and "x" stand for *read*, *write*, and *execute*. The first rwx applies to the owner of the file, the second rwx applies to the group of the file, and the last rwx applies to any user. A hyphen (-) indicates that particular permission is denied. Thus, the file ls1 in the list above can be read or executed by anyone, but it can be written only by the owner of the file. The file statfile2.c can be read or written only by the owner of the file and cannot be executed at all. On a Unix system, the permissions of a file can be changed using the chmod system program. For example:

```
ahoover@video> chmod g+w ls1.c
ahoover@video> ls -l ls1.c
-rw-rw-r-- ahoover fusion    468 May 28 20:21 ls1.c
ahoover@video>
```

This command added the write permission to the group of the file. A full description for the chmod program can be found in its man page.

Returning to the file listing, the second column identifies the owner of the file and the third column identifies the group of the file. For the example listing, all the files are owned by the user "ahoover" and belong to the group "fusion." A group is a name for a set of users working together, who may all need access to a file. The fourth column identifies the size of the file, in bytes. Thus, the file ls1 is 14,196 bytes, and the file testme.txt is only 7 bytes. The remaining columns prior to the filename indicate the date and time that the file was last modified.

This is only about half the information that a Unix system maintains about each file. All of this information is stored in tables managed by the system. The information for a file can be accessed using the stat() function call. The following program demonstrates its usage:

```
#include <stdio.h>
#include <sys/stat.h>  /* needed for stat() function */

int main(int argc, char *argv[])
{
struct stat    fileinfo;  /* returned info about file */
int            i;

if (argc != 2)
   {
   printf("Usage:  statfile filename\n");
   exit(0);
   }
```

```
i=stat(argv[1],&fileinfo);
if (i == -1)
{
printf("Unable to stat %s\n",argv[1]);
exit(0);
}
printf("size: %d\n",fileinfo.st_size);
printf("permissions: %d\n",fileinfo.st_mode);
printf("last modified: %d\n",fileinfo.st_mtime);
}
```

Notice that the program never opens the file. Instead, it calls stat() on the given filename. This is because the extra file information is not contained in the one-dimensional array of bytes that is the file; rather, it is maintained in tables managed by the system. Assuming that this code is stored in a file named statfile.c, then compiling it and executing it on the file ls1.c from above produces the following output:

```
ahoover@video> gcc -o statfile statfile.c
ahoover@video> statfile ls1.c
size: 468
permissions: 33188
last modified: 1212020479
ahoover@video>
```

The size of the file matches the size (468 bytes) displayed from the file listing. The other two fields look strange because they are encoded. For the permissions, each possible permission requires only 1 bit to store. The individual bits can be printed out using the following code:

```
    .
    .
    .
for (i=9; i>=0; i--)
  if (fileinfo.st_mode & (1 << i))
    printf("1");
  else
    printf("0");
printf("\n");
    .
    .
    .
```

Recompiling and running the program now produces the following:

```
ahoover@video> gcc -o statfile statfile.c
ahoover@video> statfile ls1.c
```

```
size: 468
permissions: 33188
0110100100
last modified: 1212020479
ahoover@video>
```

Comparing the sequence "-rw-r--r--" to the bit pattern for 33188 reveals that for each permission granted, there is a value of 1 in the related bit:

```
-rw-r--r--
0110100100
```

The last modified date for a file is also encoded. Dates on a Unix system are stored as a whole number giving the number of seconds since midnight (UTC) of January 1, 1970. Thus, approximately 1.2 billion seconds after January 1, 1970, or May 28, 2008, is when the file ls1.c was last modified.

The stat() function returns other information besides that covered in this section. A full description can be found in its man page.

5.4.3 Directories

A directory is an organizational tool for files. It is used to group together a set of files. Technically, a directory is a list of filenames and auxiliary information for each file. But it can be conceptualized as a one-dimensional array of filenames. For example, consider the following file listing:

```
ahoover@video> ls -a
./  ../  data.txt  fileseek.c  ls1  ls1.c
ahoover@video>
```

The directory for the above file listing can be written as follows:

Directory

Entry	Filename
0	./
1	../
2	data.txt
3	fileseek.c
4	ls1
5	ls1.c

The output shows ./ and ../ at the start of the list of filenames. These "filenames" are used to provide a tree-like hierarchical structure for directories. The filename ./ refers to the *current directory*, which is the directory containing the listed files. The filename ../ refers to the *parent directory*, which is the directory containing the filename of the current directory. The directory entries for these two filenames are used to link directories together, allowing one directory to be placed "inside" another.

The O/S manages directories in much the same manner as it manages files. It maintains tables that contain directory filename lists as well as additional data for each filename. These tables can be accessed using the opendir(), readdir(), and closedir() functions. For example, consider the following code:

```c
#include <stdio.h>
#include <dirent.h>

int main(int argc, char *argv[])
{
DIR              *directory;   /* the directory */
struct dirent    *entry;       /* each entry */

directory=opendir(".");
if (directory == NULL)
   {
   printf("Unable to open directory .\n");
   exit(0);
   }
while (1)
   {
   entry=readdir(directory);
   if (entry == NULL)
     break;
   printf("%s\n",entry->d_name);
   }
closedir(directory);
}
```

This program opens up the current working directory "." and reads through all its directory entries, printing out the filename for each entry. If this code is stored in a file named ls1.c, then compiling and executing it in the same directory as the example above produces the following output:

```
ahoover@video> gcc -o ls1 ls1.c
ahoover@video> ls1
.
..
data.txt
fileseek.c
ls1
ls1.c
ahoover@video>
```

The function opendir() opens the given directory table (also called a directory stream). The function readdir() reads an entry from the directory table. The system maintains a directory pointer that is automatically advanced to the next directory entry subsequent to a read. This behavior is similar to how a file pointer is advanced subsequent to the reading or writing of bytes to a file. Each directory entry contains a filename as well as other organizational information, such as whether the filename is a regular file or a directory. Finally, the function closedir() is used to close access to the directory.

5.5 • Devices

One of the neat aspects of Unix is that any peripheral, device, or piece of hardware connected to the computing system can be accessed as though it were a file. This concept is often referred to as "file-based I/O." An I/O transaction with a device is handled similarly to an I/O transaction with a file. They both make use of streams and buffers, and they both use the same I/O functions.

The following example shows how fopen() can be used to establish an I/O connection to a terminal display through the device's filename /dev/pts/1:

```
#include <stdio.h>
main()
{
FILE *fpt;
fpt=fopen("/dev/pts/1","w");
fprintf(fpt,"Hello terminal.");
fclose(fpt);
}
```

Assuming that code is stored in a file called fopen-term.c, then compiling and executing it will produce the following result:

```
ahoover@video> gcc -o fopen-term fopen-term.c
ahoover@video> fopen-term
Hello terminal.
ahoover@video>
```

The exact name of the terminal display will depend upon the system, and how many terminals are currently running. In order to determine the name of a terminal display, one can run the `tty` program at the prompt. For example:

```
ahoover@video> tty
/dev/pts/1
ahoover@video>
```

The example above can be modified accordingly using the discovered terminal display name.

The following example shows how fopen() can be used to establish an I/O connection to a mouse through the device's filename /dev/psaux:

```
#include <stdio.h>
main()
{
FILE    *fpt;
int     c,buf[4];

fpt=fopen("/dev/psaux","r");
while (1)
  {
  c=fread(buf,4,1,fpt);
  printf("Read %d bytes:  %d\n",c,buf[0]);
  }
fclose(fpt);
}
```

Assuming that code is stored in a file called `fopen-mouse.c`, then compiling and executing it will produce something like the following result:

```
root@video> gcc -o fopen-mouse fopen-mouse.c
root@video> fopen-mouse
Read 1 bytes:  65537
Read 1 bytes:  130856
Read 1 bytes:  65064
Read 1 bytes:  130856
Read 1 bytes:  130600
... [CTRL-C] ...
root@video>
```

Running this example requires some care. First, the exact name of the mouse may differ depending on the system; a common practice is to link the filename /dev/mouse to whatever device filename is actually used for the mouse. Second, the user typically must be root to run the program. The mouse device filename will typically have file permissions set so that only the root user can access it. Finally, the user must move the mouse to see something like the output shown above. Each time a mouse button is clicked, or the mouse is moved, a stream of bytes should appear. The purpose of this example is not to decode or understand the byte values but simply to demonstrate how a stream connection can be made to a mouse.

The directory /dev is normally used to store filenames for all the devices that the computing system might want to access. There are often literally thousands of filenames in that directory. Many of them are simply reserved in case a particular device is connected to the computing system, at which time it becomes accessible through its related device filename. Sometimes a single device may have multiple device filenames associated with it, where each filename provides access to a different part of the device. For example, it is common practice to access a hard drive through the filename /dev/hda, and to access its individual partitions through the filenames /dev/hda1, /dev/hda2, and so forth.

5.5.1   Device Drivers

A device driver is a set of functions used to access a device. These functions include custom versions of open(), close(), read(), write(), seek(), and a small handful of others. The functions associated with a particular device are executed when the device is accessed through its device filename.

Determining which functions to execute is controlled by something called the *major device number*. The major device number of a particular device filename can be seen by looking at the full file information for the given filename. For example:

```
ahoover@video> ls -l /dev/hda
brw-rw----  root  disk   3,   0 Aug 30  2001 /dev/hda
ahoover@video> ls -l /dev/psaux
crw-------  root  root  10,   1 May 27 14:58 /dev/psaux
ahoover@video>
```

For these filenames, notice that the column in the middle that is usually used to report the size of the file shows something different. For the file /dev/hda, part of the file listing reports "3, 0," and for the file /dev/psaux, part of the file listing reports "10, 1." For each of these number pairs, the first number is the major device number. It tells the operating system which set of device driver functions to use to access the device. When the device driver is introduced to the system (either during kernel compilation, or as a dynamically loaded module similar to the concept of "plug and play"), it must register a major device number. It is through this mechanism that a program can use a device filename to access the appropriate functions for interacting with the device.

The second number in each number pair is the minor device number. It is used to provide a unique ID for multiple device filenames that use the same device driver functions. For example, a system may have more than one hard drive of the same type connected to it. In order to allow access to both hard drives, each drive would use a different device filename with the same major device number but with a different minor device number.

Device drivers can seem complicated until a programmer attains some familiarity with them. The intent of this chapter was to provide a general understanding of how I/O works, including I/O with devices. In this context, the most important thing to remember is that devices are accessed just like files, and that device drivers are nothing more than a set of functions customized to each device. For further discussion, the interested reader is directed to the excellent book *Linux Device Drivers*, 3rd ed., J. Corbet, A. Rubini, and G. Kroah-Hartman, O'Reilly, 2005.

Questions and Exercises

1. Write out the file contents for out.txt as produced by the following code. Give specific byte values. How many total bytes will the file contain at the end of execution?

```
#include <stdio.h>
main()
{
FILE *fpt;
int x;

fpt=fopen("out.txt","w");
for (x=0; x<15; x+=2)
  fprintf(fpt,"%2d ",x);
fclose(fpt);
}
```

2. Write out the file contents for out2 as produced by the following code. Give specific values to bytes or ranges of bytes. The values of the same variable are being written using fprintf() and then fwrite(). How many bytes are written by each, and which is more efficient?

```
#include <stdio.h>
main()
{
FILE *fpt;
struct frog {
        float d;
        int x;
        } henry;

henry.d=12.73;
henry.x=81925;
fpt=fopen("out2","w");
fprintf(fpt,"%7.2f %7d\n",henry.d,henry.x);
fwrite(&henry,sizeof(struct frog),1,fpt);
fclose(fpt);
}
```

3. Write out the memory map and file contents for the following code, providing all values at the end of execution. What is the exact output produced by this program?

```
#include <stdio.h>
main()
{
double testd;
int testi;
FILE *fpt;
struct frog {
        double *x,y;
        };
struct frog turtle,*apple,tv[3];

testi=21;
apple=&turtle;
turtle.y=5.2;
fpt=fopen("out3","w");
fwrite(apple,sizeof(struct frog),1,fpt);
fclose(fpt);
```

```
apple->x=&testd;
fpt=fopen("out3","r");
fread(&(tv[1]),sizeof(struct frog),1,fpt);
fclose(fpt);
*(turtle.x)=7.3;
(*apple).y=3.6;
turtle.y=1.5;
*(tv[1].x)=6.4;
printf("%lf \n",tv[1].y);
}
```

4. Describe two ways in which shell pipelining can be useful during program development.

5. Consider the code given below. Write a custom print function "cprintf()" that implements a buffer. The function takes a single string as input and returns nothing. All bytes in the string are buffered until the percent symbol (%) is encountered. Upon encountering that symbol, all contents of the buffer should be flushed (printed to the stdout stream) and the buffer should be reset to empty. The percent symbol should not be printed; it is only a trigger. The buffer only needs to be large enough for this example, do not worry about overflow. The newline character should be printed but should not cause a flush.

```
#include <stdio.h>
#include <stdlib.h>
#include <string.h>


        /* custom function cprintf() goes here */

main()
{
cprintf("Test\n");
sleep(1);
cprintf("Re%test\n");
sleep(1);
cprintf("All done\n%");
}
```

If your function works correctly, in what chronological manner should the printed text appear? (Hint: in order to implement this function, the contents of the buffer must persist through multiple calls to the function.)

6. Using the same instructions as given in Exercise 5, there is a potential problem with flushing the buffer. If the last byte that the cprintf() function received

before the program ends is the percent symbol, then it will work fine. However, if the program ends with bytes still in the buffer, they will be lost and never appear on the stdout stream.

Discuss a way in which this could be fixed so that the buffer would also flush whenever the program ended. Your solution can take one of several approaches. Think conceptually even if you are not sure how to code your approach.

7. Consider the variable declaration below. Write code that opens a file for output and uses a single line of code to write out all of the declared variable(s).

```
struct inventory {
                char name[30];
                int count;
                float price;
        } log[75];
```

8. Write a program that reads a text file and reports the total count of words of each length. A word is defined as any contiguous set of alphanumeric characters, including symbols. For example, in the current sentence there are 10 words. The filename should be given at the command line as an argument. The file should be read one word at a time. A count should be kept for how many words have a given length. For example, the word "frog" is 4 bytes in length; the word "turtle" is 6 bytes in length. The program should report the total word counts of all lengths between 3 and 15 bytes. Words with lengths outside that range should not be counted.

9. Write a program that reads a text file and prints out any words that begin with a user-given string. The filename should be given at the command line as an argument. The program should prompt the user for the search string. The program should then read the file one word at a time and print out the word if its first N bytes match the search string, where N is the length of the search string.

10. The program listed in Section 5.3.2 did not correctly remove all the desired punctuation marks in the given test file. Debug the program and correct it. Make another test file and expected output file to use during debugging.

11. Consider the following structure template and variable definition:

```
struct rec {
                char name[30];
                double ppg;
                int years;
        } team[12];
```

Suppose there is a file in which the entire variable *team* has been written in its natural array order. Write a program that accesses the file and reads a single entry of the array as selected by the user. The program should require two arguments, one being the filename and the second being the number of the desired entry. The program should not read the entire file; it should use other methods to access only the desired entry. The retrived information should be displayed, and then the program should exit.

12. Write a program that will display text on any terminal. The program should prompt the user for the name of the device file for the terminal on which to display output, as well the output to display. It should then perform the necessary I/O operations. This process should repeat until the user decides to exit the program.

13. Write a program that allows the user to search an ASCII text file loaded into main memory. The program should be able to search by byte value, ASCII string, or address (memory, not file). The program should report the answer, surrounded by context, that is, part of the file on either side of the answer. The program should run until the user selects an option to quit.

The program must use a command line argument to discover the name of the file to load. The program must use dynamic memory allocation to create an array (remember, arrays are pointers) of bytes in which to load and process the file. The array should allow addressing of individual bytes from the file, and it should be exactly the same size (in bytes) as the file.

Once loaded, the program should go into a loop, providing the user with four options. The first option allows the user to specify a byte value (0–255). Given a value, the program displays all occurrences in the array of that value. The display should take the form of:

```
address              context value context
```

where address is the base 10 address of the location in memory (not the array index, and not the file address). The value and context should be displayed using ASCII symbols. Context should be the 5 bytes immediately preceding the value, and the 5 bytes immediately following the value. Do not be concerned if the ASCII symbols for the context or value are nonprintable characters; simply print them. However, printing of symbols should not go beyond the beginning of the array, or past the end of the array. If the context reaches past these boundaries, an appropriate message should be displayed prior to the context, or after the context, as the case warrants.

The second program option allows the user to specify an ASCII string. Given that string, the program displays all occurrences in the array of that string. The display should look exactly as it did for option 1 (with the string in place of the value). The third program option allows the user to specify an address (memory), and displays that address as for option 1. The fourth program option allows the user to quit. Appropriate error checking must take place for bounds on expected input (for example, a value must be 0–255, and an address must be within the expected range).

14. Write two programs that encode and decode plain text files. The encryption is a simple cipher, replacing each alphanumeric symbol with a shifted value. Here are two examples:

```
Dog3     => shifted +1 => Eph4
Cat...0 => shifted -1 => Bzs...9
```

Only letter (upper- and lowercase) and numeric (0–9) symbols should be affected. All other symbols should pass through encryption and decryption unaffected. The shifting of a symbol should wrap around its set. For example, the symbol "a" shifted -1 should become "z." The symbol "9" shifted +1 should become "0." The symbol "Z" shifted +2 should become "B." This is also demonstrated in the examples above.

The first program should encode text. It should prompt for one word (string) at a time, encode it, and print out the encoded version. This should continue until the single symbol "." is given as input, which should terminate the program. The first program must accept a single command line argument defining the shift delta. The value of delta must be an integer between -9 and +9, inclusive.

The second program should decode encrypted text. It should be unaware of the value of delta used to encode the text. Instead, it must figure out the value of delta by trying to decrypt using all possible values for delta and examining the resulting text. To examine the result, the program must use the dictionary stored in the linux.words file (usually found in /usr/share/dict, depending on your system's installation of ispell). It should compare every potential decrypted word with the dictionary, looking for a match. Whichever value for delta produces the most matches with words in the dictionary should be assumed to be the correct value for delta. The program should print out the decrypted text using that value of delta (and it should not print out anything else).

Assume that the message being encrypted or decrypted consists of fewer than 100 words, and that no word is longer than 30 characters.

Develop the programs using shell I/O redirection techniques, including taking stdin from a file, piping stdout from the encoder to stdin on the decoder, and placing stdout to a file. These operations should work.

15. Write a program that provides a file listing for the given directory. The program should list the filename, file size, and time last modified for each file within the directory. The program should provide the user with the option to sort the listing based on filename, on file size, or on time last modified. The program should run once and quit (it does not loop).

The syntax (usage) for the program should be

```
prog_name [directory] [[-s][-t]]
```

where -s indicates sort by file size and -t indicates sort by time last modified. These flags are optional but mutually exclusive. The directory is also optional; if it is omitted, then a default directory of "." (the current directory) should be assumed. Every possible combination of command line arguments from the above syntax should be tested.

The output should be displayed with fixed-width columns for the size and date. Column orders should be size, then date, then filename. The time last modified should be printed as a 12-character string (e.g., "Oct 10 11:37"). This can be done by manipulating the returned string from the ctime() function and printing only a portion of it.

If the given directory is not a directory—for example, if it is a single filename—then the program should report an error and quit.

Sorting of filenames should be done in a to z order. No special cases need to be handled; simple ASCII ordering is sufficient (this means for example, that uppercase A through Z comes before lowercase a through z; they do not need to be interleaved). Sorting of file sizes should be done largest to smallest. Sorting of times should be sorted most recent to least recent. Because the year is not to be shown in the printed listing, this may look out of order, but that is not an issue to be addressed in this exercise.

6

Program Management

Program management concerns the organization, building, and distribution of programs. The organization of a program involves how the code is written, including its logical and visual layout. The goals of good organization include code readability and modularity. These characteristics support good design practices and make program debugging and scaling easier. The building of a program entails how the code is compiled. Compiling involves many intermediate steps and file types that enable the construction of an executable. The distribution of a program is concerned with how the code is packaged and delivered to target systems. There are a number of tools and practices designed to facilitate program distribution and installation.

For the writers of programs, program management can seem like a chore. Management and bookkeeping tasks seemingly take time away from the job of actually writing programs. However, in the long run, having well-organized code and understanding the compilation and distribution processes make programming both simpler and more efficient. With practice, good management techniques become incorporated into all programming work. The goal of this chapter is to familiarize the reader with the tools and practices common to program organization, building, and distribution. The reader may be familiar with many of the individual concepts discussed in this chapter; however, putting them all together under the context of program management should provide new insight into how and when all these concepts and tools should best be used.

6.1 • Program Building

After a program is written, it must be built into an executable so that it can be run. Building a program consists of a series of steps. At each step, the code is transformed to produce an intermediate form. Intermediate forms include pre-processed, assembly code, object code, and libraries. Understanding these steps and the intermediate forms is important for several reasons. Each offers different strategies for saving programming time or maximizing system resources. For example, the preprocessing step provides macros for repetitive string substitution; the assembly step provides a programmer with named memory locations; and the linking step provides a way to reuse existing executable code in multiple programs. The intermediate forms can be retained between program builds to speed up subsequent rebuilds. Errors in the program can be uncovered at each program building step. This section goes through the program building process and discusses each step.

6.1.1   Object Code and Linking

Figure 6.1 presents a diagram of the basic steps in program building. The steps of compiling and linking transform a source code file into an executable file. Source code is the C program as written by the programmer. For example, assume the following code has been written:

```c
#include <stdio.h>

int OurSquareRoot(int n)
{
if (n == 4)
    return(2);
else
    {
    printf("I cannot compute the square root of %d\n",n);
    return(-1);
    }
}
```

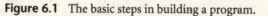

Figure 6.1   The basic steps in building a program.

If this code is stored in a file named `sqrt.c`, then it can be compiled into object code as follows:

```
ahoover@video> ls
sqrt.c
ahoover@video> gcc -c sqrt.c
ahoover@video> ls
sqrt.c  sqrt.o
ahoover@video>
```

The `-c` flag tells gcc to stop after the compile stage and not to proceed to linking. There are actually several steps during compiling, but these are addressed in the next section; for now they are considered as a whole. This creates a file named `sqrt.o` that contains object code. An object code file contains machine code, instructions that can be run on the processor. But an object code file cannot be directly executed. Object code files must be linked to become an executable program that can be run. Linking is the process of bringing together multiple pieces of object code and arranging them into an executable. Object code can come from multiple source code files, each compiled into its own object code file. To demonstrate, consider the following additional code:

```c
#include <stdio.h>

int OurSquareRoot(int);

int main(int argc, char *argv[])
{
int     x,s;

printf("Enter any integer: ");
scanf("%d",&x);
s=OurSquareRoot(x);
if (s != -1)
   printf("The square root of %d is %d\n",x,s);
}
```

If this code is stored in a file named `main.c`, then it can be compiled as follows:

```
ahoover@video> gcc -c sqrt.c
ahoover@video> gcc -c main.c
ahoover@video> ls
main.c  main.o  sqrt.c  sqrt.o
ahoover@video> gcc sqrt.o main.o
```

```
ahoover@video> ls
a.out  main.c  main.o  sqrt.c  sqrt.o
ahoover@video>
```

Through these steps, two object code files were created, main.o and sqrt.o. Following that, an executable was created, a.out, by linking together the two object code files. The executable is the file that can actually be run:

```
ahoover@video> a.out
Enter any integer: 4
The square root of 4 is 2
ahoover@video>
```

In order to further understand the difference between an executable and an object code file, consider the following:

```
ahoover@video> gcc sqrt.o
.... undefined reference to 'main'
ahoover@video>
```

The compiler was unable to create an executable because no main() function was found in the given object code. An executable can contain any number of functions, but it must contain exactly one main() function so that when the program is run, the system knows where to begin execution of the program. Other errors can also be uncovered during linking. For example:

```
ahoover@video> gcc main.o
.... undefined reference to 'SquareRoot'
ahoover@video>
```

In this case, the compiler was unable to create an executable because it could not find the object code for the SquareRoot() function.

Object code files can be created from any source language, not just C. It is possible to link object code files that were compiled from combinations of lanauges, such as C, C++, and Fortran, as well as files originally written directly in machine language. Once a source code file has been compiled into object code, the original language of the source code does not matter. The source code has been transformed into machine code that is capable of being executed on the host system.

When compiling, unless otherwise instructed, gcc will automatically proceed to linking, and then remove any object code files it created. This is done to simplify the process, so that a programmer does not need to separately perform all the compiling and linking steps. It also saves file storage space on the system by

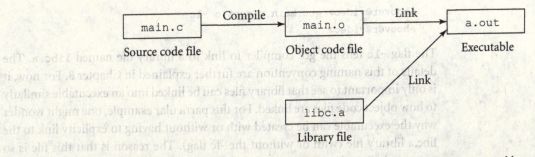

Figure 6.2 Linking a library file with an object code file to create an executable.

removing intermediate files that may not be needed. However, when compiling multiple files, it is often convenient to instruct the compiler to keep object code files, so that only changed source code files need to be recompiled. Everything else needs only to be linked. This can save time when the number of source code files comprising a program grows large. It can also help with organization, in that it helps track which files have had modifications made to them between program builds.

Linking primarily serves to bring together object code files into an executable. However, it can also bring in object code from library files. Figure 6.2 shows this in diagram form. Library files contain object code for functions that are frequently used. In this way, the source code can be compiled once and stored in a permanent place, ready to link. For example, the most commonly linked library file is libc.a, the primary library file of the C standard library. It contains the object code for the standard functions like printf(), fopen(), and strcmp(). The contents of this library file can be seen as follows:

```
ahoover@video> ls -al /usr/lib/libc.a
-rw-r--r--  1 root root 2567960 2006-03-24   /usr/lib/libc.a
ahoover@video> ar t /usr/lib/libc.a | grep print
.
.
fprintf.o
printf.o
.
.
ahoover@video>
```

Since these functions are used over and over, their object code is permanently stored in a library file, so they do not need to be recompiled every time. The following demonstrates linking to a library file:

```
ahoover@video> gcc main.o sqrt.o -lc
ahoover@video>
```

The flag -lc tells the gcc compiler to link to a library file named libc.a. The details of this naming convention are further explained in Chapter 8. For now, it is only important to see that library files can be linked into an executable similarly to how object code files are linked. For this particular example, one might wonder why the executable can be created with or without having to explicity link to the libc.a library file (with or without the -lc flag). The reason is that this file is so commonly linked, most compilers are set up to assume that it is needed and so link to it by default.

Normally, object code files are copied into an executable; all the machine code is rearranged a bit but is otherwise copied over into the executable. If this were done with the object code in a library, then there would be many redundant copies of the same machine code throughout all the executables using the library functions. To prevent this, a library can be linked dynamically, which means that the object code is not copied into the executable. Instead, when the program is run, if machine code from a library file is needed, it is loaded into memory directly from the library file. To demonstrate:

```
ahoover@video> gcc main.c sqrt.c
ahoover@video> ls -al a.out
-rwxr-xr-x  1 student student 7442    a.out
ahoover@video> gcc -static main.c sqrt.c
ahoover@video> ls -al a.out
-rwxr-xr-x  1 student student 476153  a.out
ahoover@video>
```

In the second case, the library was linked statically, causing all the needed object code to be copied into the executable (this includes the object code for printf(), for example). Notice how much larger the executable is when the library file is linked statically. There are other implications of dynamic versus static linking. Dynamically linked executables can run more slowly because multiple library files may need to be accessed. Dynamically linked executables are also fragile to the system in that, if a library file is removed, the executable will no longer run. However, dynamic linking is the default for most compilers and systems, due to the space it saves in keeping executables smaller.

6.1.2 Compiling

The compile process transforms a source code file into an object code file. Looking a little deeper, the process consists of three steps: preprocessing, compiling,

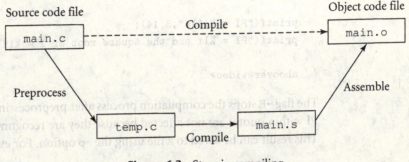

Figure 6.3 Steps in compiling.

and assembling. Figure 6.3 illustrates the process of compiling. The most complex of the three transformations is the compiling step, and so the total process of the three steps is often referred to simply as compiling.

The first step is preprocessing. Preprocessing provides mechanisms to support text substitutions, also called macros or macro substitutions. For example, it is convenient to name a value that is used often during a program. Consider the following code:

```
#include <stdio.h>

#define PI      3.14
#define SQRT2   1.7

int main(int argc, char *argv[])
{
printf("PI = %lf\n",PI);
printf("PI = %lf and the square root of 2 = %lf\n",PI,SQRT2);
}
```

The line #define PI 3.14 is a preprocessor directive. It says to replace every occurrence of PI with 3.14. The line #define SQRT2 1.7 is similar. Assume that this code is stored in a file named pre1.c. The gcc compiler can be commanded to stop after preprocessing, so that the result can be seen. For example:

```
ahoover@video> gcc -E pre1.c
.
.
.
int main(int argc, char *argv[])
```

```
{
printf("PI = %lf\n",3.14);
printf("PI = %lf and the square root of 2 = %lf\n",3.14,1.7);
}
ahoover@video>
```

The flag –E stops the compilation process after preprocessing. The occurrences of PI within quotes are not affected because they are recognized as parts of strings. This result can be saved to a file using the –o option. For example:

```
ahoover@video> gcc -E pre1.c -o temp.c
ahoover@video>
```

The compiling process can be resumed from this point, by running gcc on temp.c, and everything still turns out the same. For example:

```
ahoover@video> gcc temp.c
ahoover@video> a.out
PI = 3.140000
PI = 3.140000 and the square root of 2 = 1.700000
ahoover@video>
```

Compiling the file temp.c produces the file a.out, which can be executed.

Preprocessing text substitutions can be useful in a variety of situations. Used in place of a variable, they prevent the accidental changing of the value during program execution. They also save storage space in that a macro takes up zero bytes of data memory. Another common use for preprocessing is to copy source code that is needed repeatedly, usually from an include file. For example, consider the following code:

```
/* global variables */
int     x;
```

Assume that this code is stored in a file named globals.h. This can be used in other source code files, as follows:

```
#include "globals.h"

int main(int argc, char *argv[])
{
x=2;
printf("x=%d\n",x);
}
```

Assume that this code is stored in a file named `pre2.c`. Compiling it and stopping after preprocessing produces the following result:

```
ahoover@video> gcc -E pre2.c
.
.
.

/* global variables */
int     x;

int main(int argc, char *argv[])
{
x=2;
printf("x=%d\n",x);
}
ahoover@video>
```

This copies the file `globals.h`, line for line, exactly in place of the `#include` line. There are two places that the preprocessor can be told to search for files to include. For example:

```
#include <stdio.h>
#include "globals.h"
```

By enclosing the filename in angle brackets (< >), the preprocessor is told to search system paths for the include file. By enclosing the filename in double quotes (" "), the preprocessor is told to search within the current directory for the include file. Otherwise, both commands accomplish the same thing.

Any statement that begins with a pound symbol (#) is a preprocessor directive, not C code. Other common preprocessor directives are `#if`, `#else`, `#endif`, `#ifdef`, and `#ifndef` to allow for control of what string substitutions are performed. For example, a common method to include or exclude debugging code in a program is to use preprocessing:

```
#include <stdio.h>
#include <stdlib.h>

#define DEBUG    1       /* debugging output */

main()
{
int     x,y,s;
```

```
y=1;
s=0;
for (x=0; x<10; x++)
  {
  y=y<<1;
  s=s+y;
#if DEBUG == 1
  printf("When x=%d, y=%d\n",x,y);
#endif
  }
printf("s=%d\n",s);
}
```

Assume that this code is stored in a file named pre3.c. Changing the value of DEBUG to 0 will prevent the debugging printf() statement from executing. The same thing could be accomplished using a regular C variable, but using preprocessing prevents the code from even being included in the executable. During preprocessing, if the #if directive is not true, then the subsequent code is not copied into the intermediate form that is compiled.

The second step in the compilation process is the actual compiling, which converts the C source code into assembly code. Once again, the gcc compiler can be instructed to stop at this point. For example:

```
ahoover@video> ls pre3.*
pre3.c
ahoover@video> gcc -S pre3.c
ahoover@video> ls pre3.*
pre3.c  pre3.s
ahoover@video>
```

The -S flag tells the compiler to stop after compiling. The compiler saves the result in an assembly code file pre3.s. The contents of that file can be viewed with a text editor:

```
        .file   "pre3.c"
        .section        .rodata
.LC0:
        .string "When x=%d, y=%d\n"
.LC1:
        .string "s=%d\n"
        .text
.globl main
        .type   main, @function
```

```
main:
    pushl   %ebp
    movl    %esp, %ebp
    subl    $24, %esp
    andl    $-16, %esp
    movl    $0, %eax
    addl    $15, %eax
    addl    $15, %eax
    shrl    $4, %eax
    sall    $4, %eax
    subl    %eax, %esp
[...]
```

The assembly code is the set of instructions that will be executed on the processor. For example, movl and subl are processor-level instructions. The exact assembly listing produced by compiling will depend upon the particular processor for which the program is compiled.

The third and final step in the compilation process is called assembling. During this step, assembly code is translated into machine code to get it ready to run. Assembly code is a human-readable version of machine code, much like ASCII symbols are a human-readable version of byte values. (Imagine trying to read text looking at the raw byte values.) Each machine code instruction is actually a set of byte values telling the processor what to do. The assembly instruction is a human-readable translation of those byte values.

As seen throughout this section, the gcc compiler has several options to control where to stop the build process. Table 6.1 summarizes these options. Most compilers have similar options, as well as options that affect how compilation is performed. One of the most important options is to include debugging information in the executable. This option was introduced in Section 1.2.3. For the gcc compiler, this option is given using the –g flag. A related option is to optimize

Table 6.1 The gcc compiler options for stopping the build process at various stages (assumes code.c as input and no other options).

Stop after . . .	gcc flag	Output produced
preprocessing	-E	modified source (streamed to stdout)
compiling	-S	assembly code (code.s)
assembling	-c	object code (code.o)
linking	[none]	executable (a.out)

the code for execution speed. For the gcc compiler, this option is given using the −O flag. With this option a compiler takes slightly more time to compile the code, searching for redundancies and rearranging some lines of code in order to make them execute faster. Normally these two options (debugging and optimization) are used separately. For example, by default the Microsoft Visual C tool compiles an executable into either a Debug or Release version, where the latter is compiled with optimization flags.

6.1.3   Makefiles

For a program that is built from a single source code file, a single execution of a compiler is usually all that is necessary. A programmer will typically manually type the compile command each time the program needs to be rebuilt. However, for a program that is built from a large number of files, a number of compile commands may need to be performed. Some of these commands may involve multiple filenames and command line options. A makefile is a tool that allows a programmer to organize the compile commands and intermediate files and to execute rebuilds with less manual typing.

A makefile is a text file placed in the current working directory, usually the directory holding the source code to be compiled. By convention, the file is usually started with an uppercase "M" (Makefile) so that in a file listing it stands out from the source code and object code files. However, the file can also be started with a lowercase "m" (makefile).

A makefile has two main parts: dependencies and commands. The format of a dependency/command block is as follows:

```
file : dependency
[TAB]   command
[TAB]   command
   :
   :
```

A dependency describes a relationship between files, where if the file on the right-hand side of the dependency is changed, then the file on the left-hand side needs rebuilding. The files on the left-hand side are usually referred to as targets, while the files on the right-hand side are referred to as sources. The command(s) to perform the rebuilding are listed after the dependency. Each command line must be started with a tab character, to differentiate command lines from dependency lines.

For example, consider the program from Section 6.1.1. It was stored in two source code files named `main.c` and `sqrt.c`. A makefile can be written for that program as follows:

```
sqrt : main.o sqrt.o
        gcc -o sqrt main.o sqrt.o
main.o : main.c
        gcc -c main.c
sqrt.o : sqrt.c
        gcc -c sqrt.c
```

This makefile defines three dependency/command blocks. In the first, the executable file sqrt is defined as depending upon the two object code files main.o and sqrt.o. A command is listed for creating the executable file by linking together the two object code files. The second and third blocks give dependencies for the object code files, as well as commands to compile the source code files into the object code files.

Assuming that neither the object code files nor the executable file exists, then this makefile can be used to build the program as follows:

```
ahoover@video> ls
main.c  Makefile  sqrt.c
ahoover@video> make
gcc -c main.c
gcc -c sqrt.c
gcc -o sqrt main.o sqrt.o
ahoover@video> ls
main.c  main.o  Makefile  sqrt  sqrt.c  sqrt.o
ahoover@video>
```

The make program[1] looks for a file named Makefile (or makefile) in the current directory. It parses that file for dependencies and executes the commands for any dependency that needs updating. Updating is determined by comparing the system's last modified times for the files; if the file on the right-hand side of the dependency has been modified more recently than the file on the left-hand side, then the subsequent commands are executed. Notice that with the makefile, the only command that needs to be typed is "make"; all the others are executed automatically.

---

1. The make program is commonly installed on systems with gcc or a related compiler. An open source version of make, as well as a full manual, can be obtained at www.gnu.org/software/make/ and is managed by the GNU project.

Continuing with this example, if make is immediately executed again, nothing happens:

```
ahoover@video> make
ahoover@video>
```

This is because all of the dependencies are up to date. However, if the source code file sqrt.c is modified (the reader is encouraged to perform a simple modification on the file to see how this works), then executing make causes some actions to be taken:

```
ahoover@video> vi sqrt.c
        [... modifying file sqrt.c ...]
ahoover@video> make
gcc -c sqrt.c
gcc -o sqrt main.o sqrt.o
ahoover@video>
```

Notice that the only commands executed are those needed to update the dependant files, in this case sqrt.o and then sqrt. For programs having a large number of files and build commands, this can save a great deal of time on repeated rebuilds.

Makefiles can have other lines in them besides dependencies and commands. Comments can be written after the # character. For example:

```
# This is a comment.
sqrt : main.o sqrt.o # another comment
```

Macros can be written to define string substitutions. For example:

```
EXEC = sqrt
$(EXEC) : main.o sqrt.o
```

This example defines a macro named EXEC for the string sqrt. At any later place in the makefile, the macro can be used by giving its name inside parentheses and preceded by the $ symbol. Macros are useful for file lists that get long but are used in multiple dependencies or commands. Two of the most commonly used macros are all and clean. The former typically defines all the final targets to be created by all the commands in the makefile; the latter typically executes commands to remove all intermediate files created during building, such as object code files. Makefiles can also make use of a few special characters and default rules defined in a system wide ruleset. (The interested reader is encouraged to consult the online reference listed in footnote 1 for full details.)

6.1.4 Other Build Tools

When moving the source code for a program from one system to another, the second system may have different compilers or system programs needed for the build process. Becauase of this, the makefile for the program may need to be modified. Tools have been developed to parse system files and automatically generate a makefile using the available compilers and system programs. One of the first examples of such a tool is *imake*, although this program is no longer actively under development. Current tools with similar goals include *Automake*, managed by the GNU Project, and *CMake*, which has been used for several large open source projects.

Integrated development environments (IDEs) commonly use a graphical interface to manage the build process. Dependencies, commands, and command line options are normally configured through an interface custom to the particular IDE. However, underneath that interface, an IDE will typically create a makefile that can be manually edited by the programmer. It is not uncommon for an advanced programmer to go underneath the IDE's graphical build configuration in order to fine-tune the control of the build process.

6.2 • Code Organization

Organizing code is not easy. Programmers probably spend as much time organizing code as they do actually writing new code. Making code modular, readable, and understandable helps a programmer in several ways. First, these practices assist with design. Writing well-organized code generally leads to a cleaner program design, which in turn generally leads to fewer flaws and bugs. Second, these practices assist with debugging. It is much easier to find errors in well-organized code, particularly if a bug is uncovered long after the code was written and the author has forgotten much of the design. Third, these practices promote code reuse and future program extension. Programmers sometimes curse having to write comments and spend time doing bookkeeping chores, yet praise the fruits of those efforts when they revisit previously written code. There are several methods and tools that assist code organization. Although this section examines them from the perspective of the C programming language, the same concepts can be found in almost all programming languages.

6.2.1 Functions

Writing a program using multiple functions is the most classic approach to making a program modular. Modular code is desirable for two reasons. First, it breaks a coding problem into pieces, where each piece can be tackled independently (divide and conquer). Second, it allows code pieces to be reused in future programming tasks. For example, consider the following code:

```c
#include <stdio.h>
#include <string.h>

int main(int argc, char *argv[])
{
FILE    *fpt;
char    first[20][30],last[20][30];
int     i,j,total;

if (argc != 2)
  {
  printf("Usage: capfix [filename]\n");
  exit(0);
  }
if ((fpt=fopen(argv[1],"r")) == NULL)
  {
  printf("Unable to open %s for reading\n",argv[1]);
  exit(0);
  }

total=0;
while (1)
  {
  if (fscanf(fpt,"%s %s",last[total],first[total]) != 2)
    break;
  total++;
  }

for (i=0; i<total; i++)
  {
  if (first[i][0] >= 'a'  &&  first[i][0] <= 'z')
    first[i][0]=first[i][0]-'a'+'A';
  for (j=1; j<strlen(first[i]); j++)
    if (first[i][j] >= 'A'  &&  first[i][j] <= 'Z')
      first[i][j]=first[i][j]-'A'+'a';
  }
```

```
for (i=0; i<total; i++)
{
  if (last[i][0] >= 'a'  && last[i][0] <= 'z')
    last[i][0]=last[i][0]-'a'+'A';
  for (j=1; j<strlen(last[i]); j++)
    if (last[i][j] >= 'A'  && last[i][j] <= 'Z')
      last[i][j]=last[i][j]-'A'+'a';
}

for (i=0; i<total; i++)
  printf("%s %s\n",first[i],last[i]);
}
```

This program reads a text file containing the last and first names of people. It then checks each first name to make sure that it begins with an uppercase letter and uses lowercase for the rest of the letters. It repeats this process for the last name. Finally, the program prints out the corrected first and last names. For example, consider the following data:

```
smith john
WALTERS sally
jones STeve
```

If that data is stored in a file named data.txt, and the program code is stored in a file named capfix.c, then compiling and executing the program as follows would produce the following output:

```
ahoover@video> gcc -o capfix capfix.c
ahoover@video> capfix data.txt
John Smith
Sally Walters
Steve Jones
ahoover@video>
```

The above program was written using only a single function, main(), to do all the work. How could the code be broken into multiple functions to support modularity and good design practices? First, the code that checks each word for proper capitalization could be put into a function. It is used twice in this program, each time on a different variable. Second, the code that reads in the data from a file could be put into a function. Although it is used only once in this program, the code may find use in additional programs written in the future. When dealing with data files, it is common to have multiple programs that all need to read the particular format of that data. Encapsulating the data-reading code into a function promotes modularity and supports the reuse of the code in the future. Taking both these observations into account, the above code can be rewritten using multiple functions as follows:

```c
#include <stdio.h>
#include <string.h>

int ReadData(FILE *fpt,
             char first[20][30],
             char last[20][30])
{
int total;
total=0;
while (1)
  {
  if (fscanf(fpt,"%s %s",last[total],first[total]) != 2)
    break;
  total++;
  }
return(total);
}

void CapFix(char word[30])
{
int i;
if (word[0] >= 'a'  && word[0] <= 'z')
  word[0]=word[0]-'a'+'A';
for (i=1; i<strlen(word); i++)
  if (word[i] >= 'A'  && word[i] <= 'Z')
    word[i]=word[i]-'A'+'a';
}


int main(int argc, char *argv[])
{
FILE    *fpt;
char    first[20][30],last[20][30];
int     i,j,total;

if (argc != 2)
  {
  printf("Usage: capfix [filename]\n");
```

```
        exit(0);
    }
    if ((fpt=fopen(argv[1],"r")) == NULL)
    {
        printf("Unable to open %s for reading\n",argv[1]);
        exit(0);
    }

    total=ReadData(fpt,first,last);

    for (i=0; i<total; i++)
        CapFix(first[i]);

    for (i=0; i<total; i++)
        CapFix(last[i]);

    for (i=0; i<total; i++)
        printf("%s %s\n",first[i],last[i]);
}
```

Functions are a good tool for organizing code, but like any tool they can be used inappropriately. One mistake is to use a function for a tiny piece of code. Calling a function takes extra program execution time, both for copying values into and out of the function, and for jumping to and from the function code for execution. The extra overhead for executing a function is sometimes not worth it for a tiny piece of code. Instead, other organizational tools should be examined, such as macros (discussed in Section 6.2.5). Another mistake is to overuse functions. Just because some code *can* be encapsulated into a function doesn't mean it *should* be encapsulated into a function. Debugging and modifying code that has been "over-functionalized" can be frustrating. Imagine reading a book where every other paragraph refers to a paragraph on another page. Trying to read the book becomes an exercise in following misdirections bouncing back and forth throughout all the pages. Some references to other parts of the book can be helpful in organizing the ideas, but too many references can lead to obscurity rather than clarity.

One of the limitations of C is that it explicitly supports modularity only in functions. Sometimes, it is desirable to modularize data or bring modularity to other abstractions in programming. The C language provides some support for data modularity; for example, a structure can be used to create a new modular data type. However, other languages such as C++ and Java have pushed the modularity principle further, providing additional language constructs. Regardless of the language, the principle remains the same: tools designed to support modularity should be used thoughtfully and not just because they are available.

6.2.2 Multiple Files

As the number of functions in a program increases, it is convenient to break them up into multiple files. It makes it easier to edit a file, because there are fewer lines of source code to scroll through to find the function of interest. It also makes program building more efficient. After changing code within a single function, only the file containing that code needs to be recompiled. The other files (assuming the object code files are kept between program builds) need only to be linked to create a new executable.

A common way to group functions is by the sort of actions they accomplish. For example, functions that read and write data to files might be collectively stored in a file named `file.c`. Another way to group functions is by the type of data upon which they operate. For example, in a file named `vector.c`, one could expect to find functions that perform mathematical operations with vectors. Just as with multiple functions, the separation of functions into multiple files can be overused. Although it is common for a file named `main.c` to contain only one function (the main() function), populating a large number of files with a scarce number of functions in each is in general a bad practice.

6.2.3 Variable Scope

The scope of a variable defines which parts of a program can access and use the variable. When breaking a program into multiple functions and files, scope is a tool that can help organize variable usage. It is possible to have all variables be global variables, accessible throughout the entire program. However, providing different scope to different variables helps organize the extent to which each variable is needed. For example, some variables might be needed for only one function, others for a handful of functions, others for only part of a function, and still others for the entire program.

The scope of a variable is defined in its declarataion. A C variable declaration can have four parts:

1. Data type: `int`, `float`, `char`, `double`. These describe how many bytes of storage are used by the variable and what bit model is used to represent values.

2. Modifiers: `signed`, `unsigned`, `short`, `long`. These modify how many bytes are used and how the bits may be used.

3. Qualifiers: `const`, `volatile`. These provide information to the compiler as to how the variable will be used so that it may optimize appropriately.

4. Storage class: `auto`, `static`, `extern`. These affect the scope of the variable, that is, the visibility of the variable throughout the program.

Data types and modifiers are explained in Chapter 2. Qualifiers belong to a discussion on optimization. This section focuses strictly on scope, as defined by the storage class. We will look at each possible storage class and how it can be used.

The first storage class keyword is `auto`. An auto variable is visible only within its code block. This is the default storage class for variables inside a function, and as such the keyword `auto` is usually omitted. For example:

```
int Function1(float e)
{
int      x;
auto int y;

[...]
}
```

The variables `x`, `y`, and `e` all have the auto storage class and the same variable scope. These variables are visible only inside the function, and when the function ends, the variables (and their values) disappear.

The auto storage class can be used within a set of braces to provide an even smaller variable scope. For example:

```
main()
{
int x;
x=42;
  {
  int x;
  x=7;
  printf("x=%d\n",x);
  }
printf("x=%d\n",x);
}
```

This code defines two variables, each with the name x but each having a different scope. If this code is stored in a file named `block-scope.c`, then compiling it and executing it produces the following output:

```
ahoover@video> gcc -o block-scope block-scope.c
ahoover@video> block-scope
x=7
x=42
ahoover@video>
```

The second declaration of the variable named x takes place within a block delimited by a set of braces. Therefore, this variable has scope only inside this block. Once that block is finished, that particular variable disappears, and the variable name x reverts to the original declaration and value.

Note that the nested use of block variable scope is easy to abuse. The example given above is not to be emulated, particularly using the same variable name in nested blocks. Novice programmers are often tempted by the ease with which new variables can be declared on the fly while writing code, simply by creating a nested block with additional braces. This practice is bad for several reasons. First, it adds block delimiters not for sound principles of modularity and program design, but because a programmer is too lazy to scroll back to the top of the code block (usually a function) to declare the newly-thought-of variable. The extra block delimiters make the code less organized and readable. It also makes it more difficult to find variable declarations for others trying to read, debug, or extend the code. Using block variable scope can be a good thing, for example, when a programmer wants to modularize a piece of code without paying the execution cost of placing it in a function. However, this use of block scope should be used rarely.

The second storage class keyword is static. A static variable has a larger variable scope. The static keyword can be used in two contexts, either within a single function or within an entire file. In the first case, the static storage class makes the value of the variable persistent through consecutive function calls. For example, consider the following code:

```
#include <stdio.h>

int summer(int x)
{
static int      sum=0;

sum=sum+x;
return(sum);
}
```

```
main()
{
int     i,j;

for (i=0; i<5; i++)
  {
  j=summer(i);
  printf("%d\n",j);
  }
}
```

The variable sum has function static scope. If this code is stored in a file named function-static.c, then compiling it and executing it produces the following output:

```
ahoover@video> gcc -o function-static function-static.c
ahoover@video> function-static
0
1
3
6
10
ahoover@video>
```

Each time the function summer() is called, the value of the variable sum is retained. This can be useful when a function needs to maintain knowledge of a local variable through repeated calls. For example, a function may keep the contents of a local array, adding to it or taking from it some of its contents through successive calls.

The static storage class provides a second scope that is similarly persistent but has a larger scope. For example:

```
#include <stdio.h>

static int      sq=0;

int summer(int x)
{
static int      sum=0;
```

```
sum=sum+x;
sq=sq-1;
return(sum);
}

main()
{
int     i,j;

for (i=0; i<5; i++)
  {
  sq=sq+(i*i);
  j=summer(i);
  printf("%d %d\n",j,sq);
  }
}
```

The variable sq has file static scope. If this code is stored in a file named file-static.c, then compiling it and executing it produces the following output:

```
ahoover@video> gcc -o file-static file-static.c
ahoover@video> file-static
0 -1
1 -1
3 2
6 10
10 25
ahoover@video>
```

The value of sq is retained throughout all the function calls for this program. A file static variable has scope only for the functions that appear following its declaration; however, in practice, file static variables are normally declared at the top of the file and so are visible to all functions in the file. This can be useful when there is data that needs to be shared between multiple functions, but which needs to be protected from functions in other files. For example, in a file dealing with the reading and writing of data, a program may use file static variables to track a file pointer or buffer used to access a data file.

The third storage class keyword is extern. An extern variable is a global variable being shared between multiple files. In order to use the extern keyword, a variable must first be declared with file scope. For example:

```
#include <stdio.h>

int     x;

int main(int argc, char *argv[])
{
x=1;
printf("main: %d\n",x);
function();
printf("main: %d\n",x);
}
```

The variable x has file scope. Assume that this code is stored in a file named ext1.c. Now consider the following code:

```
#include <stdio.h>

extern int x;

void function()
{
printf("function: %d\n",x);
x=7;
printf("function: %d\n",x);
}
```

Assume that this code is stored in a file named ext2.c. In this file, the variable x is declared using the extern storage class, so that it has global scope. Compiling and executing this code produces the following output:

```
ahoover@video> gcc -o ext ext1.c ext2.c
ahoover@video> ext
main: 1
function: 1
function: 7
main: 7
ahoover@video>
```

Note that the value of x is maintained through all functions in both files. In order to create a variable with global scope, it must be declared in one file, and then referenced as an extern in all other files that want to access it. An object code linker normally tries to merge variable declarations that have the same name and all use file scope into a single variable with global scope, so that programmers sometimes omit the extern keyword. However, in order to avoid a linker doing something unexpected, and to promote code clarity, it is best to explicitly declare the scope of variables intended to be global.

6.2.4   Comments, Indentation, and Variable Names

The most basic organizational tools for a programmer involve the readability and visual layout of the code. Comments are annotations made by the programmer, like small notes used to document ideas throughout a project. Indentation refers to the amount and regularity of spacing used to start lines of code in nested blocks. Variable names should be chosen to help describe what the variable is doing, thus making the code easier to read. All of these practices promote clarity and organization.

It is important to note that there is no universally accepted "best" way to use any of these tools. The proper use of these tools is something of an art. It can be compared to the organization of a kitchen. Different people may prefer placing cooking equipment in various drawers or cupboards, organizing foodstuffs in different ways, and so on. Regardless of the organization chosen, however, the common goal is to arrange materials in a way that facilitates cooking. A cook arriving in a new kitchen may not immediately recognize or be comfortable with all the arrangements, but if the kitchen is well organized, the new cook will be able to work. Keeping code well organized is a comparable undertaking with similar rewards. Most programmers develop an individual style; consistency is an important trait regardless of the details. The following are some conventions commonly adopted.

Comments can be used throughout a program for a variety of reasons. Most functions should have a few sentences near the beginning that describe the subtask solved by the function. It is also common to describe the function inputs and outputs in comments. Within a function, code blocks may have single sentence or phrase descriptions, serving as a plain text outline for the code. The program usage, history (revisions), to-do list, and authorship are commonly commented at the top of the main source code file. Variables with overlapping names or complex uses may have comments defining their purpose or expected ranges of values. In code that is complex or critical to the problem, comments may be written line by line. The following demonstrates some of these uses:

```
/*
** This program prompts the user for a number,
** and then determines if the number is a sum
** of the squares of two unique integers.
*/
```

```
#include <stdio.h>

main()
{
int     i,j;    /* used to test all pairs of squares */
int     number;

printf("Enter a number: ");
scanf("%d",&number);
i=1;
while (i*i <= number)   /* i = 1 ... sqrt(number) */
  {
  j=1;
  while (j < i)         /* j = 1 ... i-1 */
    {
    if (i*i + j*j == number)
      printf("Found: %d + %d\n",i*i,j*j);
    j++;
    }
  i=i+1;
  }
}
```

The multiple-line comment at the beginning of the file describes the purpose of the program. The comment for the variables i and j describes their purpose, since their names are nondescriptive. Some simple comments at the beginning of each loop help describe the purpose of each clode block.

Indentation refers to the amount of space at the beginning of each line of code. In general, lines of code within the same block should be indented the exact same amount, in order to allow a programmer to more easily perceive the grouped statements. Lines of code defining the boundary of a block can be indented with the lines of code inside the block. For example:

```
i=0;
while (i < 3)
  printf("Hello turtle %d\n",i);
  i++;
  }
printf("How are you?\n");
```

This is the style used by the author throughout this book. Some programmers prefer to line up block denoters with the enclosing block instead of the enclosed block. For example:

```
i=0;
while (i < 3)
{
  printf("Hello turtle %d\n",i);
  i++;
}
printf("How are you?\n");
```

Still other programmers prefer to concatenate some block denoters with other lines of code. For example:

```
i=0;
while (i < 3) {
  printf("Hello turtle %d\n",i);
  i++;
}
printf("How are you?\n");
```

This last style increases the number of lines of code that can be seen simultaneously onscreen. All of these styles are acceptable, although some programmers (like some cooks) can remain ardent about their preferred organizational style.

Variable names should usually describe the purpose of the variable. For example:

```
int ProgramRunning=1; /* 0 => end program, 1 => continue */
```

Sometimes the variable name describes the process it manages, as in the example above, and sometimes it describes the quantity stored, such as int age. Simple, brief variables names are okay to use when the meaning is obvious. For example, loop indices often use single letters, as most programmers recognize the convention.

6.2.5   Preprocessing

Preprocessing is not strictly a C language construct; it can be supported by any language since it happens before compiling. The text substitutions provided through preprocessing can be used in several ways to support code organization. First, they can make code more readable. It is much easier to view short strings that are to be substituted by longer strings when the meaning is still clear in the shorter string. For example, it can be convenient to read that some operation is being performed on a variable instead of verifying all the details each time:

```
#define KAZAM(x)  (((x)*3/4)-2)/5)
```

Using the string KAZAM(x) throughout a program would be easier to read, understand, and debug as compared to typing out the full operation each time.

Second, a program can be written with scalability in mind by using macros. It is much easier to change a constant using a text substitution. For example:

```
#define MAX_LINES 20
```

In a program that is working with data and expects a maximum amount, coding that constant using a macro would allow it to be easily changed to a different value at a later time.

Third, text substitutions can be useful for portability. They help in compiling the same source code for different processors or operating systems. For example, an int is usually 4 bytes, but on some systems it may be 2 or 8 bytes. One can use text substitutions to name a 4-byte entity that is replaced by the appropriate data type depending on which machine the code is compiled for as follows:

```
#define four_bytes int   /* use on 32-bit machines */
#define four_bytes long int  /* use on 16-bit machines */
#define four_bytes short int  /* use on 64-bit machines */

main()
{
four_bytes  x,y,a;
    .
    .
    .
}
```

In this example, the variables x, y, and a will be 4 bytes (either an int, a long int, or a short int), regardless of the system architecture, so long as the appropriate preprocessor directive is executed before compiling. (Only one of the above directives should be kept as shown; the other two should be commented out or ommitted using additional preprocessor directives.)

6.2.6 Typedefs

A typedef is a tool in the C language for providing an alias for an existing data type. It provides a new name for a data type that already has a name:

```
typedef SomeExistingType MyNewNameForIt;
```

For example, suppose a programmer wanted int to have a second name, "frog":

```
typedef int frog;
```

Now code can be written using "frog" as an alias for int:

```
main()
{
int a;
frog b;
.
.
.
}
```

Both the variables a and b are ints; "frog" is only an alias for int.

There are two reasons why aliases for existing data types can be useful. First, they can make code more readable. For example, code involving structures can be difficult to read because structure definitions require at least two words (e.g., "struct x"). A typedef can be used to give this multiword tag a single word alias:

```
struct TemplateName {
                int field1;
                float field2;
                } ;
typedef struct TemplateName NewStructType;
```

"NewStructType" is not a variable name, it is now an alias for struct Template-Name. Variables of type struct TemplateName can now be defined in two ways:

```
struct TemplateName s1;
NewStructType s2;
```

Both variables s1 and s2 are of the same data type, struct TemplateName. A typedef and a structure definition are often clumped together:

```
typedef struct TemplateName {
                int field1;
                float field2;
                } NewStructType;
```

This has the same net result as the example above.

A second use for typedefs is portability. Typedefs are often used to achieve the same portability goals as described for preprocessing in the last section. For example:

```
typedef int        Int32; /* 4 byte variable */
typedef short int  Int16; /* 2 byte variable */
```

Now code can be written using the data type names Int32 and Int16. If the code is moved to another system architecture, only the typedef lines need to be changed.

6.2.7 Discussion

In summary, there are many tools that help a programmer organize code. When used properly, they can be a great help. When used improperly, or when not well understood, they can be a great pain. It can be frustrating trying to read code that is riddled with typedefs when the code is absolutely never going to be ported to any other system. It can be painful trying to read code that is broken up into multiple functions when the entire program is less than 20 lines. Files containing a single function are usually superfluous. Multiple levels of preprocessing text substitutions can be arduous to work with and are unnecessary when they do not provide any real flexibility. These tools do not exist to demonstrate the wit of the programmer; they exist to help organize code. They should be used, but they should be used with care and respect for the original goals of organizing code.

A related discussion concerns abstraction. Abstraction refers to the level of detail required by a programmer to implement an idea in code. The more abstract a language construct, the less a programmer needs to understand how the machine actually implements the idea. In turn, the more concrete a language construct, the more a programmer needs to understand how the machine implements the idea. The C language is not very abstract. Some of the tools developed to help organize code also attempt to abstract out the details. While this is a laudable goal, it should again be used with prudence. Abstraction does not necessarily make a program better organized. Sometimes it is better to leave the details clearly visible so that the program can be better managed.

6.3 • Program Distribution Methods

Once a program has been written, it is convenient to package the code in a manner that facilitates its distribution to other computers and systems. If the target distribution is systems that are exactly the same as the one on which the program is written, than the executable can be distributed. If the target computers run different operating systems or have different hardware, then either the source code must be compiled for all the desired platforms prior to distribution, or the source code itself needs to be distributed so that it can be compiled on the target systems. This section discusses some common methods and tools for packaging and distributing programs.

6.3.1   Archives

The most basic tool for program distribution is an archive. An archiving tool groups together a set of files into a single file called an *archive file*. An archive file contains the contents of all the individual files plus some *metadata*. The metadata usually details the sizes of the files, the last modified dates and times of the files, each file's path or subdirectory, and possibly additional information. An archive file also typically contains some parity or error checking content so that the validity of the files afer unpacking can be verified.

Most archive tools also include a lossless compression capability. As a file is added to the archive, it is compressed, so that the archive file takes up much less space than the sum of the original files. This is convenient for long-term storage as well as program distribution. Some archive tools rely upon external or postarchive compression, and therefore the entire archive file is compressed or decompressed in one step. This generally results in smaller archive files as the compression can search for redundancy across all individual files within the archive. However, it also tends to be slower to use because individual modifications or accesses to the archive must decompress and recompress the entire archive.

Example archive tools commonly found on a Unix system include ar and tar. The ar program is most commonly used for library files, placing multiple object code files into a single library file. The tar program is used more generically for almost any type of file. For example:

```
ahoover@video> ls
main.c  Makefile  sqrt.c
ahoover@video> tar cf dist.tar *
ahoover@video> ls
dist.tar  main.c  Makefile  sqrt.c
ahoover@video>
```

In this example, tar was used to create an archive file named dist.tar containing all files in the current directory. The contents of the archive file can be listed as follows:

```
ahoover@video> tar tf dist.tar
main.c
Makefile
sqrt.c
ahoover@video>
```

Other command line options can be used to extract files, add more files to the archive file, and perform a variety of other operations. Full details can be found within the man page for tar.

The tar program does not provide compression. Instead, it relies upon the gzip compression tool[2] for postarchiving compression and decompression. For example:

```
ahoover@video> ls -l
-rw-r--r--  1 ahoover  fusion  10240 Oct 15  2008 dist.tar
-rw-r--r--  1 ahoover  fusion    221 Oct 15  2008 main.c
-rw-r--r--  1 ahoover  fusion    125 Oct 15  2008 Makefile
-rw-r--r--  1 ahoover  fusion    171 Oct 15  2008 sqrt.c
ahoover@video> gzip dist.tar
ahoover@video> ls -l dist.tar.gz
-rw-r--r--  1 ahoover  fusion    485 Oct 15  2008 dist.tar.gz
ahoover@video>
```

Note that the archive file was originally larger than even the sum of the contents of the individual files inside it. This is because of the metadata information described above.

Other example archive tools include PKZIP, WinZip, and WinRar, which all include built-in compression. They are proprietary but have achieved a notable level of popularity. The .zip archive file format, whose specification is public domain, is also inherently supported by the MS Windows Explorer tool.

6.3.2 Packages

A package management system is a more advanced program distribution tool. A package file is similar to an archive file, but it contains additional information. It may describe how to compile or execute files extracted from the package file. It may describe how to install or organize files on a target system, where the exact destination of each file depends upon how the target system is configured. For example, if a target system contains an older version of a library file, but the older library file is needed by an already installed program, then the package installer may rename the extracted newer version of the library file so as to maintain versions for both programs. Typically, the dependency information for all programs installed by a package manager is kept in a local file on the target system. This file also typically contains history metadata about all the programs installed and their interdependencies.

---

2. Free versions of tar and gzip are available from the GNU Project at www.gnu.org.

Packages are usually maintained at web sites organized for specific package management tools. The packages stored there sometimes contain executables built for specific target systems. Using packages in this manner is not very different from using more traditional archive files. The advantage is that installation of such a package is quick; the disadvantage is that the build contained within the package must exactly match the specifications of the target system. In contrast, many package files contain source code and instructions on how to build executables from the extracted files. Some package management systems contain tools that automatically interact with one or more web sites to obtain packages. This further automates the program distribution process in that the target user need know only the name of the desired package, and not even necessarily where to get it. Most package management systems have graphical interface front ends to command line tools. This allows even relatively inexperienced users to use the program distribution tools.

Example package management systems include rpm, deb/dpkg, and portage/emerge. The rpm package format is used by both the Fedora (Red-Hat) and openSUSE Linux distributions. The deb package file format and dpkg software tool are used by both the Debian and Ubuntu Linux distributions. The portage package file format and emerge software tool are used by the Gentoo Linux distribution. At the time of this writing, all these Linux distributions are among the most popular; one of the main reasons (if not the main reason) for their popularity is the ease of software distribution and installation provided by their package management systems. On an MS Windows system, the proprietary tools InstallShield and WISE Installer perform similar operations. However, MS Windows systems have less diversity than Unix systems, in terms of kernels and system file arrangements, so that software distribution and installation is less complex to manage.

Questions and Exercises

1. Consider the following code:

```
#include <stdio.h>

char * Flip_A_Coin(int x)
{
if (x%2 == 0)
    return("heads");
```

```
else
  return("tails");
}
```

Assume that this code is stored in a file named `coin1.c` and compiled as follows:

```
ahoover@video> gcc -o coin1 coin1.c
```

What sort of error would you expect to see? At what stage of building the program does this error occur?

2. Consider the following code:

```
#define HEADS 0

#include "some_library.h"

char * Flip_A_Coin(int x)
{
if (x%2 == HEADS)
  return("heads");
else
  return("tails");
}

main()
{
printf("%s\n",Flip_A_Coin(1));
}
```

Assume that this code is stored in a file named `coin2.c` and compiled as follows:

```
ahoover@video> gcc -o coin2 coin2.c
```

What sort of error might you expect to see? On what situation does this error depend? At what stage of building the program does this error occur?

3. Consider the following code:

```
#define HEADS "heads"
#define TAILS "tails"

char * Flip_A_Coin(int x)
{
if (x == heads)
  return(HEADS);
```

```
    else
      return(TAILS);
    }
```

Assume that this code is stored in a file named coin3.c and compiled as follows:

```
ahoover@video> gcc -c coin3.c
```

What sort of error would you expect to see? At what stage of building the program does this error occur?

4. Write out the memory map for the following code, providing all values at the end of execution. What is the exact output produced by this program?

```
#include <stdio.h>

int x;

int Magic(int z)
{
z=x*3;
return(z);
}

int main()
{
int y;

x=4;
y=6;
x=Magic(y);
printf("%d %d\n",x,y);
}
```

5. Consider the following program:

```
#include <stdio.h>

main()
{
int a,b,c,d;

a=0;
while (1) {
printf("%d\n",a);
```

```
printf("Input? ");
scanf("%d",&c);
if (c == 0) break;
d=0;
for (b=1; b<=c; b++)
if (c%b == 0) d++;
if (d == 2 || c == 1) a=a+c;
}
}
```

What does this program do? Rewrite the code, organizing it using sound principles. Include comments and redo variable names and indentation. Use multiple functions, blocks, and/or preprocessing if you deem it necessary.

6. Write out the memory map for the following code, providing all values at the end of execution. How many total bytes does this code declare for variables?

```
#include <stdio.h>

typedef struct amount {
                        int dollars;
                        char cents;
                        } money;


main()
{
money a,*b;

a.dollars=1;
a.cents=99;
b=&a;
b->cents=75;
}
```

7. Name four methods to organize code.

8. Write out the memory map for the following code, providing all values at the end of execution. What is the exact output produced by this program?

```
#include <stdio.h>

#define MAX 5
#define MAGIC 9
```

```
main()
{
int n[MAX];
int i;

for (i=0; i<MAX; i++)
  {
  n[i]=i*i;
  printf("MAGIC = %d ? ",n[i]);
  if (n[i] == MAGIC)
    printf("yes\n");
  else
    printf("no\n");
  }
}
```

9. Write out the memory map for the following code, providing all values at the end
    of execution. What is the exact output produced by this program?

```
#include <stdio.h>

main()
{
int i,s;
int a[6];
typedef int * stair;
stair b;

a[0]=83;
a[1]=13;
b=&(a[2]);
s=0;
for (i=2; i<5; i++)
  {
  *b=a[i-2]%a[i-1];
  s+=(*b);
  b++;
  }

printf("%d\n",s);
}
```

10. Consider the lines of code below. Indicate which are invalid, meaning either they would not compile or they may produce a memory fault.

```
#define TOTAL 5
#define TURTLE 2;
typedef struct automobile {
                            char    name[TOTAL];
                            int     vehicle_id;
                            float   kpg;
                            double  *manuf_code;
                          } Entry;
Entry    list[3],*passenger;
char     who[7],a,*b;
double   *d,d2;

Entry.kpg=35.6;
list[1].kpg=39.1;
passenger->kpg=42.2;
who[TOTAL]=TURTLE
list[2].manuf_code=&d2;
list.kpg=28.7;
Entry->manuf_code=11;
list[3].name[0]=who[1];
list[TURTLE].vehicle_id=7;
list[TOTAL].vehicle_id=3;
passenger=&(list[0]); passenger->vehicle_id=3;
```

11. Write a program that displays a clipped version of the contents of a text file. The clipped display should show the first N letters of each word, with even spacing between all words. For example, if the previous sentence were clipped to three letters, it would look like this:

```
The cli dis sho sho the fir N   let
of  eac wor wit eve spa bet all wor
```

The filename to display should be given by the user as a command line argument. Punctuation marks should not be treated specially; they should be included in letter counts. The program should use preprocessing to define the number of letters to clip, the amount of extra spacing between clipped words, the number of words to display per line, and the maximum number of words to display before stopping.

12. Write a program that maintains a database of telephone book entries. An entry should be stored and processed using the following structure:

```
struct entry {
        char name[32];
        int telephone;
        char address[32];
        };
```

The program should use several different functions. One function should allow the user to add an entry to the database. Another function should allow the user to search the database for an entry. The search could be initiated from a name or telephone number; in either case, the search should return all information for the entry. A third function should allow the user to delete an entry from the database. Whenever the database is updated, another function should write the entire database to a file for storage. Whenever the program is started, it should read this file to initialize the database. The main function should provide an interactive menu of options to the user. The display of information within an entry should be handled by yet another function.

Organize the functions into at least two source code files and one header file. Program correctness is important, but a strong effort should be made to organize the code using sound principles.

13. For the program described in the preivous problem, create a makefile. The makefile should allow the user to issue the make command to initiate a rebuild for any portion of the program modified since the last build. However, it should only rebuild the portions of the program affected by modifications since the last build.

14. Write a program that asks a user for an input string and then prints it out in the following radial manner. The last letter of the word should be at the center of the printout. Horizontally, vertically, and along each diagonal, the word should be printed starting from the outside and ending with the last letter in the middle. For example, for the word "cat," the output should look like:

```
c c c
 aaa
catac
 aaa
 c c c
```

For the word "frog," the output should look like:

```
f   f   f
 r   r   r
   ooo
frogorf
   ooo
 r   r   r
f   f   f
```

Program correctness is important, but the following organizational tools should be applied appropriately. The program should use preprocessing to define a maximum word size and to test its correct usage by the user. Comments should be used, at an appropriate level of detail, to describe the method(s) for storing and/or displaying the radial printout.

15. Write a program that creates and unpacks a custom archive file. The archive file should be a simple concatenation of bytes of the individual files that are added to it. Some information should be stored at the beginning of the archive file describing the number of files within the archive file, along with the names and sizes of the individual files within the archive file. The program should use command line arguments to allow the user either to create an archive file, to list the contents of the archive file, or to unpack the archive file. Each time the program is run, only one of these three options should be allowed. For the first of these options (creating the archive file), the user should be able to specify any number of filenames on the command line. The program does not need to work with subdirectories; if any of the filenames given to archive is a directory, then the program should report an error and quit.

    Optional: include a fourth option to add files to an existing archive. In order to make this work, the information describing the contents of the archive must be updated, in addition to adding the new file(s). One way to do this is to recreate the entire archive. Another option is to make the front of the archive file large enough to hold additional contents information. Yet another option is to space contents information throughout the archive file, instead of placing it all at the beginning.

16. What is the difference between an archive file and a package file in terms of program distribution?

7

System Calls

An operating system (O/S) is a program that has two main jobs: it manages the resources of the computer, including peripherals, files, and memory, and it coordinates all other programs running on the computer. Figure 7.1 shows a conceptual diagram. In reality, an O/S is a collection of programs, the heart of which is the kernel. After bootloading (i.e., loading the O/S from a hard drive or other secondary memory), the kernel is executed. The kernel eventually runs the init process, which is what spawns all other processes. The kernel also acts as the moderator between applications and the resources of the computer.

The kernel provides a set of functions to other programs called *system calls*. System calls are used to request access to the resources of the machine, to communicate with other currently running programs, and to start new programs. A collection of system calls is sometimes referred to as an application programming interface (API). Different operating systems provide different sets of system calls. Over the years, standards have been developed to regularize at least a subset of system calls common to all systems, for example, POSIX. It is beyond the scope of this book to detail the full POSIX standard, or to contrast differences in system calls from various kernels.[1] Instead, this chapter focuses on explaining some of the primary families of operations provided by system calls. Detailed examples are provided for some families to familiarize the reader with the use of system calls. This coverage is intended to complement (or prepare for) what is typically seen in an operating systems textbook.

---

1. The interested reader is directed to *Advanced Programming in the UNIX Environment*, 2nd ed., R. Stevens and S. Rago, Addison-Wesley, 2005, ISBN 0201433079. This excellent book provides a history of many Unix APIs and provides a comparative coverage of many system calls.

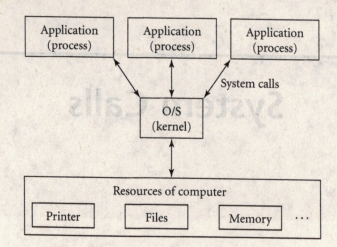

Figure 7.1   A conceptual diagram of system calls.

7.1 • Families of Operations

Modern Unix kernels provide several hundred different system calls. These system calls are typically broken up into families of functions, each of which target a specific purpose or type of operation. This section overviews some of the common taxonomy of system calls. Later sections will take a detailed look at a few of these families.

Memory management system calls ask the O/S to manipulate a block of memory in some manner, typically so that the memory can be used by an application program. Example system calls include mmap(), shmget(), mprotect(), mlock(), and shmctl(). These operations involve manipulating the low-level attributes of memory as managed by the operating system. For example, an O/S typically maintains levels of memory protection, where the lower levels (such as that used by the O/S) cannot be accessed by other programs. Some of these system calls allow the access permissions of portions of memory to be changed so that application programs can use it.

Time management system calls ask the O/S to access the system clock, in some cases taking action based upon its value. Examples include time(), gettimer(), settimer(), settimeofday(), and alarm(). These system calls either retrieve values from the system clock, or start or stop timers based upon the system clock. The alarm() function arranges for a signal (signals are discussed in Section 7.4) to be sent to a process once the given amount of time has passed.

File system calls ask the O/S to access a file or device. Example system calls include open(), read(), write(), close(), creat() (not a typo—there is no "e" at the end), lseek(), and link(). These bear a resemblance to the C standard library functions fopen(), fread(), fwrite(), and fclose(), which are covered in detail in Chapter 5. The relationship between library functions and system calls is explored in the next section.

Three families of system calls are examined in detail in later sections of this chapter. Process system calls ask the O/S to run another program, or control how it runs. Examples include fork(), execl(), execv(), and wait(). These functions are discussed in Section 7.3. Signal system calls provide a rudimentary form of interprocess communication. Examples include signal(), pause(), kill(), and sigaction(). They are typically used to send a message to a process, telling it about an error it has committed and asking it to terminate. These functions are discussed in Section 7.4. Socket system calls allow a program on one computer to communicate with a program on a second computer through a network. Examples include socket(), bind(), connect(), listen(), accept(), send(), and recv(). These functions are discussed in Section 7.5.

Other system calls include those used for message passing, shared memory, semaphores, and thread management. Some of these families of system calls have entire books devoted to their theory and usage. It is not the goal of this chapter to cover all system calls and their potential applications. The goal is to make the reader aware of system calls and show, through many examples, how and when they can be used to help solve problems.

7.2 • Libraries and System Calls

Many standard library functions are built on top of system calls, meaning that the library functions use system calls as part of their code. For example, the malloc() family of functions is built on top of the mmap() and brk() functions, meaning that the latter are called upon to get the job done. The malloc() function is in the C standard library, while mmap() is a system call. As another example, the sleep() library function is implemented by calling a few time management system calls, such as alarm(). The sleep() function provides a single function to pause a program for a specified amount of time. The fopen(), fread(), fwrite(), and fclose() library functions build on top of the open(), read(), write(), and close() system calls. This is a common hierarchical relationship between library functions and system calls.

The library functions tend to hide the details of how the resources of the system are managed, and they provide a simpler interface to application programs. This is usually advantageous for application programming. As an example, operating systems use a variety of techniques to manage the available physical memory and present it to application programs as one contiguous virtual memory. The memory management system calls allow a programmer to get into these details and manipulate memory at the lowest level. Most of the time, applications are not interested in these operations and simply want to request a chunk of memory. The malloc() family of functions in the C standard library provides this capability by building on top of the memory management system calls. However, for some types of programming, getting into the lowest level of detail is very important. The programming for a device driver, for instance, usually involves getting into the details of the machine through system calls.

Library functions sometimes provide additional capabilities not available directly through system calls. For example, the C standard library functions fopen(), fread(), fwrite(), and fclose() provide buffering, whereas the system calls open(), read(), write(), and close() generally do not. When an fread() call is made, more than the requested amount is read() from the file. The extra bytes are held in a buffer managed by the library code. When the program next calls fread(), the system may be able to satisfy the request using bytes already in the buffer, eliminating the need for another read() system call. Standard library functions often optimize operations to minimize the number of system calls, thus speeding up program execution.

Library functions tend to be more portable than system calls. They both have standards: the ANSI C standard defines many library functions, while the POSIX standard defines many system calls. However, since system calls provide direct access to the kernel, different operating systems (including different variations of Unix) will have at least slightly different system calls. Therefore, applications that are intended to be ported to many different systems are usually coded using library functions instead of system calls whenever possible.

The man pages for system calls, library calls, and system programs are all stored in different directories, often called sections or chapters. The man pages for system programs are in section 1, those for system calls in section 2, and those for library functions in section 3. Using man, the section can be specified by a command line argument. For example:

```
man 2 stat
[... provides man page for system call stat() ...]
```

```
man 3 printf
[... provides man page for library function printf() ...]
```

```
man 1 ls
[... provides man page for system program ls ...]
```

By default, the man program will start in section 1 and look upward. If the section number is omitted, the result is the lowest section number that has a man page with the given name. This can be confusing because, to take one example, there is a stat program in section 1 as well as the stat() system call in section 2.

System calls can fail for a variety of reasons. For example, a requested resource may be busy or temporarily unavailable, or the application may not have permissions to access the requested resource. When a system call fails, it typically returns a value of −1. If a programmer wants to find out why the system call failed, then the perror() function can be called to display a string associated with the error number. This is often helpful during program development and debugging.

7.3 • Process System Calls

Process system calls deal with the starting up of new programs. Example process system calls include fork(), execl(), execv(), and wait(). The paradigm behind these functions can seem a little strange. In order to start a new program, a currently running program makes a clone of itself; the clone then replaces its code with the code of the new program. All programs are therefore clone-descendants of the first program run on the system after the kernel boots. In order to understand this paradigm, this section will first provide some needed background on processes, and then look at the system calls in detail.

7.3.1 Processes

A process is a running program, that is, a program currently in execution. On a modern computing system, dozens of processes are often running concurrently.[2] Most operating systems have system programs that allow the user to look at the current process list. On a Unix system, one can run the ps program:

```
ahoover@video> ps
  PID TTY          TIME CMD
15461 pts/3    00:00:00 tcsh
15794 pts/3    00:00:00 ps
ahoover@video>
```

Each line in the output lists a process, along with some information about the process. The PID is the process identifier, a unique number assigned to each

---

2. Technically, processes swap in and out of the processor or processor cores at a rapid rate, providing the illusion that they are running concurrently.

process. The TTY is the terminal in which the program was run. The TIME is the cumulative execution time, or how long the program has been running. The CMD is the command, including command line options, that was used to start the program.

The previous example showed only two processes because by default ps will show only processes started in the current terminal. It can also be run with appropriate flags to show all processes currently running on the system:

```
ahoover@video> ps -ef
UID       PID PPID TTY        TIME CMD
root        1    0 ?      00:00:09 init [5]
root        2    1 ?      00:00:00 [keventd]
root        3    1 ?      00:00:09 [ksoftirqd_CPU0]
root        4    1 ?      00:00:00 [kswapd]
root        5    1 ?      00:00:00 [bdflush]
[...]
liy     14276 14273 pts/1 00:00:00 -tcsh
liy     14297 14276 pts/1 00:00:00 pine
[...]
root    15460   875 ?     00:00:00 /usr/sbin/sshd
ahoover 15461 15460 pts/3 00:00:00 -tcsh
ahoover 16824 15461 pts/3 00:00:00 ps -ef
ahoover@video>
```

The full listing (-e flag) is abbreviated by [...] for the sake of space. The extra columns (-f flag) provide additional information about each process. The UID is the user identifier of the user who started the process. In this listing, one can see that two users (ahoover and liy) are currently running programs on this system, as well as processes started by the root user when the machine booted. The PPID is the parent PID, which shows which process was cloned to start each new process. The init process is the first program run by the kernel after it has finished initializing, so it has a PPID of 0 and a PID of 1. It then starts a lot of other root processes, which in turn can start others, and so on. At the bottom of the listing, one can see that the shell program tcsh is the parent process of the ps program executed to generate that list. The system program top shows some of the same information, but sorts it by resources used and continuously updates it. On an MS Windows system, a similar process table can be seen by pressing CTRL-ALT-DEL and then selecting the task manager.

Within a shell, there are several commands that can be used to alter how a program is running. Table 7.1 lists the commands that affect how the process

Table 7.1 Shell commands used to alter how a program is run.

Command/key stroke	Effect
CTRL-C	terminate process currently connected to stdin
&	run program in background; stdin stream is disconnected
CTRL-Z	suspend process currently connected to stdin
bg	restart suspended process; stdin still disconnected
fg	reconnect suspended/background process to stdin
kill #	terminate the given process ID

connects its stdin stream. To demonstrate these commands, consider the following code:

```
main()
{
while (1);
}
```

This program executes an endless loop. Assuming the code is stored in a file named loop.c, then it can be compiled and executed as follows:

```
ahoover@video> gcc -o loop loop.c
ahoover@video> loop
[]
```

The square brackets represent the cursor, and the fact that the program is running indefinitely. It can now be suspended by pressing CTRL-Z:

```
ahoover@video> loop
[]
[CTRL-Z]
Suspended
ahoover@video>
```

The program is still in the process table, but it has been paused:

```
ahoover@video> ps
  PID TTY          TIME CMD
15461 pts/3    00:00:00 tcsh
16904 pts/3    00:00:01 loop
16905 pts/3    00:00:00 ps
ahoover@video>
```

Using the bg command, the program can be moved to the background with execution resumed:

```
ahoover@video> bg
[1]    loop &
ahoover@video> ps
   PID TTY         TIME CMD
 15461 pts/3   00:00:00 tcsh
 16904 pts/3   00:00:06 loop
 16906 pts/3   00:00:00 ps
ahoover@video>
```

The program can be moved back to the foreground and have its stdin stream reconnected to the keyboard, by issuing the fg command:

```
ahoover@video> fg
loop
[]
[CTRL-C]
ahoover@video>
```

The last command shown, CTRL-C, terminates a program currently running in the foreground. For a program running in the background, it must either be moved to the foreground, or be terminated using the kill command. For example:

```
ahoover@video> loop
[]
CTRL-Z
Suspended
ahoover@video> bg
[1]    loop &
ahoover@video> ps
   PID TTY         TIME CMD
 15461 pts/3   00:00:00 tcsh
 16974 pts/3   00:00:06 loop
 16975 pts/3   00:00:00 ps
ahoover@video> kill 16974
[1]   + Terminated            loop
ahoover@video> ps
   PID TTY         TIME CMD
 15461 pts/3   00:00:00 tcsh
 16976 pts/3   00:00:00 ps
ahoover@video>
```

In this example, the PID of the loop program was found by running the ps program. The PID was then used in a kill command to terminate the loop program. Finally, a program can be placed into background execution immediately upon running it from a shell using the & command:

```
ahoover@video> loop &
[1] 16909
ahoover@video>
```

The loop program is started executing in the background, and its PID (16909) is displayed by the shell.

Why would a program need to be run in the background? Some programs require no keyboard input. For example, many system programs monitor resources or record logs without ever needing input from a user. This can be seen in the longer ps listing shown earlier in the section, where several root processes have no associated terminal (they have a "?" in the TTY field). Some user application programs may also be pushed to the background. For example, suppose a program was started that was going to sort a database of millions of records, perhaps running for hours. There is no need for this program to use up the terminal keyboard and screen streams while it is running. Instead, it can be run in the background. The shell will report whenever a background process terminates.

7.3.2 fork()

The fork() system call creates a clone of the currently running program. The original program continues execution with the next line of code after the fork() function call. The clone also starts execution at the next line of code. For example, consider the following code:

```c
#include <stdio.h>
#include <unistd.h>

main()
{
int i;

printf("Ready to fork...\n");
i=fork();
printf("Fork returned %d\n",i);
while (1);
}
```

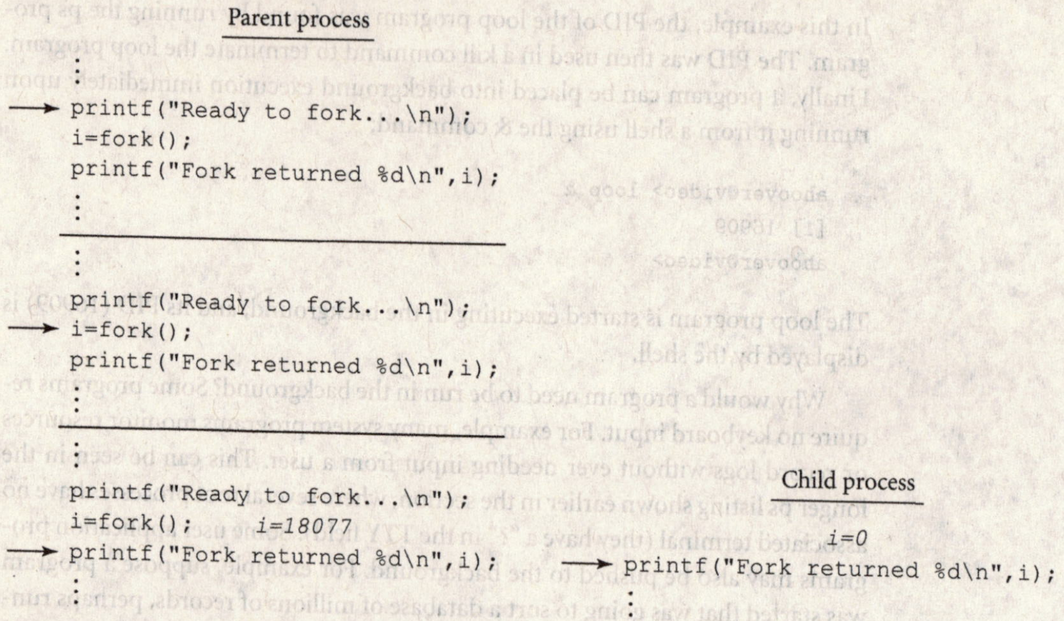

Parent process

```
printf("Ready to fork...\n");
i=fork();
printf("Fork returned %d\n",i);
```

```
printf("Ready to fork...\n");
i=fork();
printf("Fork returned %d\n",i);
```

Child process

```
printf("Ready to fork...\n");
i=fork();        i=18077
printf("Fork returned %d\n",i);                    i=0
                              printf("Fork returned %d\n",i);
```

Figure 7.2 A timeline of events during a fork system call.

This program calls the fork() function and then goes into an infinite loop. Assuming the code is stored in a file named fork1.c, then it can be compiled and executed as follows:

```
ahoover@video> gcc -o fork1 fork1.c
ahoover@video> fork
Ready to fork...
Fork returned 18077
Fork returned 0
[]
```

Figure 7.2 displays a timeline of events. The original program (the parent process) displays the output "Ready to fork . . . " and then calls the fork() function. At that point, the program is cloned (the child process starts) and there are two copies of it running. Each executes the line to display the code "Fork returned . . . ". However, notice that the return values are different. The parent process (the original) gets a different return value from fork() than the child process (the clone) does. In the parent process, fork() returns the PID of the new child process, while in the child process, fork() returns zero. Continuing the example, the foreground process can be suspended so that the process table can be seen:

```
[]
[CTRL-Z]
Suspended
ahoover@video> ps
  PID TTY          TIME CMD
15461 pts/3    00:00:00 tcsh
18076 pts/3    00:00:01 fork1
18077 pts/3    00:00:01 fork1
18078 pts/3    00:00:00 ps
ahoover@video> kill 18076
[1]  + Terminated                          fork1
ahoover@video> ps
  PID TTY          TIME CMD
15461 pts/3    00:00:00 tcsh
18079 pts/3    00:00:00 ps
ahoover@video>
```

Note that there were two copies of fork1 running. The kill command was used on the parent process, causing it to terminate, along with the child process. The termination of both processes, however, is a system-dependent behavior; on some systems, it may be necessary to kill child processes independently.

Cloning a program and running it identically is not very useful. The return value from fork() allows a program to affect which code its clone will execute. For example, consider the following code:

```
#include <stdio.h>
#include <unistd.h>

main()
{
int     i,j;

j=0;
printf("Ready to fork...\n");
i=fork();
if (i == 0)
  {
  printf("The child executes this code.\n");
  for (i=0; i<5; i++)
    j=j+i;
  printf("Child j=%d\n",j);
  }
else
```

```
{
printf("The parent executes this code.\n");
for (i=0; i<3; i++)
  j=j+i;
printf("Parent j=%d\n",j);
}
}
```

This program uses the return value from fork() to decide what to execute next. The parent and child processes will each go into different code blocks. If this code is stored in a file named fork2.c, then compiling it and executing it produces output like the following:

```
ahoover@video> fork2
Ready to fork...
The parent executes this code.
The child executes this code.
Child j=10
Parent j=3
ahoover@video>
```

The order of the lines of output will vary from run to run. This is because after the fork(), both processes are running concurrently and the order of execution is not predictable. All we know for certain is the relative order of the " . . . executes this code" and "j=" lines (the former precedes the latter for each code block). However, the important thing to note is that each process has its own variables, and they are executing different code.

The fork() function can be called iteratively, meaning that one process can start up multiple new processes, which can in turn start multiple new processes, and so on. For example, consider the following code:

```
#include <stdio.h>
#include <unistd.h>

main()
{
int     i;

i=getpid();
printf("Parent=%d\n",i);
fork();
fork();
i=getpid();
printf("Who am I? %d\n",i);
}
```

The getpid() function is a system call that returns the PID of the current process. This program calls fork(), creating a clone. Then each of those programs calls fork(), creating another clone each. Assuming this code is stored in a file named fork3.c, then compiling and executing it produces output like the following:

```
ahoover@video> gcc -o fork3 fork3.c
ahoover@video> fork3
Parent=18210
Who am I? 18210
Who am I? 18211
Who am I? 18212
Who am I? 18213
ahoover@video>
```

Again, the order of the lines of output will vary from run to run because all the processes are executing concurrently. Caution should be exercised when using fork() in a loop or nested fashion. If coded in error, it may result in a "fork-bomb" where processes are continually spawned until the process table is filled, crashing the system or bringing it to an unusable state.

7.3.3 exec() Family

The exec() family of system calls replaces the currently executing code of a process with another piece of code. The process retains its PID but otherwise becomes a new program. For example, consider the following code:

```
#include <stdio.h>
#include <unistd.h>

main()
{
char    program[80],*args[3];
int     i;

printf("Ready to exec()...\n");
strcpy(program,"date");
args[0]="date";
args[1]="-u";
args[2]=NULL;
i=execvp(program,args);
printf("i=%d ... did it work?\n",i);
}
```

This program calls the execvp() function to replace its code with the date program. If the code is stored in a file named exec1.c, then compiling it and executing it produces the following output:

```
ahoover@video> gcc -o exec1 exec1.c
ahoover@video> exec1
Ready to exec()...
Tue Jul 15 20:17:53 UTC 2008
ahoover@video>
```

The program outputs the line "Ready to exec()..." and after calling the execvp() function, replaces its code with the date program. Note that the line "... did it work" is not displayed, because at that point the code has been replaced. Instead, we see the output of executing "date -u."

If the execvp() function is unable to find or execute the replacement code, then the function fails and the original code continues execution. This can be seen by changing a line of code in the above example, as follows:

```
strcpy(program,"find_a_date");        /* changed program */
```

Recompiling and executing this program produces the following output:

```
ahoover@video> gcc -o exec1 exec1.c
ahoover@video> exec1
Ready to exec()...
i=-1 ... did it work?
ahoover@video>
```

Because the program "find_a_date" could not be found, the execvp() function failed and the original code was continued.

There are several variations in the exec() family of functions, including execl(), execlp(), execle(), execv(), and execvp(). They all achieve the same effect but differ in how the replacement code and arguments are named or called.

7.3.4   wait()

The wait() system call suspends a process, waiting for a child process to finish. This allows some control of the synchronicity actions of parent and child processes. For example, consider the following code:

```
#include <stdio.h>
#include <unistd.h>
```

```
main()
{
int    i,j;
j=0;
printf("Ready to fork...\n");
i=fork();
if (i == 0)
   {
printf("The child executes this code.\n");
for (i=0; i<5; i++)
   j=j+i;
printf("Child j=%d\n",j);
   }
else
   {
j=wait();
printf("The parent executes this code.\n");
printf("Parent j=%d\n",j);
   }
}
```

This code is very similar to an example from Section 7.3.2. However, the wait() function is executed in the block reached by the parent process. This causes the parent process to pause until the child process has finished, at which time the parent process resumes execution. If this code is stored in a file named wait1.c, then compiling and executing it produces the following output:

```
ahoover@video> gcc -o wait1 wait1.c
ahoover@video> wait1
Ready to fork...
The child executes this code.
Child j=10
The parent executes this code.
Parent j=24148
ahoover@video>
```

Unlike the similar example from Section 7.3.2, executing this code will always produce its output in this order. Note that the return value of the wait() function is the PID of the child process.

The wait() function pauses until any child process has completed. Finer control over synchronization can be obtained using the waitpid() function, which can wait on a process with a specific PID, or can wait until a process terminates in a specific manner or with a specific condition. Even finer synchronization and process control can be obtained by using mutexes and other concepts provided by a threads library, such as pthreads. However, these topics are beyond the scope of this text. The interested reader is encouraged to look at the book *UNIX Systems Programming: Communication, Concurrency and Threads*, 2nd ed., K. Robbins and S. Robbins, Prentice Hall, 2003, ISBN 0130424110, for coverage of pthreads and related system calls.

The system() function is a C standard library function that puts the fork(), exec(), and wait() functions together into a single convenient call. For example, consider the following code:

```c
#include <stdio.h>
#include <stdlib.h>

main()
{
char    text[80];

printf("Ready to system()...\n");
sprintf(text,"date -u");
system(text);
printf("Did it work?\n");
sleep(4);
printf("Indeed it did.\n");
}
```

This program prints out a "ready" message, and then uses system() to execute the date program. The sleep() function is then called to emphasize the continuing execution of the original program. The sleep() function pauses the program for the given number of seconds (in this case 4). Assuming this code is stored in a file named system1.c, then compiling it and executing it produces the following output:

```
ahoover@video> gcc -o system1 system1.c
ahoover@video> system1
Ready to system()...
Tue Jul 15 20:23:57 UTC 2008
Did it work?
Indeed it did.
ahoover@video>
```

There will be a noticeable pause between the last two lines of output, caused by the sleep() function call.

7.4 • Signal System Calls

As described at the beginning of this chapter, an operating system (O/S) has two main jobs: it manages the resources of the computer (peripherals, files, memory, etc.) and it manages all other programs running on the computer. One of the most important aspects of managing programs is supporting communication between them. Communication between running programs is called interprocess communication (IPC). Since the O/S is itself a program, there are a set of system calls designed primarily to facilitate communication between the O/S and an application. These communications are called signals. Most commonly, they are used by an O/S to tell a program that it needs to terminate.

IPC using signals is limited to an alphabet of signal types. Modern operating systems typically provide 30–40 different signal types.[3] Table 7.2 lists the names and IDs from the POSIX.1 standard for the most common signals. Each signal communication involves sending one of these signals, referenced by signal name or ID, to a process.

A process decides what to do with a signal by declaring or installing a signal handler. A signal handler is a function that is executed when a signal is received. Different signal handlers can be executed for different signal IDs. A signal handler is executed asynchronously, meaning that it interrupts the process at its current execution point and execution is jumped to the signal handler function. Each process is given a default signal handler for each signal, usually containing code that terminates the process. The following subsections explain how to set up custom signal handlers and how to send signals between processes.

7.4.1   signal()

The `signal()` function asks the O/S to install a signal handler function for a given signal. Installation means that the O/S successfully associates that function with the given signal and readies it for execution should that process receive the given signal. For example, consider the following code:

---

3. On a Unix system, the command `man 7 signal` will show a man page listing all signals for the system. They can also be listed by executing the command `kill -1`, or they can be found in /usr/include/signal.h or a derivative system header file.

```
#include <stdio.h>
#include <signal.h>

main()
{
void    f(int);    /* prototype for signal handler function */
int     i;

signal(SIGFPE,f);    /* install the handler */
for (i=-3; i<=3; i++)
  printf("%d\n",12/i);
}

void f(int signum)
{
printf("You can't divide by zero!\n");
exit(SIGFPE);
}
```

This code installs a signal handler for the SIGFPE signal. Whenever the program causes a floating point exception (a type of arithmetic error), then the function

Table 7.2 Common signal names and IDs from the POSIX.1 standard.

Name	ID	Usually used for . . .
SIGHUP	1	hangup or death of controlling process
SIGINT	2	interrupt from keyboard
SIGQUIT	3	quit from keyboard
SIGILL	4	illegal instruction
SIGABRT	6	abort signal from abort() function
SIGFPE	8	floating point exception
SIGKILL	9	kill signal (cannot be ignored/trapped)
SIGUSR1	10	user-defined signal 1
SIGSEGV	11	invalid memory reference
SIGUSR2	12	user-defined signal 2
SIGPIPE	13	broken pipe: write to pipe with no readers
SIGALRM	14	timer signal from alarm() function
SIGTERM	15	termination signal

`f()` will get executed. If this code is stored in a file named `sig1.c`, then compiling it and executing it produces the following output:

```
ahoover@video> gcc -o sig1 sig1.c
ahoover@video> sig1
-4
-6
-12
You can't divide by zero!
ahoover@video>
```

When the value of the variable `i` reaches zero, the program attempts to divide by zero, and a SIGFPE signal is generated. The program jumps to the `f()` signal handling function, and its code is executed. By tradition the `exit()` function should return the value of the signal indicating why the program terminated.

An application can also request that a signal be ignored. For example, consider the following code:

```
#include <stdio.h>
#include <signal.h>


main()
{
signal(SIGINT,SIG_IGN);  /* tell the O/S to ignore the signal */
printf("I'm running ...\n");
while (1)
  {
  printf("Still going ...\n");
  sleep(1);
  }
}
```

The second argument for signal() in this example is given the value SIG_IGN, which asks the O/S to ignore that signal. The SIGINT signal is normally generated when the user presses CTRL-C to terminate a program. If this code is stored in a file named `sig2.c`, then compiling it and executing it produces the following output:

```
ahoover@video> gcc -o sig2 sig2.c
ahoover@video> sig2
I'm running ...
Still going ...
[... CTRL-C ... nothing happens ...]
```

```
Still going ...
Still going ...
[... CTRL-\ ...]
Quit
ahoover@video>
```

This program will run indefinitely unless terminated by the user. However, when the user presses CTRL-C, nothing happens. The user can press the CTRL-\ key sequence to force the program to terminate. This generates the SIGQUIT signal, which has much the same effect as the SIGINT signal.

Finally, a program that has previously defined an alternate signal handling function can use signal() to return the signal handler to its default. For example, consider the following code:

```
#include <stdio.h>
#include <signal.h>

main()
{
int     i;

signal(SIGINT,SIG_IGN);  /* ignore the signal */
printf("I'm running ...\n");
for (i=1; i<10; i++)
  {
  printf("Still going ...\n");
  sleep(1);
  if (i == 3)
    signal(SIGINT,SIG_DFL);  /* re-install default handler */
  }
}
```

If this code is stored in a file named sig3.c, then compiling it and executing it while repeatedly pressing CTRL-C produces the following output:

```
ahoover@video> gcc -o sig3 sig3.c
ahoover@video> sig3
I'm running ...
Still going ...
Still going ...
Still going ...
Still going ...
ahoover@video>
```

The program displays the output from within the loop three times before the default signal handler is reinstalled, and then normally a fourth time before the user is quick enough to press CTRL-C and cause the program to terminate.

7.4.2   kill()

Signals can be generated by users, the operating system, or other processes. A user can generate a signal through a keyboard sequence, for example, by pressing CTRL-C. This signal is usually used by a user to ask the operating system to terminate a process. An O/S typically generates a signal when a program does something wrong, such as dividing by zero or attempting to access an invalid or restricted memory location. Usually these signals also cause the process to terminate. Another process can generate a signal by calling the kill() system function call. Such a signal is usually sent from a parent to a child process, telling the child to terminate. However, these signals can be sent in either direction and can be used to provide a limited form of interprocess communication (IPC). For example, consider the following code:

```
#include <stdio.h>
#include <unistd.h>
#include <signal.h>

int running;

main()
{
void    f(int);
int     i,j;
char    text[80];

i=fork();  /* parent & child process running now */
if (i == 0)
   {    /* child process */
   signal(SIGUSR1,f);    /* install the handler */
   printf("Child waiting...\n");
   running=1;
   while (running == 1)
     sleep(1);
   }
else
```

```
{
while (1)
    {
    sleep(1);
    printf("Command? ");
    scanf("%s",text);
    if (strcmp(text,"frog") == 0)
        kill(i,SIGUSR1);
    if (strcmp(text,"quit") == 0)
        break;
    }
}

void f(int signum)
{
printf("Child received a frog!\n");
running=0;
}
```

This program first executes a fork(), creating a child process. The child process installs a signal handler for the SIGUSR1 signal that displays a simple line of text. The child process then goes into an infinite loop. The parent process enters its own loop, asking the user for an input string. If the user enters "frog", then the parent process uses the kill() function to send the SIGUSR1 signal to the child process. If this code is stored in a file named kill1.c, then compiling it and executing it produces the following output:

```
ahoover@video> gcc -o kill1 kill1.c
ahoover@video> kill1
Child waiting...
Command? turtle
Command? frog
Child received a frog!
Command? quit
ahoover@video>
```

This program also uses a global variable to communicate between the f() signal handler function and the main() function.

The kill shell command, introduced in Section 7.3, calls the kill() system call. It allows a user to send a signal to a process from the shell. It can be used to send a specific signal to a given process through a command line argument. For example, consider the following code:

```
#include <stdio.h>
#include <signal.h>

main()
{
void  f(int),g(int);

signal(SIGUSR1,f);        /* install the handler */
signal(SIGUSR2,g);        /* install the handler */
while (1)
   sleep(1);
}

void f(int signum)
{
printf("Received a frog!\n");
}

void g(int signum)
{
printf("Received a giraffe!\n");
exit(SIGUSR2);
}
```

This program installs custom signal handlers for the SIGUSR1 and SIGUSR2 signals, and then goes into an infinite loop. If this code is stored in a file named kill2.c, then compiling and executing it produces the following output:

```
ahoover@video> gcc -o kill2 kill2.c
ahoover@video> kill2 &
[1] 20166
ahoover@video> kill -USR1 20166
ahoover@video> Received a frog!
ahoover@video> kill -USR2 20166
ahoover@video> Received a giraffe!
[1]    Exit 12              kill2
ahoover@video>
```

The program is run in the background using the & command, at which time the shell prints out the PID, 20166. The kill command is then used to send a SIGUSR1 signal to process 20166. The kill command is also used to send a SIGUSR2 to the process, which causes the process to print a line of output and exit().

7.5 • Socket System Calls

Socket system calls are used for interprocess communication over a network. They allow a process on one computer to communicate with a process on another computer. In order to communicate, each process makes some socket system calls to set itself up for sending or receiving data. Additional system calls are then made to actually send or receive the data. Finally, each process makes a system call to terminate the communication. These three steps (connect, send/receive data, terminate) bear a resemblance to basic file I/O (open, read/write data, close). The main difference is that a file and a program accessing that file are on the same system, and so the options in the communication are more limited. The socket system calls act similarly to those used for file I/O, but they provide a greater set of options to facilitate communication between processes on different machines.

In order to explain socket system calls, this section will first cover some basic networking concepts and system commands. The client-server model is then explained, and the most common socket system calls are examined. At the end of the section, two process-to-process communication problems are examined to show how the socket system calls can solve these problems. Note that this section does not provide a detailed explanation of every possible scenario or use of the socket system calls, as that is beyond the scope of this text. The interested reader is referred to *Unix Network Programming, Volume 1: The Sockets Networking API*, 3rd ed., R. Stevens, B. Fenner, and A. Rudoff, Addison-Wesley, 2003, ISBN 0131411551, for a book that covers the entire sockets API and networking background in general. The goal of this section is to introduce the reader to the concepts involved in network process communication and socket system calls.

7.5.1   Network Concepts and System Commands

The network interface of a computer is identified by its Internet Protocol (IP) address. An IP address is a numeric identifier unique to a single machine on the network. At the time of this writing, the Internet is beginning a transition from 32-bit identifiers (IPv4) to 128-bit identifiers (IPv6) to allow for the large growth in the number of computers connected to the Internet. However, most of the Internet still uses IPv4 and all the concepts are similar regardless, so the examples used in this section will be demonstrated using IPv4 addressing. The 32 bits of an IPv4 address are commonly written as a set of four 8-bit numbers separated by periods; for example, 192.168.0.100. Historically, the leading portion of an IPv4 address (usually the first two or three 8-bit numbers) has been used to designate a network of computers collocated or coadministered, while the last 8-bit number designates a specific machine on the local network, also called a subnetwork or subnet. Using the Domain Name System (DNS), an IP address is given a corresponding human readable name. For example, 130.127.69.75 has the domain name of www.clemson.edu.

A port is an identifier on a computer through which network process communication takes place. A computer may have multiple processes involved in separate network communications at the same time; each is assigned a different port number. A port is identified by a 16-bit, nonnegative integer. The port values in the range 0–1023 are generally reserved for system processes. Most of these are standardized to traditional services, such as telnet (port 23), secure shell (port 22), web server (port 80), and the like. On a Unix system, the file /etc/services contains a full list of standardized ports. The port values in the range 1024–49151 are generally assigned to applications. The port values in the range 49152–65535 are unreserved and are generally used for transient connections. The ports used on each of the two computers having a network communication do not need to match. But when establishing a connection, the calling computer must know both the IP address of the computer it wishes to call and the port number of the process to which it wishes to communicate.

There are a number of system programs that manage and report IP and port number information. On a Unix system, the ifconfig program reports the machine's IP address. For example:

```
ahoover@video> ifconfig eth0
eth0     Link encap:Ethernet  HWaddr 00:D0:09:F7:C1:07
         inet addr:130.127.24.92  Bcast:130.127.24.255 [...]
         UP BROADCAST RUNNING MULTICAST  MTU:1500 [...]
         RX packets:31351262 errors:1 dropped:0 [...]
         TX packets:34052244 errors:0 dropped:0 [...]
         collisions:0 txqueuelen:1000
         RX bytes:3858447315 (3679.7 Mb)  TX bytes: [...]
         Interrupt:5 Base address:0xf00
ahoover@video>
```

The IP address of the system, 130.127.24.92, can be seen in the second line of output (some of the output is clipped to fit the page). On an MS Windows system, the program ipconfig produces similar output. The nslookup program can be used to look up the DNS name of an IP address, or vice versa. For example:

```
ahoover@video> nslookup -silent 130.127.24.92
Server:         130.127.24.10
Address:        130.127.24.10#53

92.24.127.130.in-addr.arpa      name = video.parl.clemson.edu.

ahoover@video>
```

The name of the system, video.parl.clemson.edu, can be seen in the output. The netstat program can be used to display all the ports on a system currently being used for network process communication. For example:

```
ahoover@video> netstat --protocol=inet
Active Internet connections (w/o servers)
Proto  Local Address  Foreign Address         State
tcp    video:736      shredder:914            TIME_WAIT
tcp    video:42961    video:60000             ESTABLISHED
tcp    video:ssh      ahoover-pc.ces.cle:3260 ESTABLISHED
tcp    video:ssh      cerberus.parl.cle:39644 ESTABLISHED
tcp    video:ssh      cerberus.parl.cle:47362 ESTABLISHED
tcp    video:ssh      cerberus.parl.cle:58697 ESTABLISHED
tcp    video:ssh      cerberus.parl.cle:58699 ESTABLISHED
tcp    video:739      shredder:sunrpc         TIME_WAIT
tcp    video:737      shredder:sunrpc         TIME_WAIT
tcp    video:741      shredder:sunrpc         TIME_WAIT
tcp    video:60000    video:42961             ESTABLISHED
tcp    video:741      shredder:sunrpc         TIME_WAIT
tcp    video:60000    video:42961             ESTABLISHED
ahoover@video>
```

Each row of the output represents a different communication. The local address is the local system's name and port number. The foreign address is the remote system's name and port number. The state is used by the system to manage the opening and closing of a network communication, as well as the active communication itself.

The iptables program manages a firewall for the system. A firewall is a common security tool that can be used to block specific ports from participating in network communications. For example, a firewall could be configured to prevent any network packets addressed to port 23 on a machine from being delivered. Even if the machine is running a telnet server that is listening on port 23, it will not be able to connect to clients because of the firewall blocking that port. The iproute2 package of programs[4] is a modern rewrite of network management utilities that performs similar operations to all those just described.

---

4. The iproute2 package is freely available from the Linux Foundation at www.linuxfoundation.org/en/Net:Iproute2.

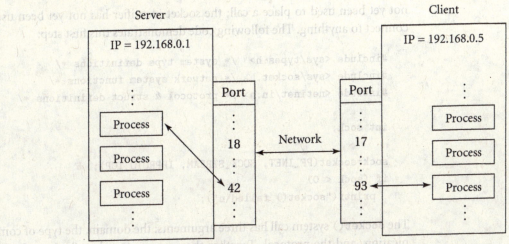

Figure 7.3 A server-client interaction.

7.5.2 Client-Server Model

Most network process communications follow a client-server model. In this model, a process on one computer acts as a server, and a process on the second computer acts as a client. The server opens up a port for listening and waits for a client to attempt to establish a connection. The client calls the server by connecting to the port on which the server is listening. When establishing a connection, a process must identify the IP and port to which it wishes to communicate. An analogy can be drawn to making a phone call to a house where multiple people live. The IP is like the phone number that identifies the house, while the port is like the name of the person to which the caller wishes to speak. Figure 7.3 shows a diagram of the idea. In this example, a server process is listening on its local port 42. The client process uses its local port 93 to attempt a connection. In the connection call, it specifies that it wishes to communicate with a process at 192.168.0.1:42, indicating both the server IP and port on which the server process is listening.

The following subsections explain the steps in creating, using, and closing a network communication from the perspectives of both a server and a client.

7.5.2.1 socket()

The first step in establishing a network communication is to create a socket. A socket provides an integer identifier through which a network communication is going to take place. The newly created socket is analogous to a telephone that has not yet been used to place a call; the socket identifier has not yet been used to connect to anything. The following code demonstrates this first step:

```
#include <sys/types.h>  /* system type definitions */
#include <sys/socket.h> /* network system functions */
#include <netinet/in.h> /* protocol & struct definitions */


int sock;


sock=socket(PF_INET, SOCK_STREAM, IPPROTO_TCP);
if (sock < 0)
  printf("socket() failed\n");
```

The socket() system call has three arguments: the domain, the type of communication, and the protocol. Together these parameters describe how the socket will be used for communication. It is beyond the scope of this text to explain all possible values for these arguments; that would involve a detailed study of network protocols and layers. However, the values listed in this example provide the most common, stable connection for an IPv4 network communication.

7.5.2.2 bind()

The second step in establishing a network communication depends upon whether the process will act as a server or a client. A server will typically bind the socket, defining the IP and port on which it will listen for connections. For example:

```
int                  i,sock;
struct sockaddr_in   my_addr;
unsigned short       listen_port=60000;

          /* ... socket has been created ... */

          /* make local address structure */
memset(&my_addr, 0, sizeof (my_addr));  /* clr structure */
my_addr.sin_family = AF_INET;    /* address family */
my_addr.sin_addr.s_addr = htonl(INADDR_ANY); /* my IP */
my_addr.sin_port = htons(listen_port);

          /* bind socket to the local address */
i=bind(sock, (struct sockaddr *) &my_addr, sizeof (my_addr));
if (i < 0)
  printf("bind() failed\n");
```

The struct sockaddr_in holds information about the connection, including the IP and port number. It is then used in the bind() function to give the socket the equivalent of a telephone number. At a detailed level, the structure is first zeroed out (all bytes in the structure given a value of zero) using the memset() function. This is done to ensure that all unused portions of the structure have a value of zero. The structure is then filled with information about how the socket will be used. The htonl() function is one of a family of functions that makes sure bytes are in the correct order for network transport. In a bind() function call, the value of INADDR_ANY as an address indicates that the socket should be bound to the IP of the machine on which the process is currently executing. In this example, the server will look for communication on its own IP on port number 60000.

7.5.2.3 listen()

After binding, a server will typically call the listen() function to await communication:

```
int i,sock;

    /* ... socket has been created and bound ... */

    /* listen */
i=listen(sock,5);
if (i < 0)
    printf("listen() failed\n");
```

The second parameter of the listen() function describes how many connections can be queued while the server is handling another communication. In this example, the operating system will queue up to five connection attempts before returning an error value to additional clients trying to connect.

7.5.2.4 connect()

A client performs a step similar to binding, but instead of listening, it actively makes a call, establishing a connection. For example:

```
int                   i,sock;
struct sockaddr_in    addr_send;
char                  *server_ip="130.127.24.92";
unsigned short        server_port=60000;

    /* ... socket has been created ... */
```

```
                    /* create socket address structure to connect to */
        memset(&addr_send, 0, sizeof (addr_send)); /* clr structure */
        addr_send.sin_family = AF_INET; /* address family */
        addr_send.sin_addr.s_addr = inet_addr(server_ip);
        addr_send.sin_port = htons(server_port);

                    /* connect to the server */
        i=connect(sock, (struct sockaddr *) &addr_send,
                    sizeof (addr_send));
        if (i < 0)
          printf("connect() failed\n");
```

In this example, the struct sockaddr_in is filled with information about the server to which the client wishes to connect. The connect() function is used to call the server in an attempt to establish a connection.

7.5.2.5   accept()

Once a server has received an incoming connect attempt, it can accept the connection. For example:

```
        int                     i,sock,sock_recv,addr_size;
        struct sockaddr_in      recv_addr;

            /* ... socket created, bound and listening ... */

            /* incoming xion -- get new socket to receive data on */
        addr_size=sizeof(recv_addr);
        sock_recv=accept(sock, (struct sockaddr *) &recv_addr,
                    &addr_size);
```

The accept() function returns a second socket (in this example, sock_recv) on which data will be transmitted. This allows the original socket (in this example, sock) to continue to listen for additional connections.

7.5.2.6   send() and recv()

After a connection has been established between the client and server, data can be transmitted and received. For example, the client could execute the following code:

```
        int sock,bytes_sent;
        char text[80];

            /* ... socket has been created and connected ... */
```

```
                    /* send some data */
            printf("Send? ");
            scanf("%s",text);
            bytes_sent=send(sock,text,strlen(text),0);
```

The send() function call takes four arguments: the socket identifier, an address pointing to data, the number of bytes to send, and a flags setting. Normally the flags value is set to zero. The server executes similar code, receiving the sent data. For example:

```
            int sock_recv,bytes_received;
            char text[80];

                    /* ... socket created, bound and accepted ... */

                    /* receive some data */
            bytes_received=recv(sock_recv,text,80,0);
            text[bytes_received]=0;
            printf("Received: %s\n",text);
```

The parameters for the recv() function call are similar to those for send(), except that the third argument (in this example, 80) indicates the maximum number of bytes that can be received. Both the server and client can execute send() and recv(); the communication can go both ways. Also note that the data does not have to be text. The send() and recv() functions are similar to the fread() and fwrite() functions in that the arguments define an address and a number of bytes, rather than the type of data at the given address.

7.5.2.7 close()

Once communication is finished, both the server and client should close their respective sockets. For example:

```
            int i,sock_recv;


                    /* ... socket communication is finished ... */
            i=close(sock_recv);
            if (i < 0)
              printf("close() failed\n");
```

A close() system call initiates a series of operations within the O/S to terminate the connection. Thus, the socket may still appear in a netstat listing for several seconds, until the O/S has finished the close.

7.5.3   Examples

In the previous section, an analogy was made between initiating a network communication and placing a telephone call. Unlike telephony, however, in which communications are mostly one person to one person, in the case of network programming, there are a variety of situations besides one-to-one network process communications. The caller may want to broadcast an announcement, calling a whole subnetwork of computers at the same time. The caller may open a socket and use it to communicate with several remote processes at the same time. The server may take only one call at a time, or open itself up to multiple simultaneous calls. The calls may be managed all through the same port, or the server might take multiple incoming calls on one port and then manage the communication for each on a different transient port. These are only some of the situations for which socket system calls can be used. The following two examples demonstrate two specific situations and detail a client and server program for each.

7.5.3.1   Single server-client connection

The following programs put together all the ideas from Section 7.5.2 into a server program and a client program. The server listens on port 60000 for a client. When a client connects, the server reads any incoming data as text and prints it out one line at a time. If the server receives the string "shutdown," then it closes the socket and exits.

The following code is for the server:

```
#include <stdio.h>
#include <sys/types.h>    /* system type definitions */
#include <sys/socket.h>   /* network system functions */
#include <netinet/in.h>   /* protocol & struct definitions */

#define BUF_SIZE       1024
#define LISTEN_PORT    60000

int main(int argc, char *argv[])

{
int                       sock_listen,sock_recv;
struct sockaddr_in        my_addr,recv_addr;
int                       i,addr_size,bytes_received;
fd_set                    readfds;
struct timeval            timeout={0,0};
```

```
int                      incoming_len;
struct sockaddr          remote_addr;
int                      recv_msg_size;
char                     buf[BUF_SIZE];
int                      select_ret;

      /* create socket for listening */
sock_listen=socket(PF_INET, SOCK_STREAM, IPPROTO_TCP);
if (sock_listen < 0)
  {
  printf("socket() failed\n");
  exit(0);
  }
      /* make local address structure */
memset(&my_addr, 0, sizeof (my_addr));  /* clr structure */
my_addr.sin_family = AF_INET;    /* address family */
my_addr.sin_addr.s_addr = htonl(INADDR_ANY); /* current IP */
my_addr.sin_port = htons((unsigned short)LISTEN_PORT);
      /* bind socket to the local address */
i=bind(sock_listen, (struct sockaddr *) &my_addr,
       sizeof (my_addr));
if (i < 0)
  {
  printf("bind() failed\n");
  exit(0);
  }
      /* listen ... */
i=listen(sock_listen, 5);
if (i < 0)
  {
  printf("listen() failed\n");
  exit(0);
  }

      /* get new socket to receive data on */
addr_size=sizeof(recv_addr);
sock_recv=accept(sock_listen, (struct sockaddr *) &recv_addr,
       &addr_size);

while (1)
  {
```

```
    bytes_received=recv(sock_recv,buf,BUF_SIZE,0);
    buf[bytes_received]=0;
    printf("Received: %s\n",buf);
    if (strcmp(buf,"shutdown") == 0)
      break;
    }

close(sock_recv);
close(sock_listen);
  }
```

Note that the server does not manage multiple clients. It lets a single client connect and communicates with that client only.

The following code is for the client:

```
#include <stdio.h>
#include <sys/types.h>
#include <sys/socket.h>
#include <netinet/in.h>

#define BUF_SIZE        1024
#define SERVER_IP       "130.127.24.92"
#define SERVER_PORT     60000

int main(int argc, char *argv[])

{
int                     sock_send;
struct sockaddr_in      addr_send;
int                     i;
char                    text[80],buf[BUF_SIZE];
int                     send_len,bytes_sent;

    /* create socket for sending data */
sock_send=socket(PF_INET, SOCK_STREAM, IPPROTO_TCP);
if (sock_send < 0)
  {
  printf("socket() failed\n");
  exit(0);
  }
```

```
                     /* create socket address structure to connect to */
memset(&addr_send, 0, sizeof (addr_send)); /* clr structure */
addr_send.sin_family = AF_INET; /* address family */
addr_send.sin_addr.s_addr = inet_addr(SERVER_IP);
addr_send.sin_port = htons((unsigned short)SERVER_PORT);

        /* connect to the server */
i=connect(sock_send, (struct sockaddr *) &addr_send,
        sizeof (addr_send));
if (i < 0)
  {
  printf("connect() failed\n");
  exit(0);
  }

while (1)
  {
      /* send some data */
  printf("Send? ");
  scanf("%s",text);
  if (strcmp(text,"quit") == 0)
    break;

  strcpy(buf,text);
  send_len=strlen(text);
  bytes_sent=send(sock_send,buf,send_len,0);
  }

close(sock_send);
}
```

The client attempts to connect to a server at a specific IP and port. If that connection is successful, then the client prompts the user for text, sending each line of text to the server. If the user provides "quit" as input, then the client closes its socket and exits.

7.5.3.2   Multiple simultaneous clients

This example operates similarly to the previous example, but the server manages multiple concurrent connections on the same port. The server creates a socket and binds exactly as in the previous example. However, instead of using the listen() function, the server uses the select() function to listen for traffic on the socket. The select() function is given a timeout value of zero so that it does not block. If nothing has been received on the socket, the program continues. If something has been received, then the server uses the recvfrom() system call to read the incoming data directly. It does not create a second socket on which to manage the communication. This allows the server to receive data from any number of clients on a single socket.

The following is the code for the server:

```
#include <stdio.h>
#include <sys/types.h>    /* system type definitions */
#include <sys/socket.h>   /* network system functions */
#include <netinet/in.h>   /* protocol & struct definitions */

#define BUF_SIZE          1024
#define LISTEN_PORT       60000

int main(int argc, char *argv[])

{
int                       sock_recv;
struct sockaddr_in        my_addr;
int                       i;
fd_set                    readfds;
struct timeval            timeout={0,0};
int                       incoming_len;
struct sockaddr_in        remote_addr;
int                       recv_msg_size;
char                      buf[BUF_SIZE];
int                       select_ret;

                /* create socket for receiving */
sock_recv=socket(PF_INET, SOCK_DGRAM, IPPROTO_UDP);
if (sock_recv < 0)
  {
  printf("socket() failed\n");
  exit(0);
  }
                /* make local address structure */
memset(&my_addr, 0, sizeof (my_addr));  /* clr structure */
```

```
        my_addr.sin_family = AF_INET;    /* address family */
        my_addr.sin_addr.s_addr = htonl(INADDR_ANY); /* current IP */
        my_addr.sin_port = htons((unsigned short)LISTEN_PORT);
                    /* bind socket to the local address */
        i=bind(sock_recv, (struct sockaddr *) &my_addr, sizeof (my_addr));
        if (i < 0)
        {
            printf("bind() failed\n");
            exit(0);
        }


            /* listen ... */
        while (1)
        {
        do
          {
          FD_ZERO(&readfds);              /* zero out socket set */
          FD_SET(sock_recv,&readfds); /* add socket to listen to */
          select_ret=select(sock_recv+1,&readfds,NULL,NULL,&timeout);
          if (select_ret > 0)        /* anything arrive on any socket? */
            {
            incoming_len=sizeof(remote_addr); /* who sent to us? */
            recv_msg_size=recvfrom(sock_recv,buf,BUF_SIZE,0,
                   (struct sockaddr *)&remote_addr,&incoming_len);
            if (recv_msg_size > 0)     /* what was sent? */
              {
              buf[recv_msg_size]='\0';
              printf("From %s received: %s\n",
                     inet_ntoa(remote_addr.sin_addr),buf);
              }
            }
          }
        while (select_ret > 0);
        if (strcmp(buf,"shutdown") == 0)
          break;
        }


    close(sock_recv);
    }
```

In addition to allowing multiple clients to communicate with the server simultaneously, this example also demonstrates a different type of network communication. In the socket() system call, the communication type is SOCK_DGRAM and the protocol is IPPROTO_UDP. These values make the communication slightly less reliable, but also faster because it uses less protocol overhead. This can be useful on a local network where congestion is known and controlled, or for applications that do not require perfect delivery of data, such as streaming multimedia.

The following is the code for the client:

```c
#include <stdio.h>
#include <sys/types.h>
#include <sys/socket.h>
#include <netinet/in.h>

#define BUF_SIZE        1024
#define SERVER_IP       "130.127.24.92"
#define SERVER_PORT     60000

int main(int argc, char *argv[])

{
int                     sock_send;
struct sockaddr_in      addr_send;
char                    text[80],buf[BUF_SIZE];
int                     send_len,bytes_sent;

    /* create socket for sending data */
sock_send=socket(PF_INET, SOCK_DGRAM, IPPROTO_UDP);
if (sock_send < 0)
  {
  printf("socket() failed\n");
  exit(0);
  }

    /* fill the address structure for sending data */
memset(&addr_send, 0, sizeof(addr_send));  /* clr structure */
addr_send.sin_family = AF_INET;  /* address family */
addr_send.sin_addr.s_addr = inet_addr(SERVER_IP);
addr_send.sin_port = htons((unsigned short)SERVER_PORT);
```

```
while(1)
  {
  printf("Send? ");
  scanf("%s",text);
  if (strcmp(text,"quit") == 0)
    break;

  strcpy(buf,text);
  send_len=strlen(text);
  bytes_sent=sendto(sock_send, buf, send_len, 0,
             (struct sockaddr *) &addr_send, sizeof(addr_send));
  }

close(sock_send);
}
```

The client creates a socket but does not use the connect() system call to talk to the server. Instead, it uses the sendto() system call with an appropriately filled struct sockaddr_in that contains the IP and port for which the data is to be sent. The client program can be run multiple times, concurrently, and each will communicate simultaneously with the server.

Questions and Exercises

1. What is a system call? For what are system calls used?

2. Write out the memory map for the following code, providing all values at the end of execution. It can be written using multiple maps, or areas of memory, one for each process. What is the exact output produced by this program?

```
#include <stdio.h>
#include <unistd.h>

main()
{
int     i,j,k;

k=0;
for (j=0; j<4; j++)
   k=k+j;
i=fork();
```

```
if (i == 0)
  for (i=3; i<k; i++)
    j=j-i;
else
  i=k%3;
printf("%d %d %d\n",i,j,k);
}
```

3. What is a signal? What are signals most commonly used for?

4. What is the exact output of the following code?

```
#include <stdio.h>
#include <unistd.h>

main()
{
int      i,j;

i=fork();
for (j=0; j<3; j++)
  {
  if (i == 0  &&  j == 0)
    {
    sleep(3);
    printf("Cats\n");
    }
  else if (i == 0)
    {
    sleep(2);
    printf("Dogs\n");
    }
  else
    {
    sleep(2);
    printf("Raining\n");
    }
  }
}
```

5. Which of the following is the code for a set of functions, and which is not? (a) library, (b) device driver, (c) application programming interface (API).

6. What is the exact output of the following code? (Hint: a SIGSEGV is generated on an illegal storage access.)

```
#include <stdio.h>
#include <signal.h>

main()
{
void    f(int);
int     i;
double  *t,x[5];

signal(SIGSEGV,f);
x[0]=0.0;
t=0;
for (i=1; i<5; i++)
{
x[i]=(double)i+11.0;
if (x[i-1] > 12.0)
*t=42.3;
printf("Ok\n");
}
}

void f(int signum)
{
printf("Bad!\n");
exit(SIGSEGV);
}
```

7. Write a C program that uses a system function call to sort itself, piping the sorted version to a file called `sorted-code`. For sorting, the system call should use the `sort` system program. Assume that your code is saved in a file named `code.c`.

8. Write a program that spawns and controls multiple processes. The program should use system calls such as fork(), wait(), execvp() to manage the processes. The program should use signal system calls to communicate between the processes. The processes should coordinate a simple command structure where the main process is "base" and the child processes are "planes".

   The base process is the main process. It should run in a simple loop, prompting the user for an input command. Valid input commands include "launch", "bomb N", "status", "refuel N", and "quit". Invalid commands should produce a suitable error message. Upon receiving the command to quit, the program should end.

The launch command should cause a child process to start. All child processes should execute the same code. A child process should execute a simple loop, counting "fuel" downward from 100 at a rate of 5 fuel/second. Every 3 seconds it should report its fuel status by printing out the line "Bomber N to base, # fuel left," where N is the child's process ID. Upon receiving the signal SIGUSR1, the child process should print out the line "Bomber N to base, bombs away!" where N is the child's process ID. Upon receiving the signal SIGUSR2, the child process should "refuel," resetting its fuel value to 100. Upon reaching zero fuel, the child process should send the signal SIGUSR2 to the main process, and then exit.

The main process must maintain a list of process IDs of the child processes. Given the bomb N command, the main process should send the signal SIGUSR1 to child process ID = N. Given the refuel N command, the main process should send the signal SIGUSR2 to child process ID = N. Given the status command, the main process should list the child processes IDs. Upon receiving the SIGUSR2 signal, the main process should print out "SOS! Plane has crashed!" The main process will not know which child process sent the signal, so if this happens the status list will thereafter be in error.

9. What is a socket? What does it mean to bind a socket?

10. The `htons()` and related functions convert the byte orders of multibyte integers for network transport, making sure that, on the network side, they are always stored most-significant-byte first. Write a program that queries the user for a 32-bit integer value. The program should then print out the value of the same bytes but sorted in reverse order. For example, if the user inputs 257, the program should print out 16842752. (Hint: what should the program print out if the user inputs 16842752?)

11. Write two programs, a client and a server, that implement file transfer through a network. Upon startup, the server should listen and wait for a client to connect to it. The client should connect to the server and then go into a loop. In this loop, the user should be able to type "get [file]", "put [file]", or "quit". The first option should cause the server to send the bytes contained in the named file. The client should open a file locally with the same name and save the received bytes. The second option should work the same but in reverse, resulting in a copy of the file being saved at the server. The third option exits the client. Both programs can be run on the same system and have their IPs and ports hard-coded, but they should be run in separate directories so that file operations can be tested. The client should report an appropriate error message if the requested file does not exist, or if it cannot connect to the server.

8

Libraries

A library is a set of functions, packaged as a system resource and intended for use by other programs on the system. Normally, a library is not written for a single program but is intended for use by many programs. By packaging the functions as a system resource, the code does not need to be rewritten for every program that uses it. Although a library may include any number of functions, it does not include one important function: main(). A library is not an executable program. A library consists of functions that can be combined with a main() to form a complete executable program.

On a typical computing system, there are many libraries. A single library tends to contain functions concerning a single topic, such as mathematical calculation, memory debugging, network operations, or graphics. Some libraries are small, containing 10 or so functions, while other libraries may contain a thousand functions. Some libraries are considered standard, having become common to a large number of computing systems. Examples include the C standard library and the X library. Some libraries are developed by individuals or companies to support their specific product line and are found only on computing systems related to those products.

When using a library, a program need not use every function inside it. A program may call only a single function within that library, or it may use them all, or any number in between. A program may use multiple libraries. A library may be built on top of another library, calling upon its functions. In the latter case, a program using the top-level library must also make use of the lower-level library. Graphics libraries, in particular, have developed this way.

This chapter covers libraries from the perspective of a system resource. A serious programmer must know how and when to use libraries. Using a library saves time in programming, because a programmer can make use of existing code. Library code tends to be written by experts and thus tends to have good design and performance. Because a library is used by many programmers, it is usually debugged by a wide audience, and so a programmer can use it with confidence.

Basic knowledge of some of the common libraries is also useful. In order to understand how libraries work, and to become comfortable with them, this chapter will describe three libraries in some detail. The C standard library provides hundreds of functions for common text processing and mathematical operations. The curses library provides functions for creating a character-based graphical interface. The X library provides functions for a pixel-based graphical interface, including windows and mouse interaction. However, the coverage of these libraries is not intended to turn the reader into an expert with these particular libraries. Rather, they are intended to familiarize the reader with the process of using a library. A programmer typically becomes an expert with a specific library only through exposure to extensive code or product development that makes use of that library. Such familiarity is generally a goal only when tackling a specific job.

8.1 • Using a Library

There are two basic steps to using a library. First, one or more header files must be included in the C program code. Second, the library must be linked into the executable. These concepts can be demonstrated with the following code example:

```
#include <stdio.h>
#include <math.h>

main()
{
double x,s;
s=8.0;
x=sqrt(s);
printf("%lf\n",x);
}
```

In this example, we are making use of the `sqrt()` function, which is one of the functions in the math library. Assume that this code is stored in a file named `sq.c`. First, the header file `math.h` is included in order to use the math library. Second, when compiling, we must link to the math library:

```
gcc -o sq sq.c -lm
```

The command line argument `-lm` tells the compiler to link (`-l`) to a library file named `m`. This library file is what actually contains the code for the sqrt() function and all the other functions in the math library. In the following two sections, we take a look at what is inside a header file and why it is needed, and at a library file and how it works.

8.1.1 Header Files

A header file does not contain the code for any of the functions in the library. That code is contained in the library file, which is brought in during linking. Why then do we need to include the header file? For example:

```
#include <math.h>
```

One can think of a header file as the *instructions for how to use the library*. It contains function prototypes, which describe the inputs and outputs of all the functions, including how many and what types of parameters each function takes, and what type of value each function returns. For example, in `math.h` we can trace the following code:[1]

```
double sqrt(double x);
```

This prototype tells us that the sqrt() function takes in one argument, a double, and also returns a double. By including the header file into our own program, we inform the compiler of how the function works so that it can properly compile our use of the function. Remember, our program does not include the code for the sqrt() function. Therefore the compiler needs the function prototype in order to properly align our code, which calls the function.

A header file can also contain constants. For example, within `math.h` we can find the following code:

```
#define M_PI          3.14159265358979323846  /* pi */
```

---

1. Function prototypes are often written using nested preprocessing substitutions to provide for flexibility in implementation and system independence. However, the net effect of expanding the preprocessing substitutions is to produce a line of code like the one given here.

This provides a constant value for pi, often used in trigonometric and other mathematical calculations. A programmer can use this constant without having to redefine it for every program. Within the header file X.h, the primary include file for the X library, we find another use for constants:

```
#define KeyPress        2
#define KeyRelease      3
#define ButtonPress     4
#define ButtonRelease   5
#define MotionNotify    6
/* ... list continues for 34 entries ... */
```

These constants provide phrases in plain English for values commonly passed to and from functions within the library. This particular list continues, defining 34 different possible values for a common function parameter. Programmers typically find it easier to remember text phrases, as opposed to numeric values, for oft-used parameter values. For example, one could write the following code:

```
if (SomeEvent.type == 2)
    /* process key press event */
```

However, it is more common to write that code as follows:

```
if (SomeEvent.type == KeyPress)
    /* process key press event */
```

This code takes advantage of the constant definitions in the header file to make the code easier to write, and more readable.

A header file may use typedef and struct definitions to create library-specific aliases for common data types or to create new data types. For example, within the X.h header file, we find:

```
typedef unsigned long Mask;
```

This code creates an alias called "Mask" for the unsigned long int. Why is this done? The X library uses bitwise operations to send and receive data through many functions. Since a bitmask will be used as a parameter for many of these functions, the X library provides a data type named "Mask" to promote code readability, by more strongly identifying what a particular variable is intended to do.

Another example can be seen in the FILE data type. By including the header file stdio.h, we eventually find the following lines of code:

```
struct _IO_FILE {
    int _flags;
    int _fileno;
    int _blksize;
    /* ... many additional fields not printed here ... */
}

typedef struct _IO_FILE FILE;
```

This code defines a structure that contains information about accessing a file. The code then defines an alias for that structure to simplify writing code. These lines of code explain the commonly seen:

```
#include <stdio.h>
```

```
FILE *fpt;
```

First, without including the stdio.h header file, the compiler will not understand the keyword "FILE". Second, by tracing through the definition, we find that the variable fpt is nothing more than a pointer to a structure. When using a library, it is common to make use of seemingly exotic and unknown data types. However, they are nothing more than typedefs, aliases, and structure definitions, written out within the header file, to make code more readable and portable.

Header files for the C standard libraries are usually stored in /usr/include on a Unix system. On an MS Windows system, the storage location depends on which compiler is being used. Different compilers store the header files in different locations. The MS Visual C compiler typically places those header files in C:\Program Files\Microsoft Visual Studio\VC98 \Include. It does not particularly matter where header files are placed, as long as the compiler knows where to find them. By default, a compiler will look in its preferred location(s), defined during installation. If a header file is placed in a different location, for example, by installing a new library in a nonstandard location, then the compiler must be told where to find the header file. Using the gcc compiler, this is accomplished by using the -Ipath command line argument. For example:

```
gcc -o sq sq.c -I/usr/include/mathlib -lm
```

The option -I/usr/include/mathlib tells the compiler to look in the /usr /include/mathlib directory, in addition to the standard locations, for any requested include files. We will see this again when we look at the X library.

8.1.2 Library Files

A library file contains the actual code for the functions in the library. During compiling, we must link to the library file to bring the code together with our own, to make the executable program. In the example at the beginning of section 8.1, we used the command line argument −lm while compiling to tell the compiler to link to the m file, which is the math library file. But where is this m file, and what exactly is inside it?

On a Unix system, library files are typically stored in /usr/lib. Unix systems use the following convention for naming library files: they begin with the letters lib and have a filename suffix of .a. The only part of a library filename that is unique lies in between these parts. Thus, the math library file, which we called m when compiling, is actually named libm.a on the system. We can find it as follows:

```
ls -l /usr/lib/libm.a
-rw-r--r--  1 root  root  3092430  Sep 4 2001 /usr/lib/libm.a
```

Notice that the file is fairly large, about 3 MB (file size will vary from system to system). This shows that there is quite a bit of code in the library file. The math library contains dozens of functions, some of which are quite complex.

On an MS Windows system, library files have no fixed prefix, but they do all end with either the .lib or .dll suffix. They may be found in several directories, including C:\Winnt\system32, C:\Winnt\system, and a \lib subdirectory installed as part of a compiler (for the MS Visual C compiler, this would be C:\Program Files\Microsoft Visual Studio\VC98\Lib).

When linking, a compiler knows to look for library files in the standard directories, usually defined when the compiler is installed. It is also aware of any naming conventions, such as expanding m to libm.a. However, some library files may be stored in nonstandard directories. For example, a new library may be added to a system and stored in its own folder to make maintenance of the library easier. The X library is commonly stored in /usr/X11R6, with subdirectories for its include (/usr/X11R6/include) and library (/usr/X11R6/lib) files. In order to link with that library, we must tell the compiler to look in that directory, in addition to the standard directories, when looking for library files:

```
gcc -o xprog1 xprog1.c -lX11 -L/usr/X11R6/lib
```

The command line argument −L/usr/X11R6/lib tells the compiler to add the path /usr/X11R6/lib to the set of directories in which to find library files.

A library file contains the actual code for all the functions in the library. The code for the library functions is static, in the sense that it is not expected to change (ignoring for the moment library upgrades). Therefore, it is precompiled and stored in an intermediate format called a library file. For the present discussion, the detailed format of a library file is not important; it is enough to know that it is code that has previously been compiled and is ready to be linked. If one tries to open the file /usr/lib/libm.a with a text editor, it will look like garbage, since it is not source code (ASCII text).

8.2 • Purpose of Libraries

There are several reasons to package a set of functions into a library:

Convenience, repetition. An example in this category is the string function library. Many of the string functions are easy to code. For example, the `strlen()` function is only a couple lines of code. However, string functions are used frequently, and even though they may be easy to code, it is convenient to put them in a library to avoid rewriting them every time a new program is written.

Difficult to code. An example in this category is the math library. The functions in the math library, such as `sqrt()` and `cos()`, are iterative in nature and very difficult to code. For example, to solve for the square root of a number, one could continually multiply a number by itself, lowering or raising the value, until it is close enough to the value whose square root is being sought. Because these functions are difficult to write, we prefer to utilize the expertise of people who have studied these problems extensively and have already written code for us to use. While we might be able to write a method that works, the experts have written more efficient, precise methods based on a detailed study of computational mathematics.

Hardware/system independence. An example in this category is a graphics library, such as the X library or the OpenGL library. In order to access a piece of hardware, a program must go through a device driver in the O/S (see Chapter 5 on I/O). The program can call the `open()` function for the specific piece of hardware, and then call the `write()` function to send it data. If we were developing an application only for one system (defined as the O/S plus hardware), then this is a viable method for graphical output. However, most of the time, we want an application to be capable of running on a variety of graphics displays or graphics cards.

Figure 8.1 shows an example. Suppose that on system A we have a state-of-the-art graphics card that can render three-dimensional primitives with shaded

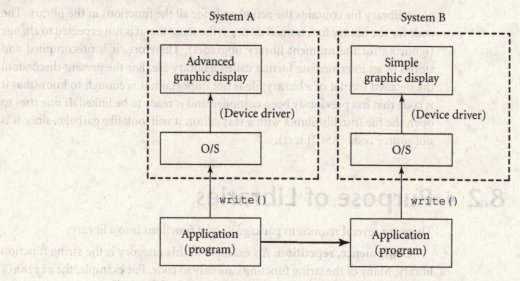

Figure 8.1 A program must be written to work with multiple device drivers if it is intended to work on different hardware or systems.

lighting, textures, and other advanced features. System B, on the other hand, has an inexpensive, low-resolution, straight pixel display card. Each of these systems uses a different device driver, specific to its hardware. The data that is sent via a write() function call on system A will look very different from the data that is sent using write() on system B. Should the application need to know about different device drivers, and change how it calls write() depending on what hardware is available?

Instead, we use a graphics library to perform this job. Figure 8.2 demonstrates the process. The graphics library contains generic graphics functions, such as "DrawLine()." Within its functions, a graphics library implements the code specific to different graphics hardware to carry out that operation. The details of how and when the graphics library calls write() to actually implement DrawLine() are hidden from us. This is very similar to how the details of the write() function call are hidden in the device driver.

Graphics libraries primarily provide us with hardware independence, but they can also provide us with O/S independence. Some of the more generally accepted and popular graphics libraries are available on a variety of operating systems, and support a large variety of hardware. Examples include the X library and the OpenGL library.

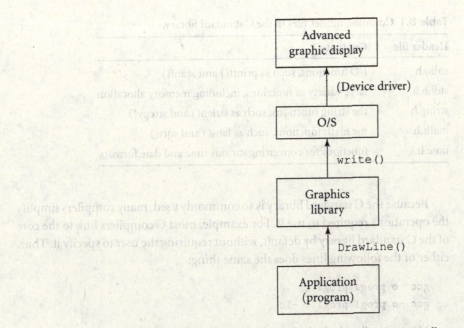

Figure 8.2 A graphics library allows an application to call system or hardware-independent functions.

8.3 • The C Standard Library

The most important library in C programming is called the C standard library. It includes hundreds of functions for doing common operations, such as basic text I/O, file I/O, string manipulation, and mathematical calculations. Its functions include many of the most well known: printf(), strlen(), fopen(), and sqrt(). Very few programs are written without making at least some use of this library.

The C standard library is really a collection of libraries that have been grouped together. It makes use of multiple header files (24 as of the 1999 ANSI standard) and multiple library files (depending on system implementation). Because it includes functions covering a wide variety of topics, and because it is organized into multiple files, different parts of it are sometimes referred to in isolation. For example, it is not uncommon to call the math functions portion of the C standard library as simply the "math library." Similarly, it is not uncommon to call the string functions portion as simply the "string library." Table 8.1 summarizes the most commonly used parts of the C standard library.

Table 8.1 Common header files in the C standard library.

Header file	Contents
stdio.h	I/O functions, such as printf() and scanf()
stdlib.h	large variety of functions, including memory allocation
string.h	the string functions, such as strlen() and strcpy()
math.h	the math functions, such as fabs() and sqrt()
time.h	functions for converting various time and date formats

Because the C standard library is so commonly used, many compilers simplify the operations required to use it. For example, most C compilers link to the core of the C standard library by default, without requiring the user to specify it. Thus, either of the following lines does the same thing:

```
gcc -o prog1 prog1.c
gcc -o prog1 prog1.c -lc
```

Most compilers include the option -lc by default so that a programmer does not have to type it every time a program is compiled. Some compilers also include the most common C standard library header files by default. While both of these practices are convenient for experienced programmers, they often confuse novice programmers. Hiding the basic steps necessary in using a library can cause a novice programmer to make simple mistakes when moving on to additional libraries.

One of the most common mistakes is to forget to include a header file. This can lead to some unexpected and often confusing behavior on the part of a program. For example:

```
main()
{
double a,b;

b=9.0;
a=sqrt(b);
printf("%lf\n",a);
}
```

On some systems, compiling and executing this code may produce the following output:

```
1075970687.000000
```

This, of course, is not the square root of 9. A novice programmer, upon seeing this, is often confused by the source of the error. Where did the garbage value come from? The answer is that the header file math.h was not included, so that the compiler did not know the type of value returned by the sqrt() function. By default, the compiler assumes that all functions return an int. However, the sqrt() function actually returns a double. This causes a mismatch, where the return value is interpreted erroneously, causing the garbage value to appear.

Some compilers will warn of this potential problem. For example, a compiler may produce the following warning:

```
main.c(8) : 'sqrt' undefined; assuming extern returning int
```

With a little practice, a programmer will come to recognize this type of warning as a potentially serious problem, and will try to alleviate its cause. However, some programmers take advantage of the "int-by-default" return value and code without proper function prototypes or header-file usage. An experienced programmer should be aware of this practice and prepared to work with code written in that manner.

8.4 • The Curses Library

Curses[2] is a basic graphics library for use on a character terminal screen. It provides the lowest level of graphics and dates back to the time when most computer displays could print only text (they could not display images or other graphics). These displays were called terminals. Although most modern computer displays can show images and other graphics, the curses library and character graphics are still useful. For example, many computing systems use a "boot loader" when first powered. This boot loader runs before the O/S is loaded. Without the O/S, and its device driver used to operate the advanced graphics functions, the computing system is only capable of character graphics. Similarly, when installing an O/S, the more advanced graphics capabilities are typically not yet available. In some embedded systems, a simple character-based display may be all that is required. A library like curses is useful in all these cases.

The following code serves to demonstrate the basic operations of the curses library:

2. The ncurses library is managed by the GNU project. The library and online documentation can be found at www.gnu.org/software/ncurses/ncurses.html.

```
#include <curses.h>

main()
{
initscr();        /* turn on curses */

clear();          /* clear screen */
move(10,20);      /* row 10, column 20 */
addstr("Hello world");  /* add a string */
move(LINES-1,0);        /* move to LL */


refresh();        /* update the screen */
getch();          /* wait for user input */


endwin();         /* turn off curses */
}
```

If this code is stored in a file called hello.c, then the following compiles the program:[3]

```
gcc -o hello hello.c -lncurses
```

Note that the header file curses.h must be included, and that the library is linked through the command line argument -lncurses (ncurses is the "new curses" library, a rewrite of the traditional curses library and the most current at the time of this writing).

Most graphics libraries use a function to initialize their internal global variables. For example, the library might discover what sort of graphics card or capability the system has, open the device driver for it, and initialize some variables recording its size and other properties. These values will in turn be available to the program using the library through those variables. In the case of curses, the function initscr() performs the initialization. After that, the program can access the global variables COLS and LINES to see the size of the terminal. The program can also access the variable stdscr as the default "window," which can be thought of as the library's name for the terminal. The library is closed (the device driver is closed, and any dynamic memory allocated is freed) through the endwin() function call. Curses functions cannot be used prior to calling initscr(), and a program should always call endwin() to close out use of the library.

---

3. The reader is strongly encouraged to run this program, and all examples in this section, to better learn the concepts.

The basic functions in curses are:

```
move(10,20);        /* move cursor to row=10, column=20 */
addstr("Hello");  /* draw string Hello at cursor location */
```

While drawing text, the cursor is moved ahead (incremented one column) per character drawn, similar to standard typing.

8.4.1   I/O Control

There are three important concepts in I/O control: buffering, echoing, and blocking. This section studies each of these concepts and shows how they can be implemented using the curses library.

8.4.1.1   Buffering

Buffering refers to the process of temporarily storing bytes on a stream, and grouping them up before transferring them to the destination. Figure 8.3 demonstrates the process. A buffer can be used on any stream; this particular example shows buffers on both the input and output streams.

By default, characters sent to the curses output window are buffered. This means that the characters are not actually displayed until the buffer is flushed, sending all the characters to the terminal display. Flushing is accomplished by the refresh() function call.

Character input is unbuffered by default. This means that functions which read the keyboard, such as getch(), return immediately after any key is pressed. This differs from how the C standard input function, scanf(), works. The scanf() function is line buffered, meaning that it does not return until the user presses [ENTER]. The advantage to line buffering is that a user can correct typing mistakes using the backspace or delete key before actually committing the input to the program. These operations are handled by the O/S working on the data in the

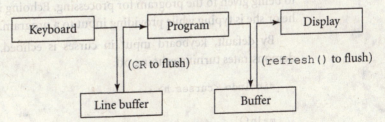

Figure 8.3   Buffering on both the input and output streams.

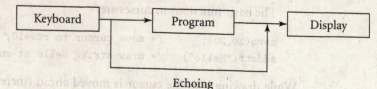

Figure 8.4 Echoing the input stream to the output stream.

buffer. Line buffering can be turned on in curses using the `nocbreak()` function. For example:

```
#include <curses.h>

main()
{
initscr();        /* turn on curses */
nocbreak();       /* turn on line buffering */
                  /* by default keyboard input is unbuffered */
getch();          /* wait for user input */
endwin();         /* turn off curses */
}
```

Seemingly, this program waits for one character of input from the user and then terminates. However, when this program is run, the user can type any number of keystrokes; the program will not end until [ENTER] is pressed. This is because the input is line buffered. Line buffering can be turned off by calling the `cbreak()` function.

8.4.1.2 Echoing

Echoing refers to the process of copying bytes from the input stream to the output stream. Figure 8.4 shows the process. When echoing is turned on, every byte that appears on the input stream is copied directly to the output stream, in addition to being given to the program for processing. Echoing is how a user can see what he or she is typing while providing input to a program.

By default, keyboard input in curses is echoed. The following example demonstrates turning echoing off:

```
#include <curses.h>

main()
{
int     i;
```

```
initscr();
noecho();          /* turn off echoing */
for (i=0; i<5; i++)
  getch();         /* wait for user input */
endwin();
}
```

The `noecho()` function call turns echoing off. When this program is run, characters typed are not seen on the screen. Echoing can be turned back on using the `echo()` function.

8.4.1.3 Blocking

Blocking refers to the process of how the program will wait for bytes to appear on the input stream. Figure 8.5 shows the process. When blocking is turned on, every function call for input will wait until data appears on the input stream. The program will not continue until input is received. When blocking is turned off, the function call will check to see if data is present. If data is present, the read occurs normally, just as if blocking were turned on. However, if no data is present, the function call will return immediately and inform the program that no data was present. This allows the program to continue whether input data is present or not.

By default, the `scanf()` function is a blocking function; it will wait until input is received. The same is true of the curses library. The following example demonstrates turning blocking off:

```
#include <curses.h>

main()
{
int i;
```

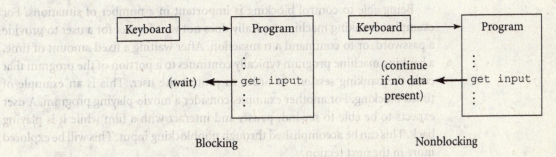

Figure 8.5 Types of blocking on an input stream.

```
initscr();
nodelay(stdscr,TRUE);    /* turn off blocking */
for (i=0; i<5; i++)
  {
  getch();        /* wait for user input? */
  sleep(1);
  }
endwin();
}
```

When this program is run, even if the user does not touch the keyboard, the program finishes in 5 seconds.

Blocking does not have to be on (indefinite) or off (immediate). Blocking can occur for a preselected amount of time, allowing the program to continue if no input is received during that time. The following example demonstrates timed blocking:

```
#include <curses.h>

main()
{
int    i;
initscr();
halfdelay(5);   /* blocking = 5/10 second */
for (i=0; i<5; i++)
  getch();        /* wait for user input */
endwin();
}
```

In this example, blocking is set to 0.5 seconds. Each getch() function call will wait 0.5 seconds for input to appear, but if nothing appears in that time, the function returns and the program continues. Thus, if this program is run without touching the keyboard, it will run for 2.5 seconds and then end.

Being able to control blocking is important in a number of situations. For example, a banking machine typically does not wait forever for a user to provide a password, or to command a transaction. After waiting a fixed amount of time, a banking machine program typically continues to a portion of the program that ends the banking session, in order to protect the user. This is an example of timed blocking. For another example, consider a movie-playing program. A user expects to be able to rewind, pause, and interact with a film while it is playing back. This can be accomplished through nonblocking input. This will be explored more in the next section.

8.4.2   Dynamic Graphics

The curses library is most commonly used for menus and basic user interaction. However, it can be used to create dynamic or moving graphics, albeit of a limited nature. In this section, we study a few techniques to create dynamic graphics. Although the techniques are demonstrated using the curses library, the same techniques can be applied using other graphics libraries as well.

8.4.2.1   Motion

The most basic technique in creating a moving graphic is to erase the screen at the graphic's previous location, immediately redrawing it at an adjacent location. Repeating this process over and over provides the illusion of motion. The following code demonstrates the technique:

```
#include <curses.h>

main()
{
int    i;

initscr();
clear();          /* clear screen */

for (i=0; i<30; i++)
  {
move (10,i);
addstr("Hello world");
refresh();              /* flush buffer */
usleep(100000);         /* pause 0.1 seconds */
move (10,i);            /* back to previous spot */
addstr("           ");  /* draw empty space */
  }
getch();
endwin();
}
```

Running this program, the user will see the phrase "Hello world" move horizontally across the screen. The usleep() function call is used to control the rate of motion. The usleep() function pauses the program for the given number of microseconds, allowing for finer control of pausing as compared to the sleep()

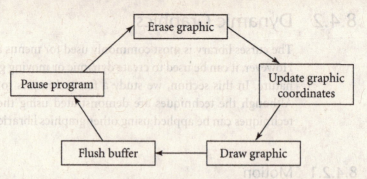

Figure 8.6 Steps in creating a moving graphic. It is often convenient to start the loop with the "erase graphic" step.

function. Note that the output buffer must be flushed (using the refresh() function) at the appropriate time or the technique will not work. If the refresh() function call were moved to the bottom of the loop, then the graphic would never be seen. The same is true of the pause (using the usleep() function). The correct order of operation is (1) draw the graphic, (2) flush the buffer, (3) pause the program, (4) erase the graphic, and (5) move to a new location. Figure 8.6 illustrates these steps. Because it is cyclical, the process can be started at any point. It is often convenient to put all the code involving a single graphic together, with the flush and pause at the end. In this case, the loop would start with the step that erases the graphic. We will see this again below.

8.4.2.2   User Input During Motion

Moving graphics generally require loops, as described above. The graphic stays in motion only as long as the loop keeps iterating. If we require that the user be able to provide input to the program while the graphic is in motion, then we must turn blocking off. Otherwise, any function call for input will wait until input is received. Meanwhile, the motion of the graphic will seem to pause. Using a fixed time blocking is also generally a bad idea, unless the fixed-time is very small. Otherwise, during iterations where the user immediately provides input, the graphic will move faster than during iterations where the program waits for the blocking to time out.

The following code demonstrates *polling* for user input while a graphic is in motion. Polling refers to the process of using a nonblocking function call to check for user input, and acting upon the input if given, but otherwise continuing program execution.

```
#include <curses.h>

main()
{
int     i,row;
char    ch;

initscr();
clear();
nodelay(stdscr,TRUE);   /* turn off blocking */
row=10;

for (i=0; i<30; i++)
  {
  move (row,i);
  addstr("Hello world");
  refresh();
  usleep(100000);
  move (row,i);
  addstr("            ");
  ch=getch();            /* poll for input */
  if (ch == 'z')         /* act on input */
    row++;
  }
getch();
endwin();
}
```

This program works similarly to the last example, but if the user presses "z," then the graphic will move down a line. With or without input, the graphic will continually move rightward across the screen. Executing this program, the user will notice that when the input "z" is given, it is also displayed on the screen, near the moving graphic. This is a consequence of echoing. In most programs that use dynamic graphics, echoing is turned off. This feature can easily be added to this example by calling noecho() before the loop starts.

8.4.2.3 Varying-Rate Graphics

Using the basic loop structure outlined above, graphics move at the rate defined by the amount of time spent paused in each iteration. Increasing the usleep() causes the graphics to move more slowly, while decreasing the usleep() causes the graphics to move faster. However, if multiple graphics are displayed, they would all move at the same rate. How can different graphics be moved at different rates?

One answer is to use modulus arithmetic on the loop counter to control when the motion of each graphic occurs. If one graphic moves every iteration, but another graphic moves only every other iteration, then the first graphic is moving twice as fast as the second. The following code demonstrates this technique:

```
#include <curses.h>

main()
{
int     i;

initscr();
clear();

for (i=0; i<30; i++)
  {
  move (10,i);
  addstr("     ");
  move (10,i+1);
  addstr("Hello");
  if (i%2 == 0)  /* every 2nd iteration */
    {
    move (12,i/2);
    addstr("     ");
    move (12,i/2+1);
    addstr("world");
    }
  move (LINES-1,0);
  refresh();
  usleep(100000);
  }
getch();
endwin();
}
```

As mentioned previously, it is convenient to start the loop with the step that erases the graphic. In this way, all the code involving a single graphic can be grouped together, and the flush and pause happen at the end of the loop. The line move(LINES-1,0); puts the cursor at the bottom left corner of the screen so that it does not bounce around following the graphics as they move.

8.5 • The X Library

In order to understand the X library,[4] this section first describes how graphics libraries in general have developed. It is beneficial to examine the graphics libraries used on both a Unix system and an MS Windows system. There are many similarities and some differences, which help to highlight some things a system programmer needs to know.

In Section 8.2, we saw that a graphics library serves as a standarized set of function calls between an operating system (in particular, a device driver) and an application. This allows the same application to work with different graphics displays having varying capabilities. Recent times have seen a tremendous growth in these capabilities, from simple two-dimensional raster buffering to full texturing, lighting control, and complex rendering of three-dimensional objects and scenes. Applications depend upon graphics libraries to implement all of these capabilities, either in hardware (if supported by the available graphics hardware) or in software in the library itself.

As graphics hardware capabilities have expanded, a hierarchy of graphics libraries has evolved that somewhat resembles the progression of capabilities. Figure 8.7 shows this hierarchy and some of the popular graphics libraries. On a Unix system, the X library is at the bottom level. The X library provides for the creation and manipulation of windows. Each window can serve as a separate "screen" or "display." This allows a user to run a number of different applications at the same time, each having its own graphical display, even though the system itself has only one monitor or hardware display. This capability has become so commonplace that users of desktop computers expect it by default. However, it would not be available without the X library or an equivalent.

In addition to windows functions, the X library provides functions for drawing simple two-dimensional graphics, such as lines, circles, and rasters (images). The basic properties of these primitives can be manipulated, for example, line color, width, and type (e.g., dotted, dashed, or solid). The X library also provides functions for interacting with user input devices, particularly a keyboard and a

---

4. There are several distributions of the X library. At the time of this writing, the most prevalent distribution is maintained by the X.Org Foundation. The library and documentation can be found at www.x.org/wiki/.

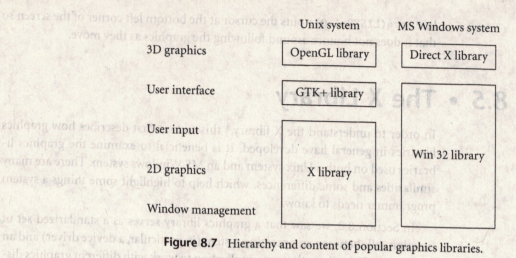

Figure 8.7 Hierarchy and content of popular graphics libraries.

mouse. Most important, input can be directed to the appropriate window (and program) depending on how the user is interacting with the overall system.

The equivalent library on an MS Windows system is the Win32 library. It provides all the above-described capabilities: window creation and manipulation, drawing of two-dimensional graphics, and control of user input. However, it provides an additional capability not available in the X library: the *user interface*. On an MS Windows system, all menus look and operate similarly. All dialog and message boxes look and operate similarly. When opening a file, the interface looks similar from application to application. This is because the Win32 library provides a set of functions to create and interact with menus, dialog boxes, message boxes, and other aspects of a standard user interface. The X library does not provide an equivalent set of functions. The developers of the X library wanted all parts of the system to remain modular. Any system operator is free to install and set up the user interface of his or her choice. Since there are no functions available in the X library for a standard user interface, additional libraries have been developed that provide different user interfaces. These libraries include GTK+, Motif, and Qt. While this initially seemed like a good idea, and in the spirit of modular system development, it turned out to be problematic. Only a small percentage of computer users want the capability to change the standard user interface. Most application developers rely upon a standard user interface. Even experienced system programmers typically prefer to rely upon a standard user interface. Many users take advantage of the capability to fine-tune or adjust a user interface to suit individual preferences, but there does not seem to be any advantage to providing completely unique user interfaces to all users. At the time of this writing, the GTK+ library is a popular user interface library on a Unix system, but there is no consensus standard.

Another important difference between the X library and the Win32 library is the separation of "display" from the hardware. Using the X library, an application can open a window and interact with a user on hardware that is separate from the hardware on which the application is running. This is accomplished through networking. For example, a user can remotely log into a machine, run an application on that machine, and yet graphically display its output on the local monitor. This process can also be done in reverse, displaying output on a remote machine. The Win32 library does not provide for separation of window and display. The library can only interact with hardware directly connected to the system. While this capability can sometimes be useful, it is rarely used by system programmers. As emphasized throughout this book, experienced system programmers prefer to interact with programs through a shell interface. A remote text-display capability is usually sufficient for interacting with programs through a network.

As three-dimensional graphics have become popular, particularly for games, another level of libraries has developed to satisfy the need for hardware-independent application development. On a Unix system, the OpenGL library is commonly used. It provides functions for manipulating and rendering three-dimensional meshes, applying textures, and controlling lighting. On an MS Windows system, the DirectX library is commonly used. It provides a similar set of functions for manipulating and displaying three-dimensional graphics. Although primarily developed for specific systems, there are implementations of both libraries available for other platforms. The main difference is that the OpenGL library is open source while the DirectX library is proprietary. At the time of this writing, both are available for free.

There is one last important difference to discuss between a Unix system and an MS Windows system. On an MS Windows system, not only is the user interface standardized but the system interface is standardized as well. All windows look and operate similarly. The titlebar is a standard size with a standard font. The application menu always lists from the top-left corner, rightward, and each is a pull-down menu. The system menu for each window always appears in the top-right corner and consists of three consistent icons: lower horizontal line (minimize window), square (maximize window), and X (close window). The mouse always uses the same cursor. The overall system menu is always in the bottom-left corner, and the clock is always displayed in the bottom-right corner. Right-clicking on the background (or desktop) brings up a menu to control desktop appearance, while left-clicking on the desktop allows the user to drag icons or start applications. On a Unix system, the system interface is not standardized. The gnome desktop is popular, but at the time of this writing, there is no consensus standard.

The lack of standardization on Unix systems is a result of modular development. This allows users maximum flexibility and, to some degree, provides for more consistent interfacing between the various parts of the system. The system software for an MS Windows system is largely monolithic and integrated. The advantage to this approach is that a user can expect a system and its applications to appear and operate in a somewhat predictable manner. This typically decreases the time necessary for a user to become proficient with a new computer, or even a new application. The user does not need to spend time becoming familiar with new icons, menu operations or placements, or appearances. This is one of the strengths of an MS Windows system; it helps allow relatively inexperienced users to operate the system. At the time of this writing, there is growing momentum toward standardizing the Unix user and system interfaces. These decisions, of course, have direct impact upon the libraries a system programmer can expect to use.

8.5.1 Windows

The basic construct in X library programming is a *window*. A window is a virtual monitor or display created for a program. It allows multiple programs to operate sharing the same physical monitor or display, each using its own window. In this paradigm, a program must create and manage a window where the output will be displayed. The window also controls input to the program. Typically, a system will send keyboard and mouse input to a program only when the program's window is *active*. Commonly, a window is active when the user selects the window by clicking on it, or when the user moves the mouse into the onscreen area of the window. Window activation depends upon the particular system interface.

The following code demonstrates the basic steps involved in a program using the X library to create a window:

```
#include <stdio.h>
#include <stdlib.h>
#include <X11/Xlib.h>          /* X library definitions */

main(int argc, char *argv[])
{
Display      *Monitor;        /* screen to display on */
Window       DrawWindow;      /* the window to be created */
GC           WindowGC;        /* graphics context */
```

```
                /* First, every X program must connect to a display */
        Monitor=XOpenDisplay(NULL);
        if (Monitor == NULL)
        {
        printf("Unable to open graphics display\n");
        exit(0);
        }

                /* Create a window - describe a few attributes */
        DrawWindow=XCreateSimpleWindow(Monitor,RootWindow(Monitor,0),
                10,10,                    /* x,y on screen */
                100,50,                   /* width, height */
                2,                        /* border width */
                BlackPixel(Monitor,0),    /* foreground color */
                WhitePixel(Monitor,0));   /* background color */

                /* Create a default graphics context */
        WindowGC=XCreateGC(Monitor,DrawWindow,0,NULL);

                /* Place the window onscreen, and flush buffer */
        XMapWindow(Monitor,DrawWindow);
        XFlush(Monitor);

                /* wait 2 seconds, then close X library */
        sleep(2);
        XCloseDisplay(Monitor);
        }
```

Assuming this code is stored in a file called window.c, then the following command compiles the code:

```
gcc -o window window.c -L/usr/X11R6/lib -lX11
```

The -L/usr/X11R6/lib command tells the compiler to search in the path /usr/X11R6/lib for additional library files. Depending on how the compiler is configured, this option may or may not be necessary (the compiler may already have that path added to its default list of places to look for linking to library files). The command -lX11 tells the compiler to link to the X11 library file.

In the example above, the first function called is XOpenDisplay(), which initializes the library for use by the program. The function also creates a connection to a physical display (this example uses the default display), discovering its properties and using them to initialize the library. The second function called is XCreateSimpleWindow(), which creates a window for use by the program. There are several function calls that create a window, with varying degrees of control over the window's appearance. This one is the simplest. The third function called is XCreateGC(), which creates a *graphics context*. A graphics context contains information about how graphics should be drawn in the window. This information includes things like which font to use, how thick to draw lines and other primitives, and which color to use when drawing. This example demonstrates creating a graphics context having all default values. The XMapWindow() function call draws the window on the given display (remember that in the X library, the concepts of window and display are separated, such that a window can be drawn on multiple different displays). Since the output display is buffered, the XFlush() function call is needed to force flushing of the buffer, to insure that the window actually appears onscreen. Finally, the example program sleeps for 2 seconds and then closes its use of the X library.

Both Window and GC (graphics context) variables are actually structures. Each contains a list of variables, the former about how the window appears, and the latter about how to draw into the window. A program can create any number of windows and graphics contexts, each having a different variable name. It is possible to use a single graphics context for all windows.

When running this program, it is possible that the window will not appear at the specified location (10,10). This is due to the involvement of a *window manager*. A window manager is a program that runs on the system and actually controls the placement of windows. It typically tries to place windows so that they all have minimal overlap. It may therefore override a program's request for a specific window location, in favor of another position. There are function calls in the X library that can override the window manager, and force placement of the window according to the program's specifications, such as XSetWMHints(). These functions are beyond the scope of this text.

8.5.2 Two-Dimensional Graphics

There are a large number of functions in the X library that draw two-dimensional graphics. The following code demonstrates the drawing of a line:

```
#include <stdio.h>
#include <stdlib.h>
#include <X11/Xlib.h>
```

```
main(int argc, char *argv[])
{
Display      *Monitor;
Window       DrawWindow;
GC           WindowGC;
int          x1,y1,x2,y2;

Monitor=XOpenDisplay(NULL);
DrawWindow=XCreateSimpleWindow(Monitor,RootWindow(Monitor,0),
       10,10,           /* x,y on screen */
       100,50,          /* width, height */
       2,               /* border width */
       BlackPixel(Monitor,0),
       WhitePixel(Monitor,0));
WindowGC=XCreateGC(Monitor,DrawWindow,0,NULL);
XMapWindow(Monitor,DrawWindow);
XFlush(Monitor);

while (1)
  {
  printf("Line coordinates? ");
  scanf("%d %d %d %d",&x1,&y1,&x2,&y2);
  if (x1 == -1)
     break;
  XDrawLine(Monitor,DrawWindow,WindowGC,x1,y1,x2,y2);
  XFlush(Monitor);
  }

XCloseDisplay(Monitor);
}
```

After initializing the library and creating and mapping a window, this program goes into a loop. The loop uses the traditional printf() and scanf() functions to get the desired endpoints of the line segment from the user. It then calls XDrawLine() with the given coordinates. The origin of the coordinate system is the top left, with the x-axis positive rightward and the y-axis positive downward. Units are pixels; for reference, the window created in this example is 100×50 pixels in size.

Additional functions for drawing two-dimensional graphics include XDraw-Rectangle(), XDrawPoint(), and XDrawArc(). The latter can be used to draw a circle, an ellipse, or any portion of an arc.

8.5.3   Graphics Properties

The properties controlling how graphics are drawn are stored in the graphics context (GC). The Win32 library has a similar construct called a device context (DC). The following code demonstrates changing the color of the lines drawn from the default (black) to blue:

```c
#include <stdio.h>
#include <stdlib.h>
#include <X11/Xlib.h>

main(int argc, char *argv[])
{
Display          *Monitor;
Window           DrawWindow;
GC               WindowGC;
int              x1,y1,x2,y2;
XGCValues        GCValues;
unsigned long    GCmask;
int              i;

Monitor=XOpenDisplay(NULL);
DrawWindow=XCreateSimpleWindow(Monitor,RootWindow(Monitor,0),
        10,10,
        100,50,
        2,
        BlackPixel(Monitor,0),
        WhitePixel(Monitor,0));
WindowGC=XCreateGC(Monitor,DrawWindow,0,NULL);
XMapWindow(Monitor,DrawWindow);
XFlush(Monitor);

        /* change the foreground color to blue */
GCmask=GCForeground;
GCValues.foreground=0x0000FF; /* red is 0xFF0000 .... */
i=XChangeGC(Monitor,WindowGC,GCmask,&GCValues);
if (i == 0)
   {
printf("Unable to change GC values\n");
exit(1);
   }
```

```
while (1)
  {
  printf("Line coordinates? ");
  scanf("%d %d %d %d",&x1,&y1,&x2,&y2);
  if (x1 == -1)
    break;
  XDrawLine(Monitor,DrawWindow,WindowGC,x1,y1,x2,y2);
  XFlush(Monitor);
  }

XCloseDisplay(Monitor);
}
```

The XChangeGC() function call takes in three relevant arguments: the GC in which values are to be changed, a new set of values, and a mask. The new set of values is stored in an XGCValues variable, which is another structure. The mask variable indicates which values in that structure are to be used to change the given GC. Multiple values can be changed in a single XChangeGC() function call. For example:

```
GCmask=GCForeground | GCLineStyle | GCLineWidth;
GCValues.foreground=0x0000FF;
GCValues.line_style=LineDoubleDash;
GCValues.line_width=4;
      /* man XChangeGC to see all GC properties */
XChangeGC(Monitor,WindowGC,GCmask,&GCValues);
```

This code changes the foreground color, the line style, and the line width. The man page for XChangeGC() or a similar reference can be used to see all the properties that are changeable in a graphics context.

8.5.4 User Input

Using the X library, user input is provided to a program through *events*. An event occurs every time the user manipulates an input device. This includes keypresses, key releases, mouse motion, and mouse button presses and releases. An event can also be generated by the operating system in response to actions taken by another program. For example, if a program ends, destroying its window and thereby uncovering another window, the operating system will send an event to the program associated with the newly uncovered window.

The following code demonstrates using events to obtain user input:

```
#include <stdio.h>
#include <stdlib.h>
#include <X11/Xlib.h>

main(int argc, char *argv[])
{
Display    *Monitor;
Window     DrawWindow;
GC         WindowGC;
XEvent     SomeEvent;
long int   EventMask;


Monitor=XOpenDisplay(NULL);
DrawWindow=XCreateSimpleWindow(Monitor,RootWindow(Monitor,0),
          10,10, 100,50, 2,
          BlackPixel(Monitor,0),
          WhitePixel(Monitor,0));
WindowGC=XCreateGC(Monitor,DrawWindow,0,NULL);
XMapWindow(Monitor,DrawWindow);
XFlush(Monitor);

      /* Tell X server which events to pass to program */
EventMask=ButtonPressMask;
XSelectInput(Monitor,DrawWindow,EventMask);

while (1)
  {
XNextEvent(Monitor,&SomeEvent);   /* get user input */
if (SomeEvent.type == ButtonPress)
   printf("Button pressed!\n");
  }


XCloseDisplay(Monitor);
}
```

In this example, if a mouse button is pressed, then the program prints out a message to the user. The XSelectInput() function call tells the system which events the program is interested in receiving. For example, a program may use only the mouse, and so would not include keyboard-related events in its event mask. The XNextEvent() function can be used to obtain input from the user. Once it returns, a program can decide what to do with the given event.

There are several functions that vary in how events are received by a program. The XNextEvent() function is a blocking function; it will not return until an event has been received. The XPeekEvent() function can be used with appropriate coding to implement nonblocking input polling.

A program can request that multiple types of events be sent to it, and then process them differently. For example:

```
EventMask=ButtonPressMask | KeyPressMask | PointerMotionMask;
        /* see /usr/include/X11/X.h for list of all masks */
XSelectInput(Monitor,DrawWindow,EventMask);


while (1)
  {
  XNextEvent(Monitor,&SomeEvent);
      /* man XEvent, and its derivatives (e.g., XButtonEvent)
      ** for complete lists of event types and contents */
  if (SomeEvent.type == ButtonPress)
    printf("Button pressed!\n");
  if (SomeEvent.type == KeyPress)
    printf("Key pressed!\n");
  if (SomeEvent.type == MotionNotify)
    printf("Mouse is moving!\n");
  }
```

Using these concepts, we can use mouse input to control the drawing of lines. The following code can replace the text-based interface from the example in Section 8.5.2:

```
int    WhichPoint;

WhichPoint=0; /* 0=>first point, 1=>second point */
while (1)
  {
  XNextEvent(Monitor,&SomeEvent);
  if (SomeEvent.type == ButtonPress)
    {
    if (WhichPoint == 0)
      {
      x1=SomeEvent.xbutton.x;
      y1=SomeEvent.xbutton.y;
      WhichPoint=1;
      }
```

```
    else
    {
    x2=SomeEvent.xbutton.x;
    y2=SomeEvent.xbutton.y;
    WhichPoint=0;
    if (x1 == x2  &&  y1 == y2)
      break;    /* exit loop and program */
    XDrawLine(Monitor,DrawWindow,WindowGC,x1,y1,x2,y2);
    XFlush(Monitor);
    }
  }
}
```

8.5.5   Fonts

A terminal display uses a fixed grid of character graphics. Characters can be drawn only inside the grid cells. For example, a character cannot be drawn halfway between two lines of text. In addition, the font is fixed and is typically Courier, in which every character fills the same amount of space. With the X library, a program can draw text at any location in a window, using any font. There is no character grid; instead, the units of location are pixels. In order to draw text using a specific font, a program must first set up the graphics context to know how to draw with that font. The following code demonstrates using the X library to draw text:

```
#include <stdio.h>
#include <string.h>
#include <X11/Xlib.h>

main(int argc, char *argv[])
{
Display        *Monitor;
Window         DrawWindow;
GC             WindowGC;
int            x1,y1;
XGCValues      GCValues;
unsigned long  GCmask;
XEvent         SomeEvent;
char           text[80];
Font           NewFont;
```

```
Monitor=XOpenDisplay(NULL);
DrawWindow=XCreateSimpleWindow(Monitor,RootWindow(Monitor,0),
          10,10, 100,50, 2,
          BlackPixel(Monitor,0),
          WhitePixel(Monitor,0));
WindowGC=XCreateGC(Monitor,DrawWindow,0,NULL);
XMapWindow(Monitor,DrawWindow);
XFlush(Monitor);

NewFont=XLoadFont(Monitor,"r14");

GCmask=GCForeground | GCFont;
GCValues.foreground=0xFF0000;
GCValues.font=NewFont;
XChangeGC(Monitor,WindowGC,GCmask,&GCValues);

XSelectInput(Monitor,DrawWindow,ButtonPressMask);

while (1)
  {
  XNextEvent(Monitor,&SomeEvent);
  if (SomeEvent.type == ButtonPress)
    {
    x1=SomeEvent.xbutton.x;
    y1=SomeEvent.xbutton.y;
    strcpy(text,"Hello!");
    XDrawString(Monitor,DrawWindow,WindowGC,x1,y1,
            text,strlen(text));
    XFlush(Monitor);
    }
  }

XCloseDisplay(Monitor);
}
```

This program will draw "Hello!" at the current mouse location whenver the user presses a mouse button. The program uses the XLoadFont() function to load information from the system about the "r14" font. It then assigns that font to the graphics context for the created window. The program uses the XDrawString() function to actually draw the text. The properties of the text are controlled by the values previously set in the graphics context.

The information about how to draw text using a particlar font is stored in a font file on the system. Font files use a variety of formats, but they all contain the same basic information: the appearance of all characters in the given font. In order to use a font, a program must identify that font by its name. The X library provides functions to identify the fonts available on a system. The following code demonstrates these functions:

```c
#include <stdio.h>
#include <X11/Xlib.h>

main()
{
char            text[80],partial[80];
char            **AvailableFonts;
int             font_count,i;
Display         *Monitor;

Monitor=XOpenDisplay(NULL);
printf("Enter a string to search: ");
scanf("%s",partial);
sprintf(text,"*%s*",partial);
AvailableFonts=XListFonts(Monitor,text,10,&font_count);
for (i=0; i<font_count; i++)
  printf("%s\n",AvailableFonts[i]);
XFreeFontNames(AvailableFonts);
XCloseDisplay(Monitor);
}
```

The XListFonts() function searches the system for fonts matching the given string, and returns a list of all font names that partially match. The example program asks for at most 10 matches and prints them out. The XFreeFontNames() function should be called to free up the memory allocated for storing the font names in the XListFonts() function. There are additional functions related to loading and handling fonts; however, they are beyond the scope of this text.

8.6 • Making a Library

Creating a library involves a handful of steps. First, source code for the desired functions must be compiled and stored in object code files. Second, the object code files are packaged together to create a library file. Third, an include file is normally written defining the prototypes of the functions in the library file. The include file may also define constants, structure definitions, macros, and global variable definitions used within the library. Once completed, the include and library files can be used like any other library.

The following code will be used to demonstrate the creation of a library:

```
int Largest(int first, int second)
{
if (first > second)
  return(1);
else if (second > first)
  return(2);
else
  return(0);
}
```

This function takes two integers as input, and returns 1 if the first is larger than the second, 2 if the second is larger than the first, and 0 if they are equal. If this code is stored in a file named largest.c, then it can be compiled into object code as follows:

```
ahoover@video> ls
largest.c
ahoover@video> gcc -c largest.c
ahoover@video> ls
largest.c  largest.o
ahoover@video>
```

Normally, a library contains multiple object code files. The following additional code will be used to demonstrate:

```
void HelloWorld()
{
printf("Hello world\n");
}

double SevenPointSeven()
{
return(7.7);
}
```

The code for these two functions does not do anything particularly useful; it is used here only to demonstrate the creation of a library. If this code is stored in a file named two.c, then it can be compiled into object code as follows:

```
ahoover@video> gcc -c two.c
ahoover@video> ls
largest.c  largest.o  two.c  two.o
ahoover@video>
```

On a Unix system, the program ar is most commonly used to package object code files into a library file. For example:

```
ahoover@video> ar r libcustom.a largest.o two.o
ahoover@video> ls
largest.c  largest.o  libcustom.a  two.c  two.o
ahoover@video>
```

In this example, the library file libcustom.a was created. The ar program can also be used to list the contents of a library file. For example:

```
ahoover@video> ar t libcustom.a
largest.o
two.o
ahoover@video>
```

The following code defines the prototypes of the functions in the library file:

```
int Largest(int,int);
void HelloWorld();
double SevenPointSeven();
```

Assume this code is stored in a file named custom_lib.h.

After the above steps have been completed, programs can be written that use the newly created library. For example, consider the following code:

```
#include <stdio.h>
#include "custom_lib.h"


int main()
{
printf("%lf\n",SevenPointSeven());
HelloWorld();
}
```

This code calls two of the functions in the custom library. The file custom_lib.h is included in order to provide function prototypes. Note that it is surrounded by quotes, indicating the search path is the current directory rather than the system include path. Assuming this code is stored in a file named testprog.c, then it can be compiled and linked to the custom library as follows:

```
ahoover@video> gcc -o testprog testprog.c -lcustom -L.
ahoover@video>
```

The command line option -lcustom tells gcc to link to the library file libcustom.a, while the command line option -L. tells gcc to search for libraries in the current directory in addition to the usual system library path. Executing the program produces the following output:

```
ahoover@video> testprog
7.700000
Hello world
ahoover@video>
```

If the library is intended to be used repeatedly, it is common practice to copy the library and include files to the appropriate system directories, to simplify the compiling of programs that use them.

8.7 • Library Pitfalls

Once a programmer gets used to the idea of using libraries, it is easy to get enthralled by them. They save time and allow us to code things that might otherwise be very difficult. It is important to remember that a library is just a tool. Libraries should be used to help overcome problems, not just because they are available. A programmer can make the mistake of using a library when its utility to a given problem is minimal. This is bad, because now an application is tied to a library that it doesn't really need. Programs can become bloated and difficult to maintain simply because they have been linked to too many libraries.

Another common pitfall is to spend too much time looking for a library to solve a problem. It can be enticing to think that somebody "out there somewhere" has already written code to tackle the problem at hand. This leads to a programmer's reluctance to solve a given problem from scratch, and a dependence on searching for existing library-supported solutions. Searching can end up taking more time than simply writing code from scratch. It can also cause a programmer to use a library that does not quite fit the problem at hand, but which can be forced to provide a hacked solution. This leads to inefficient and sometimes error-prone applications.

A library is just another tool in the arsenal of an experienced system programmer. Like a debugger, a shell, or a system call, a library is there to help solve problems. A carpenter may use a hammer, a wrench, or a screwdriver to work on something, but (hopefully) only in the appropriate circumstances. Similarly, a programmer should only use the tools at hand when the job calls for them.

Questions and Exercises

1. During the writing and compiling of a program, what two steps must be taken to make use of a library?

2. A program has been written that makes use of both the math library and a custom widget library. The code for the program is stored in a file named myprog.c. The math library file resides in a standard system directory but the widget library file, named libwidget.a, resides in a custom directory /lib/widget. For the gcc compiler, write the command necessary to compile the code and build an executable, including all command line arguments.

3. What, if any, are the similarities and differences between a device driver and a system library?

4. The following code snipet contains some unfamiliar text:

```
#include <stdio.h>
#include <stdlib.h>
#include <wintrust.h>

/* ... */

WINTRUST_FILE_INFO FileData;
memset(&FileData, 0, sizeof(FileData));
FileData.cbStruct = sizeof(WINTRUST_FILE_INFO);
FileData.pcwszFilePath = pwszSourceFile;
FileData.hFile = NULL;
FileData.pgKnownSubject = NULL;
```

How could one go about discovering the definition of WINTRUST_FILE_INFO, and how to interpret it?

5. The following formula can be used to describe how an investment increases in value over time through the accumulation of compound interest:

$$F = Ie^{ry}$$

where I is the amount initially invested, r is the interest rate, y is the number of years of interest accumulation, and F is the final value accumulated. For example, given an initial investment I of 941.76, accumulating interest at a rate r of 0.03 for a period y of 2 years results in a final value F of 1000.00. Write a program that calculates the needed initial investment given values for the other three variables. The program should prompt the user for the needed values, and then report the needed initial investment. The program should make use of the math library for the value of e (use the macro defined as M_E) and the pow() function to calculate the power.

6. The following formula can be used to describe the dimensions of a loading ramp:

$$sin(\theta) = \frac{h}{l}$$

where θ is the incline angle of the ramp, h is the height of the ramp, and l is the length of the ramp. Write a program that calculates the needed length of a ramp given a desired incline and height. For example, given an incline of 9.5 degrees and a height of 0.5 m, a ramp needs to be 3.03 m in length. The program should prompt the user for the needed values and calculate and report the required length. The program should make use of the math library for the sin() function, and should use the macro M_PI for the value of π to convert degrees to radians (radians = degrees $\times \frac{\pi}{180}$).

7. Write a program that makes use of the math library to solve triangles. A triangle has six values of interest, which are the lengths for each of its sides, and the angles of each corner:

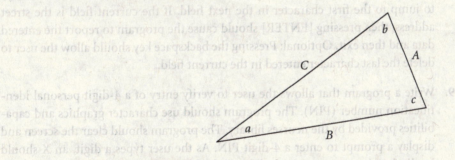

The Law of Cosines states that

$$A^2 = B^2 + C^2 - 2BC \cos a$$
$$B^2 = A^2 + C^2 - 2AC \cos b$$
$$C^2 = A^2 + B^2 - 2AB \cos c$$

(8.1)

The Law of Sines states that

$$\frac{A}{\sin a} = \frac{B}{\sin b} = \frac{C}{\sin c}$$

Given any three of the six unknown values, it is possible to solve for the remaining three values using these equations. That is the goal of the program. The program should be menu driven, with options for entering a value for a triangle's side or angle, displaying the known values, solving for the unknown values, resetting (so that all values are unknown), and exiting. No graphics are expected; everything should be text driven. When solving for the unknown values, the program should check to make sure that exactly three values have been entered; any more or less and the program should provide the user with an appropriate error statement. It should also check for and reject values for negative lengths or angles, all equal lengths, one length greater than the sum of the other two, and angles outside allowed ranges.

8. Write a program that allows the user to enter data into a form. The program should use character graphics and capabilities provided by the ncurses library. The program should display the prompts of the form continuously in the same positions (the specific prompts and positions are at the discretion of the programmer). After each keypress by the user, the data entered into the form should be updated and displayed. The fields of the form should include the first name, last name, and street address for a person. The two name fields should be limited to 20 characters, the street address field should be limited to 30 characters. Pressing the [ENTER] key should cause the cursor (current point of data entry) to jump to the first character in the next field. If the current field is the street address, then pressing [ENTER] should cause the program to report the entered data and then exit. Optional: Pressing the backspace key should allow the user to delete the last character entered in the current field.

9. Write a program that allows the user to verify entry of a 4-digit personal identification number (PIN). The program should use character graphics and capabilities provided by the ncurses library. The program should clear the screen and display a prompt to enter a 4-digit PIN. As the user types a digit, an X should be displayed to represent each digit. Only the characters 0 through 9 should be accepted, any others should be ignored. If the user presses the backspace key, then the last digit entered should be deleted and the display updated to reflect the deletion. When the user presses [ENTER], the system should compare what has been entered (may be 0 to 4 digits) against the value 5309. If it matches, the program should report success and end; otherwise the program should report that the code entered is incorrect, and then start over from the beginning.

10. Write a program that uses the curses library to let the user play a video game. The game should use character graphics and capabilities provided by the ncurses library. The action is to be modeled after the classic *Space Invaders* game. The basic action is that a ground tank controlled by the user fires at aliens that are attempting to land.

All objects in the game, including the tank, the aliens, and any shots fired, should occupy 1 character of space each. Use easily identifiable characters for all objects. The tank should be made to move left or right on the bottom row of the screen by using the arrow keys of the keypad. The tank should also be made to fire a shot by using the spacebar. The initial position of the tank should be the center bottom. The initial position of any shot fired should be immediately above the tank. Shots fired should move upward only, one position at a time. The tank should move horizontally only, one position at a time. The game should limit the user to having three shots active at any time. If the spacebar is pressed while three shots are still active, nothing should happen. Upon reaching the top of the screen, shots should disappear. Tank motion should be bounded by the edges of the screen.

Aliens should appear immediately when the game starts. They should initially number 30 in count. They should be positioned in three rows, 10 per row, starting on the second row. The first row is reserved (as discussed below). On each row they should be somewhat spaced out—they cannot be side by side. The exact configuration is left to the programmer. Every alien should move sideways only, starting by moving to the right, until it hits an edge. Upon hitting an edge, the alien should drop down one row and change directions, moving toward the other side. Thus, the overall motion is zig-zag across the screen. Aliens should randomly drop bombs. There should be a 1% chance of an alien dropping a bomb each time it moves to a new location. Bombs should fall vertically downward one position at a time. Upon reaching the bottom of the screen, bombs should disappear.

Bombs should pass through (not affect) other aliens or shots fired by the tank. Similarly, shots fired by the tank should not affect bombs. If a shot fired by the tank occupies the same location as an alien, the alien dies (disappears). If a bomb dropped by an alien occupies the same location as the tank, the tank dies. The game is won when the user kills all the aliens. The game is lost if the tank dies, or if an alien reaches the ground.

A score should be reported on the top (first) row of the screen, in the leftmost position. The score should give 20 points for each alien killed, minus 1 point for each shot fired by the tank. The cursor should be kept unobtrusively out of the action, located at the top right corner of the screen. The user should be able to press "q" at any time to quit the game.

The keyboard control of the tank should be nonechoing, unbuffered, and nonblocking. The overall speed of the game, as defined by an iteration in which objects move and user input is polled, should be a variable with a fixed value in milliseconds. This can be controlled by a usleep() function call each iteration, with the appropriate value. Object speeds should be integer scalars of the timing of the main loop. For example, if the tank motion scalar is 3, then the tank would move every third iteration through the loop. The control values include the overall speed of the game, the speed of alien motion, the speed of the tank shots, the speed of the alien bombs, and the percentage chance of an alien dropping a bomb. These control values should all be set to fixed values.

11. Write a program that uses the X library to display a screen saver. The screen saver should show a circle bouncing vertically in the window. The window should be large enough to fill most of the screen, but a specific size is not required. The circle should start in the center of the window, moving upward. The radius of the circle is at the discretion of the reader. The center of the circle should move 1 pixel per 0.1 seconds, controlled via use of the `usleep()` function. The circle should be "erased" (drawn in the background color) and then redrawn (in the foreground color) to create the illusion of motion. When the boundary of the circle hits the boundary of the window (top or bottom), then the circle should reverse direction. The program should run indefinitely.

12. Write a program that uses the X library to display a clock. The program should use the `ctime()` function to obtain the current time. The time should be display as text in HH:MM:SS format, where HH is the current hour, MM is the current minute, and SS is the current second. The display should be updated once per second, controlled using the `sleep()` function. The time should be displayed using the `XDrawString()` function in the center of a window created by the program. The program should run indefinitely.

13. Write a program that uses the X library to allow the user to paint simple two-dimensional primitives in a window. Various properties of the primitives should be selectable through mouse clicks in a second window. The program should run indefinitely until the user presses the system "X" to close a window, thus killing the program.

The program should open two windows. Neither window should fill the entire screen; both windows should be of reasonable size to accommodate the desired content. The first window will serve as a canvas in which to draw; it should otherwise be empty. The second window will serve as a palette, containing icons. These icons will allow the user to select various properties to control the drawing. There should be four groups of icons. The exact appearance and distribution of the icons is left to the reader.

The first set of icons should show a straight line, an arc, and a circle. This set controls what shape the user is drawing. If a line is selected, the user draws a line by pressing any button twice, once for each endpoint. If an arc is selected, the user draws an arc by pressing any button four times, first and second for the corners of the bounding box, and second and third for the beginning and ending angles of the arc (see XDrawArc() for how this works). If a circle is selected, the user draws a circle by pressing any button twice, first at the center, then at any point on the radius.

The second set of icons should show two line styles, solid and dotted. The third set of icons should show four line thicknesses, from 1 to 4 pixels. The fourth set of icons should show a set of four colors (reader's choice). Any primitive drawn should use the selected line style, thickness, and color. All currently selected icons should be highlighted, by drawing a red rectangle around it. Exactly one choice per set of icons should be active at any time, including a default selection at startup.

14. Create a library. The library should contain two functions, Hello() and World(). Calling the Hello() function should print out the string "Hello"; calling the World() function should print out the string "World." The library should use a flag (implemented using a static global variable) that keeps track of which string was last printed. A call to the Hello() function should print out "Hello" only if "World" was the last string printed, and vice versa. The flag should be updated at the end of each function call. Each function should return 1 if the string was printed, 0 otherwise. Write a simple program that uses the library and tests for the correct working of the functions.

15. Describe two problems that can arise when libraries are overly relied upon or used improperly.

9

Scripting Languages

A scripting language is a very high-level programming language, usually targeted toward a specific type of programming work. For example, the shell scripting languages provide mechanisms that simplify operations on lists of files. Consider a weekly task where a system administrator wants to search user directories for large files, and then email each user with a personalized list of their files as part of an announcement to reduce network storage. The system administrator could use a shell scripting language to quickly write a program to get that task done. It would take less time to write the program using a shell scripting language, as compared to the C language, because of the mechanisms that a shell scripting language provides to simplify coding for those sorts of tasks. From this point of view, the main reason for using a scripting language to write a program is to save coding time.

Scripting languages provide a higher level of abstraction than standard programming languages. The biggest distinction is in data and type definitions. Most scripting languages do not distinguish between integers, real values, strings, and other data types. They rely upon context and built-in converters to implicitly change the bit patterns used to store values and perform computations. This makes it easier to write programs that deal with numbers and text, because the programmer does not have to keep track of how the values are actually stored or how computations on them are actually performed. However, it can also be dangerous because without explicit declarations and type casting, unexpected results can occur. What makes this work is that most script programs are small and tend to have a small number of variables of homogeneous type. Thus, a programmer can save coding time by being less strict with variables.

Script languages tend to be good for automating the execution of other programs, for example, running daily backups or creating log files. They can be useful for rapid prototype programming, where the goal is to see how a particular program might look or operate. Script languages are also good for writing a program that is going to be used once and then discarded. These sorts of programs do not need to be rigorously defined or maintained. Good code organization techniques should still be followed, but for a program that is going to be written, used once, and then deleted, all within the span of an hour, commenting and many other organization practices can be skipped. Similarly, the program is likely to be short, so that functions and other organization techniques are not needed. Some script programs end up being useful for a longer time, in which case more sound code organization principles should be followed. However, the majority of script programs are "quick and dirty," where the main goal is to get the program written quickly.

Most scripting languages use C-like syntax and are therefore somewhat readable to experienced C programmers. However, they also use a lot of shortcuts, such as using on-the-fly variable declaration. They tend to use short sequences of text or symbols to implement common operations, such as reading data from a file or testing variables for various types of equality. Thus, they can be difficult to follow in detail. Even experts can have a hard time, because most scripting languages provide many ways to accomplish the same thing, depending on which shortcuts are used.

Scripting languages use interpretation to run programs. There is no compile step and no executable file separate from the source code file. Some quasi-compile the source code file as it is loaded into the interpreter, so that those parts of the program accessed more than once (e.g., loops) will execute more quickly. However, in general, script programs run more slowly than those written in the C programming language. Execution speed is not the primary concern, because it is expected that the program will be run only once or that the job will be relatively quick. Instead, program writing time is the primary concern.

There are a number of different scripting languages, including shell scripting (which itself has many varieties), Perl, Python, Tcl, PHP, Ruby, JavaScript, and VBScript. Most scripting languages were developed for a specific type of work. A particular language may include additional abstraction features, such as hashes or graphical user interface widgets, that facilitate a certain type of programming work. This chapter looks at three scripting languages in some detail. Shell scripting is most commonly used for system administration tasks. Perl is most commonly used to "glue" together other programs, especially for web server/client and database interactions. MATLAB[1] is most commonly used for batch processing of tabular data and for generating large numbers of plots. The goal is not to make the reader an expert with these three languages. The goal is to make the reader familiar with the sorts of tasks for which scripting languages are a useful tool. Scripting languages are so diversified and varied, with new ones appearing every few years, that it is virtually impossible to become fluent in all of them. But they share many common design goals and features. By exploring these three scripting languages, the reader will be prepared to become fluent in any scripting language.

9.1 • Using Scripting Languages

Scripting languages use interpreter programs to execute script code. For many scripting languages, the interpreter program can be run interactively. For example:

```
ahoover@video> python
Python 1.5.2 (#1, Jul  5 2001, 03:02:19)
>>> x=7
>>> print x
7
>>> print "Hello from python"
Hello from python
>>>
>>> [CTRL-D]
ahoover@video>
```

This example demonstrates the use of the Python scripting language. After the python script interpreter is started, it displays >>> as its prompt. Python statements can be entered at this prompt, and the results will be displayed interactively. The key sequence CTRL-D exits the Python interpreter.

Shells work similarly; most of the examples throughout this book have already shown interactive usage of a shell. A shell can also be used to start another shell. For example:

```
ahoover@video> sh
sh-2.05$ ls
hello.pl  hello.py  hello.sh
```

---

1. GNU Octave, a free open source program similar to MATLAB and capable of running the same examples in this chapter, is available at www.octave.org.

```
sh-2.05$ mkdir temp
sh-2.05$ ls
hello.pl  hello.py  hello.sh  temp
sh-2.05$ exit
exit
ahoover@video>
```

In this example, the prompt ahoover@video> is used by the tcsh shell interpreter. Running the program sh starts the Bourne shell, which displays sh-2.05$ as its prompt. Standard shell statements can then be entered with the results displayed interactively. The exit command quits the Bourne shell interpreter, which in the above example returns to the tcsh shell interpreter.

Although scripting languages can be used interactively, they can also be used as programming languages. In this case, a *script* of statements is written and saved in a file. For example:

```
@filenames=<*>;
$count=@filenames;
if ($count > 5) {
  print "large directory\n";
}
else {
  print "small directory\n";
}
```

This is a Perl script that finds the number of files in the current directory; if the number of files is greater than five, then it reports "large directory"; otherwise, it reports "small directory." If the above statements are stored in a file named dirsize.pl, then they can be executed as follows:

```
ahoover@video> ls
dirsize.pl  hello.pl  hello.py  hello.sh
ahoover@video> perl < dirsize.pl
Small directory
ahoover@video>
```

Running the script in this manner pipes the statements from the script file into the interpreter. The script can also be executed like this:

```
ahoover@video> perl dirsize.pl
Small directory
ahoover@video>
```

Running the script in this manner provides the script filename as a command line argument to the interpreter. Although script files can be run in these ways, the most common way of running a script file is to start it with a line identifying the interpreter. For example:[2]

```
#!/usr/local/bin/perl
print "Hello from perl\n";
```

The first line of a script file has a unique syntax. The #! sequence tells the system that the remainder of the line is the name of the program that should be used to execute the rest of the statements in the file. If these statements are stored in a file named hello.pl, then they can be executed as follows:

```
ahoover@video> hello.pl
Hello from perl
ahoover@video>
```

In this case, the system finds the script interpreter from the first statement in the script file.

The last examples showed three different ways to run a script file. The paradigm of having multiple ways to get something done is found throughout script programming. Also in these examples, the number of keystrokes necessary to execute the script was reduced from the first to the last example. This is another paradigm found throughout scripting languages, where the goal is to save programming time by reducing the amount of code or keystrokes necessary to accomplish a task.

In order for the last example to work correctly, the script file must have executable permission. This can be checked and changed as follows:

```
ahoover@video> ls -l hello.pl
-rw-r--r-- ahoover  fusion  49 Sep  4 15:18 hello.pl
ahoover@video> chmod 755 hello.pl
ahoover@video> ls -l hello.pl
-rwxr-xr-x ahoover  fusion  49 Sep  4 15:18 hello.pl
```

Text editors typically save new files with read/write permissions only, so that chmod must be used to add executable permission. At this point, programmers typically stop thinking of script files as lists of statements and start thinking of them as programs. The dividing line is tenuous, and the distinctions can be

---

2. The exact path may differ from system to system. The which command (e.g., which perl) can be used to find the exact path for a script interpreter on a system.

murky. The most common distinction involves interpretation versus compilation. Many scripting languages are purely interpretive, meaning that they analyze statements one at a time as they are reached in the script file. If the statement is valid for the language, then it is executed, and interpretation proceeds to the next line. However, some scripting languages perform a type of compilation, converting the entire script file to an intermediate form before beginning execution. Perl works in this way. If any statement in a Perl script is invalid, then the Perl interpreter will report the error before beginning execution. Both of these forms of execution can be contrasted with C program compilation, where the source code is compiled to machine code and saved in a separate file for execution. An advantage with scripting languages is that the compilation step is skipped, making the distribution and use of a script program simpler. A disadvantage is that script programs run more slowly than machine code because of the interpretation. In any case, the rest of this chapter will refer to scripts as programs, and all example script files will be assumed to have executable permission.

A common error encountered by novice script writers and users involves the correct path and spelling of the script interpreter on the first line. For example, consider the following code:

```
#!/urs/local/bin/perl
print "Hello from perl\n";
```

If this code is stored in a file named hello2.pl, then executing produces the following output:

```
ahoover@video> hello2.pl
hello2.pl: Command not found.
ahoover@video>
```

The error message is unfortunate, implying that the file hello2.pl could not be found. This is not the case. Instead, the problem is that the interpreter given on the first line in the script file could not be found. Usually this is because it was spelled incorrectly (as in this case), or the path is incorrect. The result is that the system does not know how to execute the script because it cannot find the script interpreter.

A large number of scripting languages have been developed that overlap in the ways they can be used. For example, consider the following python script:

```
#!/usr/bin/env python
print "Hello from python"
```

If this code is stored in a file named hello.py, then it can be executed as follows:

```
ahoover@video> hello.py
Hello from python
ahoover@video>
```

The following Bourne shell script does the same thing:

```
#!/bin/sh
echo "Hello from sh"
```

If this code is stored in a file named `hello.sh`, then it can be executed as follows:

```
ahoover@video> hello.sh
Hello from sh
ahoover@video>
```

A Perl script for accomplishing the same thing was shown in a previous example. The point is that there are many scripting languages and it is unlikely that a programmer will become proficient in all of them. This chapter is not intended to make the reader an expert with any individual scripting language. Instead, this chapter explores three examples in order to demonstrate how scripting languages can be used to save time for some programming tasks.

9.2 • Shell Scripting

While shells are most commonly used interactively, they can also be used as programming environments. Shell scripting refers to the running of a script, as a program, on a shell. Certain aspects of system administration can often be accomplished more quickly using shell scripts. For example, account management, such as the making and deletion of accounts as well as the monitoring of account usage, can be simplified. Other popular uses for shell scripts include the configuration of applications during installation, and operations involving the management of large numbers of files.

There are many different shells, and each has its own scripting language. The three most popular shells are sh, csh, and ksh. In chronological order of development, sh is the oldest, and historically it was the default shell for the root user. The second oldest is csh, the syntax of which most closely resembles that of the C programming language. The ksh shell is the newest of the three and the most rich in terms of the number of programming features it supports. In addition to these three, there are other derivative shells that have achieved notable popularity, such as tcsh (a derivative of csh) and bash (a derivative of sh). At the time of this writing, the default shell on most Unix systems is bash, with sh commonly linked to bash.

Different shell scripting languages can be thought of as different dialects of a human language. There are differences between all the dialects, but there is a great deal of commonality in the core syntax of all shell scripting languages. If a programmer is fluent with that core, then most shell scripts can be read and understood with at least some modicum of familiarity.

This section will focus on the Bourne shell (sh) scripting language. The Bourne-again shell (bash) scripting language is a superset of the sh scripting language, so the syntax discussed here is applicable to both. In order to explain how it is used, the primary features of the language will be discussed. Examples will highlight how it can be used to save time and effort to accomplish certain programming tasks.

9.2.1   Input/Output

The basic I/O statements for the Bourne shell are *echo* for displaying text and *read* for reading input from the keyboard. For example, consider the following code:

```
#!/bin/sh
echo Name a fruit?
read FRUIT
echo Vegetable?
read VEGGIE
echo $FRUIT and $VEGGIE are healthy foods
```

If this code is stored in a file named foods.sh, then it can be executed[3] as follows:

```
ahoover@video> foods.sh
Name a fruit?
apple
Vegetable?
potato
apple and potato are healthy foods
ahoover@video>
```

The read statement takes all characters typed until the [ENTER] key is pressed and stores them into the given variable. For example:

```
ahoover@video> foods.sh
Name a fruit?
apple pie
Vegetable?
```

---

3. It is assumed that file permissions have been set correctly, as explained in Section 9.1.

```
ice cream cake
apple pie and ice cream cake are healthy foods
ahoover@video>
```

The echo statement will print multiple arguments as demonstrated above. By default, echo eliminates redundant whitespace (spaces and tabs) and leaves a single space between arguments. For example:

```
ahoover@video> foods.sh
Name a fruit?
apple   pie
Vegetable?
ice      cream         cake
apple pie and ice cream cake are healthy foods
ahoover@video>
```

This is one of the shortcuts that shell programming provides. It is assumed that a programmer is most likely displaying text and would benefit from a default behavior where spacing was singularized. This behavior can be suppressed in the echo statement by enclosing the desired output within double quotes. The string of multiple words is then treated as a single argument. For example, the last line of the above program can be changed as follows:

```
echo "$FRUIT and $VEGGIE are healthy foods"
```

Running this new program produces the following output:

```
ahoover@video> foods2.sh
Name a fruit?
apple   pie
Vegetable?
ice cream            cake
apple   pie and ice cream       cake are healthy foods
ahoover@video>
```

Note that the extra spaces have been preserved.

There are a handful of symbols that affect how output is displayed. As just mentioned, double quotes group multiple words into a single argument, preventing the collapsing of whitespace. The following code demonstrates some other special symbols:

```
#!/bin/sh
# This is a comment
# Special symbols include # $ \ ' {}
HI=Hello
```

```
echo HI          # displays HI
echo $HI         # displays Hello
echo \$HI        # displays $HI
echo '$HI'       # displays $HI
echo "$HIJ"      # displays nothing?
echo "${HI}J"    # displays HelloJ
```

The # symbol starts a comment, where everything after it is considered part of the comment. The $ symbol indicates that the rest of the string is the name of a variable. The \ symbol is an escape sequence and indicates that the next character should be displayed literally; this allows for the display of the reserved symbols in output. The use of single quotes (') indicates that everything inside them should be displayed literally including any special symbols. The braces ({}) can be used to enclose the name of a variable when it is to be displayed adjacent to other text; in this manner, the shell knows the extent of the variable name. In the second to last line in the example above, the shell tries to display the value of the variable HIJ, which is undefined and hence displayed as empty.

9.2.2 Variables

Variables do not need to be explicitly declared before being used. The first time a new variable name is seen, the shell programming environment allocates space for it automatically. For example:

```
#!/bin/sh
ROCKS=4
echo Price?
read PRICE
echo $ROCKS rocks for sale, $PRICE each
```

If this code is stored in a file named rocks.sh, then it can be executed as follows:

```
ahoover@video> rocks.sh
Price?
$1.25
4 rocks for sale, $1.25 each
ahoover@video>
```

This can seem quite strange to someone familiar with C programming or other high-level languages. It is one of the shortcuts provided by shell programming. The idea is to save the programmer the time required to write explicit variable declarations, allowing variables to be declared on-the-fly.

The type of data held by the variable is also unimportant. In a shell program, there is only one type of variable, and no distinction is made between text and numeric data, or between different types of numeric data. All variables are stored as strings. Numeric operations can be performed upon variables, but the variables are passed to the appropriate operator as strings and then converted before the numeric operation is performed. If a numeric result is stored in a variable, it is automatically converted back to a string before storage. This is another shortcut provided by shell programming. The idea is to relieve any burden upon the programmer with regards to explicit data typing.

By convention, variables are often named using all uppercase letters. This allows them to be seen more easily and differentiated from other code. If a variable is named using two or more words, then by convention the underscore character is often used to separate the words. For example:

```
#!/bin/sh
AUTHOR_NAME="Douglas Adams"
```

Some variables are declared automatically. For example:

```
#!/bin/sh
echo Run with $# arguments
echo First three command line arguments:
echo $0
echo $1
echo $2
echo PID is $$
```

If this code is stored in a file named vars.sh, then executing it produces output like the following:

```
ahoover@video> vars.sh turtle frog tree
Run with 3 arguments
First three command line arguments:
vars.sh
turtle
frog
PID is 23061
ahoover@video>
```

The command line arguments are stored similarly to how they are stored for a C program. The process ID can be useful if multiple copies of the script are executed concurrently. Each process can use its PID to uniquely name temporary storage files or other constructs that would otherwise collide.

Most scripts do not use a large number of variables. The idea behind all these shortcuts and conventions in shell programming is to save time while writing a program. Most scripting languages remove or limit the need for variable declaration, type casting, and data conversion. Some scripting languages go so far as to eliminate the need for naming variables at all. This will be seen in some examples for the Perl scripting language.

9.2.3 Loops

There are two simple loops in Bourne shell programming: *for* and *while*. The for statement iterates a variable through a list of values, executing one iteration per value. For example:

```
#!/bin/sh
for i in 1 2 5 tree frog
do
  echo "file${i}.txt"
done
```

If this code is stored in a file named loop1.sh, then executing it produces the following output:

```
ahoover@video> loop1.sh
file1.txt
file2.txt
file5.txt
filetree.txt
filefrog.txt
ahoover@video>
```

The for statement provides a convenient shortcut method for creating a list of strings that differ only in part, as shown in this example. This is often useful for creating, moving, or renaming a large number of files.

The while statement executes a loop until a test condition has been satisfied. For example:

```
#!/bin/sh
NAME=Unknown
while [ $NAME != "Fred" ]
do
  echo Who are you?
  read NAME
```

```
        echo Let me see ...
    done
    echo Found you!
```

If this code is stored in a file named loop2.sh, then executing it produces output like the following:

```
ahoover@video> loop2.sh
Who are you?
Joe
Let me see ...
Who are you?
Fred
Let me see ...
Found you!
ahoover@video>
```

The while statement is used in shell scripting as it is used in many languages, namely, for the processing of data of unknown length.

9.2.4 Conditionals

The *if* statement is the primary method of program flow control in shell scripting. For example:

```
#!/bin/sh
NAME="Fred"
if [ $NAME = "Fred" ]; then
    echo Matches
fi
```

If this code is stored in a file named if1.sh, then executing it produces the following output:

```
ahoover@video> if1.sh
Matches
ahoover@video>
```

The if statement tests a condition; if the condition is true, then the code inside the delimiters *then* and *fi* is executed.

The if statement can contain *else* clauses, similar to most programming languages. For example:

```
#!/bin/sh
NAME="Joe"
if [ $NAME = "Fred" ]; then
  echo Matches
else
  echo No match
fi
```

If this code is stored in a file named if2.sh, then executing it produces the following output:

```
ahoover@video> if2.sh
No match
ahoover@video>
```

Multiple if statements can be chained using the *elif* statement, similar to other programming languages.

The if statement, and the while statement from the previous section, most commonly use the test program to evaluate a condition. The test program can be called by its full name, "test," or by a convenient shorthand alias using square brackets. For example:

```
#!/bin/sh
NAME="Joe"
if test $NAME = "Fred" ; then    # one test syntax
  echo Hello Fred
fi
if [ $NAME = "Joe" ]; then       # another test syntax
  echo Hello Joe
fi
```

If this code is stored in a file named if3.sh, then executing it produces the following output:

```
ahoover@video> if3.sh
Hello Joe
ahoover@video>
```

Each of the two syntaxes is equivalent,[4] but the square brackets syntax is usually preferred because it is shorter and somewhat easier to read. Note that when the square bracket syntax is used, all arguments within the square brackets must have

---

4. The interested reader is encouraged to type which [at the shell prompt to see the relation between the two syntaxes.

preceding and succeeding spaces. These spaces can look redundant when compared to other programming languages, but in shell scripting they are necessary in order to separate all the arguments correctly.

The test program provides a shorthand method for evaluating simple string equivalencies, as shown in the previous examples. Strings can also be tested for nonequality and other conditions. For example:

```
#!/bin/sh
NAME="Fred"
GHOST=""
if [ "$NAME" != "Joe" ]; then
  echo Where\'s Joe?
fi
if [ -z "$GHOST" ]; then
  echo Boo!
fi
if [ -n "$GHOST" ]; then
  echo I'm not a ghost.
fi
```

If this code is stored in a file named if4.sh, then executing it produces the following output:

```
ahoover@video> if4.sh
Where's Joe?
Boo!
ahoover@video>
```

The -z option tests if a string is empty, while the -n string tests if a string is not empty. Note that in this example all the variables are placed within double quotes. This is a good practice, because if a variable is an empty string, then it will not appear as an argument to the test program and the result will likely differ from what was expected.

Numeric comparisons can be performed with the test program. For example:

```
#!/bin/sh
i=7
j=9
if [ "$i" -lt "$j" ]; then
  echo Lesser
fi
if [ "$i" -gt "$j" ]; then
  echo Greater
fi
```

If this code is stored in a file named if5.sh, then executing it produces the following output:

```
ahoover@video> if5.sh
Lesser
ahoover@video>
```

The flag -lt tests if the first argument is less than the second; the flag -gt tests if the first argument is greater than the second. The flags -le and -ge also test for equality but include the case where the arguments are equal in the evaluation.

File properties can be evaluated using the test program. For example:

```
#!/bin/sh
FILE=if6.sh
if [ -f "$FILE" ]; then
  echo FILE exists
fi
if [ -x "$FILE" ]; then
  echo FILE is executable
fi
```

If this code is stored in a file named if6.sh, then executing it produces the following output:

```
ahoover@video> if6.sh
FILE exists
FILE is executable
ahoover@video>
```

The flag -f tests whether or not a file with the given name exists. The flags -r, -w, and -x test whether or not the read, write, and execute permissions for the file are set. The flag -d tests if the given filename is a directory. Other flags test additional properties of files.

Together, the if statement and test program give a convenient shorthand method for control flow. For example, these methods would be suitable to write a program that searches a set of text files in some nontrivial manner. Compared to writing the same program in C, using these methods in a shell script would likely save programming time.

9.2.5 Shell External Programs

The Bourne shell interpreter has only a few built-in commands and language constructs. In order to write shell scripts, a programmer typically takes advantage of a number of other programs external to the shell. A shell script calls external programs by invoking them as commands. This is done by enclosing the name of the program to be run, along with any arguments, using back quotes (`). The entire back quote–enclosed string is replaced with the output that results from running that command. For example:

```
#!/bin/sh
FILES=`ls`
echo $FILES
```

If this code is stored in a file named `backquotes.sh`, then executing it produces the following output:

```
ahoover@video> ls
backquotes.sh
ahoover@video> backquotes.sh
backquotes.sh
ahoover@video>
```

This mechanism is commonly used in shell script programming. It lets a script use other programs to do some work, placing the result into a variable in the script or using the result to control program flow.

The `test` program introduced in the last section is an example of an external program. However, the test program does not produce any output. It only evaluates true/false expressions, and uses its exit (return) code to report the evaluation. Therefore, programming using the test program does not require the back quotes mechanism. A more complex expression evaluation program is `expr`. For example:

```
#!/bin/sh
i=3
j=7
a=`expr $i + $j`
b=`expr $j / $i`
echo "$a $b"
```

If this program is stored in a file named `expr1.sh`, then executing it produces the following output:

```
ahoover@video> expr1.sh
10 2
ahoover@video>
```

The expr program can perform the evaluation of a variety of numeric and string expressions. Since the result of the evaluation is output to stdout, back quotes are placed around the command in order to assign the result to a variable. The following is another example:

```
#!/bin/sh
files=`ls`
i=1
for name in $files
do
    echo "File $i is $name"
    i=`expr $i + 1`
done
```

If this code is stored in a file named expr2.sh, then executing it produces the following output:

```
ahoover@video> ls
backquotes.sh  expr1.sh  expr2.sh
ahoover@video> expr2.sh
File 1 is backquotes.sh
File 2 is expr1.sh
File 3 is expr2.sh
ahoover@video>
```

The expr program is the main tool used in shell script programming for arithmetic operations.

There are a handful of programs that are commonly used for string processing. For example, the tr program can be used to perform character substitutions. The following data will be used to demonstrate:

```
The cat went up the tree
```

If this data is stored in a file named data1.txt, then the following command performs a simple substitution:

```
ahoover@video> tr e o < data1.txt
Tho cat wont up tho troo
ahoover@video>
```

The tr program replaces all occurrences of the first command line argument with the second command line argument. It operates on data received on the stdin stream and places output on the stdout stream. The following demonstrates using tr in a shell script:

```
#!/bin/sh
files=`ls`
```

```
for name in $files
do
  newname=`echo $name | tr "[:lower:]" "[:upper:]" `
  if [ "$newname" != "$name" ]; then
    mv "$name" "$newname"
  fi
done
```

This program looks at all the filenames in the current directory and renames them to use all uppercase letters. The tr program is used to perform the character substitution from any lowercase letter to its equivalent uppercase letter. If this code is stored in a file named upper.sh, then executing it produces the following output:

```
ahoover@video> ls
upper.sh  This_Is_A_Test.txt
ahoover@video> upper.sh
ahoover@video> ls
UPPER.SH  THIS_IS_A_TEST.TXT
ahoover@video>
```

This type of program provides a convenient shortcut for renaming a large number of files according to a desired convention. It also provides a convenient shortcut for minor alterations of the contents of a large number of files, for example, removing extra newline or carriage return characters.

The cut program can be used to parse lines of text, reformatting it for a desired style of output. The following data will be used to demonstrate:

```
The cat went up the tree
The dog chased the stick
The turtle took a nap
```

If this data is stored in a file named data2.txt, then it can be processed using the cut program as follows:

```
ahoover@video> cut -d " " -f 2 data2.txt
cat
dog
turtle
ahoover@video>
```

The -d argument tells the cut program to use the following character (in this example, the space character) as the delimiter between fields. The -f 2 argument pair tells the cut program to display the second field only. The following demonstrates using the cut program in a shell script:

```
#!/bin/sh
# adds up the size of all files
sizes=`ls -l | cut -b 29-38`
total=0
for i in $sizes
do
  total=`expr "$total" + "$i"`
  echo $i
done
echo $total
```

If this code is stored in a file named sizes.sh, then executing it produces the following output:

```
ahoover@video> ls -l
-rw-r--r--  ahoover  fusion       72 Sep  2 18:05 data2.txt
-rwxr-xr-x  ahoover  fusion      176 Sep  3 15:57 sizes.sh
ahoover@video> sizes.sh
72
176
248
ahoover@video>
```

This example uses the cut program to parse the characters in positions 29–38 on each line into the variable sizes. It then uses the expr program to total the sizes and prints out the total.

Two more advanced string processing programs are sed and awk. They are actually complex enough to be considered scripting languages by themselves. It is possible to write script programs entirely in sed or awk. However, sed and awk are more commonly used as shell external programs. The sed program is like an advanced version of the tr program; it can be used to search for and replace strings within the given input data, displaying the results. The following example uses the file data2.txt from above:

```
ahoover@video> sed s/e/o/g < data2.txt
Tho cat wont up tho troo
Tho dog chasod tho stick
Tho turtlo took a nap
ahoover@video>
```

The command line argument to sed in this example says to search for the string "e" and replace it with the string "o," globally across all occurrences. The sed program can be used with similar commands to insert, append, and delete text; however, the usage just shown is the most common. The awk program is like an advanced version of the cut program; it can be used to parse lines of text, displaying them in the desired format. For example:

```
ahoover@video> ls -l
-rw-r--r--  ahoover   fusion       72 Sep  2 18:05 data2.txt
-rwxr-xr-x  ahoover   fusion      176 Sep  3 15:57 sizes.sh
ahoover@video> ls -l | awk '{print $4;}'
72
176
ahoover@video>
```

The awk program provides more powerful formatting capabilities than the cut program, similar to those provided by the printf() statement in the C programming language.

From these few examples of shell external programs, it is easy to see the wealth of options available to shell script programmers. A list of dozens of shell external programs is provided in Appendix C. Many of them overlap in what they can accomplish, but the common goal remains the same: save programming time. Once a programmer becomes familiar with a handful of these programs and methods, they can often be a useful tool for repetitive work.

9.2.6 Other Features

There are a number of features of Bourne shell programming that were not covered in this section. Features not covered include exit codes, pattern matching (wildcards), exporting variables to other scripts or shells, the case statement, and functions. When combined with the large number of shell external programs available, there are a lot of ways to get tasks accomplished. Collectively they can be thought of as a large set of shortcuts. Individual programmers tend to become familiar with a handful of the available shortcuts, and to use them whenever opportunities arise. It is unlikely that even an advanced shell programmer would ever use all these tools, or even become fluent with the complete syntax of some of the more advanced (e.g., sed and awk). Each shell external program has a man page that can be consulted to find the details of its syntax. The main goal for a programmer is to understand how these programs interact with shell script programming. If a programmer faces performing a repetitive task, it may be worth the time to find a way to accomplish the task using shell scripting. This is most commonly how new tools and uses for shell scripting are learned.

9.3 • Perl

Perl is a scripting language that is similar to shell scripting. However, it includes many more built-in features than shell scripting. Some of these features are equivalents of capabilities that shell scripting gets by calling external programs. For example, Perl has a built-in *tr* command for transliterating characters that works similarly to the system program `tr`. Another built-in command, *substr*, performs operations similar to the system program `cut`. The capabilities to evaluate true/false expressions and to check file properties, provided by the system program `test`, are built in to Perl. Perl also includes some features that are not found in shell scripting, such as hashes and references. In general, Perl is a more feature-rich scripting language than the shell scripting languages.

The Perl interpreter program is not run interactively. When it is started, it scans the entire Perl script and compiles it into an intermediate form called a "syntax tree." A syntax tree is not machine code, but it is quicker to interpret than the original Perl code (some limited optimizations are also performed during the compilation phase). Thus, a Perl program tends to run more quickly than an equivalent shell script program, but still not as fast as an equivalent C program.

Perl gained in popularity with the proliferation of web servers and web-related applications. It is often used to write programs that work in between web servers, database programs, and clients. For example, consider a situation where a client sends some form data to the server initiating a transaction. The server wants to customize how the next web page looks based upon the form data. A Perl program could work in the middle to perform the customization. As another example, consider where a web server needs to access a database based upon some received form data. Again, a Perl program could work in the middle to perform the access. For these sorts of tasks, Perl is sometimes referred to as the "glue language" of the Web because it is used to write smaller programs that work in between the primary programs. It is important to note that these sorts of programs could be written using shell scripting or other programming languages. However, Perl provides a number of programming shortcuts and features that make writing such programs quicker.

This section explains some of the basics of the Perl language and how it is used for programming. The goal is to familiarize the reader with the concepts that save programming time, not to serve as a reference. There are a number of books that teach Perl more fully or serve as a reference. The interested reader is referred to *Learning Perl*, 5th ed., R. Schwartz, T. Phoenix, and b. foy, O'Reilly, 2008, ISBN 0596520107; or *Beginning Perl*, 2nd ed., J. Lee, Apress, 2004, ISBN 159059391X.

9.3.1   Input/Output

The basic I/O statements for the Perl language are *print* for displaying text and *<STDIN>* for reading input from the keyboard. For example, consider the following code:

```
#!/usr/local/bin/perl
print "Name an animal: ";
$a1=<STDIN>;
print "Name another animal: ";
$a2=<STDIN>;
print "A $a1 and a $a2 go for a walk ...\n";
```

If this code is stored in a file named animals1.pl, then it can be executed as follows:

```
ahoover@video> animals1.pl
Name an animal: turtle
Name another animal: frog
A turtle
 and a frog
 go for a walk ...
ahoover@video>
```

The <STDIN> statement reads all input from the stdin stream until the [ENTER] key is pressed and stores it in the given variable. Unlike most other programming languages, Perl includes the [ENTER] key (newline character) in the set of characters stored in the variable. This can be convenient for line-based test processing, where the newline character is treated like any other. The newline character can be removed by the *chomp* operator. For example:

```
#!/usr/local/bin/perl
print "Name an animal: ";
chomp($a1=<STDIN>);
print "Name another animal: ";
chomp($a2=<STDIN>);
print "A $a1 and a $a2 go for a walk ...\n";
```

If this code is stored in a file named animals2.pl, then it can be executed as follows:

```
ahoover@video> animals2.pl
Name an animal: turtle
Name another animal: frog
A turtle and a frog go for a walk ...
ahoover@video>
```

The chomp operator can be used in a separate assignment statement, but it is more often combined as written in the above example. The special symbols used for formatting strings in shell scripting (' $ \ {}) are treated similarly in Perl. A semicolon is used to separate lines of Perl code, and is generally placed at the end of each line.

In order to provide more control over the formatting of output, Perl provides the *printf* operator. It is modeled after the C function of the same name. For example:

```
#!/usr/local/bin/perl
$t=4;
$s="turtles";
$f=1.3;
printf "The %d %s move at %f kph ...\n",$t,$s,$f;
```

If this code is stored in a file named animals3.pl, then it can be executed as follows:

```
ahoover@video> animals3.pl
The 4 turtles move at 1.300000 kph ...
ahoover@video>
```

Most of the symbols available in C for formatting printf() statements are also available in the Perl version of printf, and they follow the same conventions.

Perl provides the *open* and *close* statements for accessing files. For example:

```
#!/usr/local/bin/perl
$n=42;
open DATA, ">data1.txt";
print DATA "History of the world\n";
printf DATA "Answer: %d\n",$n;
close DATA;
```

Executing this program produces a file named data1.txt with the following contents:

```
History of the world
Answer: 42
```

The open and close statements work similarly to the C functions fopen() and fclose(), but with a slightly different syntax. The type of I/O to be performed on the file is indicated by pipelike symbols preceding the filename: < for read, > for write, and >> for append. The analog to the C file pointer is called a filehandle in Perl and can be used in print and printf statements to indicate the stream to which bytes are to be written. Data can be read from a file using the diamond operator (<>) surrounding the filehandle name. For example:

```perl
#!/usr/local/bin/perl
open WORLD, "<data1.txt";
$s=<WORLD>;        #the diamond operator
print "(1) $s";
close WORLD;
```

If this program is stored in a file named readdata.pl, then executing it produces the following output:

```
ahoover@video> readdata.pl
(1) History of the world
ahoover@video>
```

Each time the diamond operator is used to read a stream, an entire line of text is read, including the newline character.

9.3.2 Variables

There are two main types of variables in Perl: scalars and arrays. A scalar variable name is preceded by the dollar sign ($).[5] The type of data stored in a variable is unimportant. Internally, all data is stored as strings and all numeric expressions are evaluated using double floating point precision, but most operators interpret and typecast the data in variables automatically. For example:

```perl
#!/usr/local/bin/perl
# This is a comment
$x=3;
$y=7.2;
$z="14frog";
$a=$x+$y;
$b=$x+$z;
```

---

5. In shell script programming, the $ symbol is omitted when the variable is on the left-hand side of an assignment but included when the variable is used in an expression or statement; in Perl script programming, it is always used regardless of the context. This can be confusing when going back and forth between scripting languages.

```
$c=$y+$z;
print "$a $b $c\n";
```

If this code is stored in a file named vars1.pl, then executing it produces the following output:

```
ahoover@video> vars1.pl
10.2 17 21.2
ahoover@video>
```

Any line or portion of a line beginning with the hash (#) is considered a comment. When a variable holding string data is used in an arithmetic operation, the operator tries to convert the data to a numeric value. In this example, the first two characters were used to form the value 14 that was subsequently used in the operation. Other convenient shortcuts include the ability to replicate and concatenate strings. For example:

```
#!/usr/local/bin/perl
$x="turtle";
$y="frog" x 3;
$z=$x . $y;
print "$y $z\n";
```

If this code is stored in a file named vars2.pl, then executing it produces the following output:

```
ahoover@video> vars2.pl
frogfrogfrog turtlefrogfrogfrog
ahoover@video>
```

The cross (x) operator replicates the preceding text a given number of times. The dot (.) operator concatenates strings.

An array variable name is preceded by the at sign (@). An array variable works similarly to a C language array, holding a number of consecutive integer-indexed values. For example:

```
#!/usr/local/bin/perl
@a=("green frog", "orange tiger", "turtle");
print "@a[0] @a[1] @a[2]\n";
$f=@a[2];
print "$f\n";
```

If this code is stored in a file named vars3.pl, then executing it produces the following output:

```
ahoover@video> vars3.pl
green frog orange tiger turtle
turtle
ahoover@video>
```

A scalar variable can take on the value of any single element within an array variable. The *qw* operator provides a convenient shortcut for initializing an array with a list of single words. For example:

```
#!/usr/local/bin/perl
@a=qw / frog tiger turtle /;
print "@a[0] @a[1] @a[2]\n";
print "@a\n";
```

If this code is stored in a file named vars4.pl, then executing it produces the following output:

```
ahoover@video> vars4.pl
frog tiger turtle
frog tiger turtle
ahoover@video>
```

There are several syntaxes that accomplish the same thing, as shown in the two print statements for this example. The paradigm is that a programmer should use whatever syntax saves the most time while writing the code; for example, the second syntax is preferable to the first in this example. However, there are a lot of shortcuts in Perl. It is unlikely that a beginning Perl programmer will write the shortest possible code; as more experience is gained, program size and writing time generally decreases until a certain level of familiarity is reached.

As with most scripting languages, variables in Perl do not need to be declared before being used. However, Perl does provide a way to enforce variable declaration. For example:

```
#!/usr/local/bin/perl
use strict;
my $x;
$x=3;
$y=7;
```

The *use strict* statement tells Perl to require that every variable be declared before it is used. A variable is declared by using the *my* statement. If this code is stored in a file named vars5.pl, then executing it produces the following output:

```
ahoover@video> vars5.pl
Global symbol "$y" requires explicit package name [...]
Execution of vars5.pl aborted due to compilation errors.
ahoover@video>
```

An error is given because the variable y was not explicitly declared. This is useful for avoiding typos in variable names, among other things.

There are a few default variables. For example, the array variable @ARGV holds the command line arguments given by the user when the program is executed. Of particular interest is $_, the default variable name used when no variable name is given. In some contexts, a programmer can skip using a variable name altogether, and Perl will by default put the result of an operation in this variable. This will be seen in the next section.

9.3.3 Loops and Conditionals

The Perl language has the familiar *for* and *while* loop programming statements. For example:

```
#!/usr/local/bin/perl
for ($i=0; $i<5; $i++)
    {
    $t=$t+$i;
    }
print "$t\n";
$j=0;
while ($j < 5)
    {
    $t=$t+$j;
    $j++;
    }
print "$t\n";
```

If this code is stored in a file named loops1.pl, then executing it produces the following output:

```
ahoover@video> loops1.pl
10
20
ahoover@video>
```

The syntax for these loop statements is similar to the syntax for the C programming statements with the same names. The only difference is that the braces ({})

surrounding the code block for the loop are required, even if the block consists of only one line of code. The *next* statement can be used to jump execution of a loop to the next iteration, while the *last* statement can be used to exit the loop. These are similar to how the continue and break statements work in C programming.

Note in the previous example that the value of $t was not defined prior to its use for summation in the loop. This is a shortcut provided by Perl. If an undefined variable is used in a numeric operation, then its value is assumed to be zero. If an undefined variable is used in a string operation, then its value is assumed to be an empty string. This shortcut allows a programmer to skip variable initialization in addition to the variable declaration step already being skipped.

Sometimes in loop programming, a loop is needed to step through all the values of a list. Perl provides the *foreach* statement to do this. For example:

```
#!/usr/local/bin/perl
foreach $i (1,2,3,4)
  {
  $t+=$i;
  }
print "$t\n";
```

If this code is stored in a file named `loops2.pl`, then executing it produces the following output:

```
ahoover@video> loops2.pl
10
ahoover@video>
```

The syntax of a foreach statement is to give the first argument (in this example, $i) each of the values in the second argument (in this case, 1, then 2, then 3, then 4), iterating through the body of the loop each time. The second argument can be formed in a number of ways. For example, if a range of values is desired, it is usually shorter to type using the following syntax:

```
foreach $i (1..4)
```

This accomplishes the same thing as the previous example. The list does not need to be consecutive values; in fact, it does not need to be numerical values at all. For example:

```
#!/usr/local/bin/perl
foreach $i (1,2,"frog","turtle")
  {
  print "tiger\n";
  }
```

This code simply prints "tiger" four times. Finally, the first argument can be omitted entirely, using the default variable name. For example:

```
#!/usr/local/bin/perl
foreach (1..4)
{
$t+=$_;
}
print "$t\n";
```

This code outputs "10," the same as in the above examples. Instead of defining a variable name to use to hold the list value in each iteration, it uses $_, the default variable name. This shortcut is frequently used in Perl programming.

The $_ default variable can also be used in while loops that are reading data from a stream. For example:

```
#!/usr/local/bin/perl
while (<STDIN>)
  {
  print "$_";
  }
```

In order to demonstrate, this example makes use of the data file data1.txt created previously. If this code is stored in a file named default1.pl, then executing it produces the following output:

```
ahoover@video> default1.pl < data1.txt
History of the world
Answer: 42
ahoover@video>
```

Using this syntax, the while statement reads from the given stream (in this example, STDIN) until no more data is available. The default variable $_ is given the contents of the input line each iteration. This provides a compact syntax for a task that is done frequently.

The Perl language has the familiar *if* conditional statement. For example:

```
#!/usr/local/bin/perl
foreach (1,2,"turtle","frog")
  {
  if ($_ >= 2)
    {
    print "number\n";
    }
```

```
if ($_ eq "frog")
    {
    print "animal\n";
    }
}
```

If this code is stored in a file named if1.pl, then executing it produces the following output:

```
ahoover@video> if1.pl
number
animal
ahoover@video>
```

The syntax of the if statement is similar to the C language if statement, except that the braces surrounding the code block are required. If the condition to be tested is numerical, then mathematical symbols (< <= == != > >=) are used for operators. If the condition to be tested is textual, then text strings (lt le eq ne gt ge) are used for operators. The Perl language also has *else* and *elsif* statements that can be used in conjunction with an if statement.

9.3.4 Pattern Substitution

One of the most popular features in the Perl language is pattern matching and substitution. In its most basic form, this works like a search-and-replace function in a word processing program. For example:

```
#!/usr/local/bin/perl
$a="Hello Mr. Frog, how are you?";
$a =~ s/Frog/Turtle/;
print "$a\n";
```

If this code is stored in a file named pattern1.pl, then executing it produces the following output:

```
ahoover@video> pattern1.pl
Hello Mr. Turtle, how are you?
ahoover@video>
```

The operation s/Frog/Turtle/ searches for the string Fred and replaces it with the string Turtle. The =~ symbol pair is called the binding operator, and it asks Perl to work the operation on the right-hand side using the variable on the left-side.

The search-and-replace operation is often performed upon text received on the STDIN stream. This allows a Perl programmer to use shortcuts involving the default variable name. The following data will be used to demonstrate:

```
Hello Mr. Frog, how are you?
Fine!  Thank you Mr. Frog.
How are you Mr. Turtle?
I've seen a lot of frogs today...
Is it a holifrog day?
```

Assume this data is stored in a file named data2.txt. The following code takes input from the STDIN stream and does the same substitution as in the previous example:

```
#!/usr/local/bin/perl
while (<STDIN>)
{
s/Frog/Turtle/;
print;
}
```

Neither the while statement, the search-and-replace statement, nor the print statement indicate a variable name, so Perl performs all these operations using the default variable name $_. This compact notation can seem confusing, but one of the goals of Perl program writing is to shorten program code as much as possible. If this code is stored in a file named pattern2.pl, then executing it on the data2.txt file produces the following output:

```
ahoover@video> pattern2.pl < data2.txt
Hello Mr. Turtle, how are you?
Fine!  Thank you Mr. Turtle.
How are you Mr. Turtle?
I've seen a lot of frogs today...
Is it a holifrog day?
ahoover@video>
```

Both occurrences of Frog were replaced by Turtle.

More powerful expressions can be written for both the search and replace patterns. For example:

```
#!/usr/local/bin/perl
while (<STDIN>)
{
s/ (F|f)rog/ Turtle/;
```

```
    print;
}
```

If this code is stored in a file named `pattern3.pl`, then executing it on the `data2.txt` file produces the following output:

```
ahoover@video> pattern3.pl < data2.txt
Hello Mr. Turtles, how are you?
Fine!  Thank you Mr. Turtle.
How are you Mr. Turtle?
I've seen a lot of Turtles today...
Is it a holifrog day?
ahoover@video>
```

The | symbol indicates *or* and the () symbols indicate precedence, so that the search pattern is a space followed by either F or f followed by rog. The space is included to prevent substitution where Frog or frog appears midword, such as in holifrog.

A large number of symbols and operators can be used to build complex search-and-replace patterns. For example, assume the following variable has been declared:

```
$a="Hello Mr. Frog, how are you?";
```

The following is a list of some symbols that provide shortcuts for patterns:

```
$a =~ s/r./oo/g;        # Hello Moo Foog, how aoo you?
$a =~ s/r\./rs\./;      # Hello Mrs. Frog, how are you?
$a =~ s/el*o/ezo/;      # Hezo Mr. Frog, how are you?
$a =~ s/l+/z/;          # Hezo Mr. Frog, how are you?
```

The . symbol matches any character except for a newline character. The g character at the end of the statement indicates that the search-and-replace should be performed globally across all occurrences in the variable; otherwise, it is performed only on the first occurrence. The \ symbol provides an escape mechanism so that the next character is interpreted literally. The * symbol indicates that the previous character should be matched zero or more times. The + symbol indicates that the previous character should be matched one or more times. Other shortcuts include \d for any digit character, \w for any word character, and \s for any whitespace character. Patterns or portions of patterns can be negated by various mechanisms, meaning that the match is the opposite of what is described. Patterns can be searched or replaced left-to-right, right-to-left, or with special circumstances such as starting only from the beginning of a line.

The full language of all these shortcuts is beyond the scope of this text. The point is to understand the kinds of operations for which Perl provides good programming shortcuts to accomplish. For example, suppose a task required parsing an HTML[6] file and removing all the markup tags. These tags consist of text enclosed in <> symbol pairs. The following simple program accomplishes this task:

```
#!/usr/local/bin/perl
while (<STDIN>)
  {
  s/<.*>//;
  print;
  }
```

This program takes only moments to write. Accomplishing the same task using the C language would likely take many minutes, even for an experienced programmer.

9.3.5   Other Features

The Perl language includes features beyond those discussed here. Perl provides *hashes*, which are like arrays but allow indices to take on arbitrary values as opposed to integers. This tool is useful for creating lists of pairs of data, for example, first and last name, IP address and DNS name, or city and state. Perl provides a system function call that works similarly to the C function of the same name, allowing other programs to be called. External programs can be run using the back quotes mechanism similarly to how it is done in shell scripting. Perl provides *references*, which are much like pointers in the C language. There are also a large number of operators that were not discussed here, including pop, push, reverse, and sort, and other shortcuts for working with list variables.

For advanced Perl programming, modules are an important tool. They act much like libraries for C programming, providing additional sets of functions for programmers. Two important examples are the Common Gateway Interface (CGI) and Database Independent (DBI) modules. These modules make it easier to write Perl programs that work with web servers and database programs by providing standard function calls and interfaces.

---

6. HTML stands for HyperText Markup Language and is the base language in which web pages are written.

9.4 • MATLAB

MATLAB is a software package designed for mathematical work, such as solving geometry, trigonometry, linear algebra, and statistics problems. Like a shell, it can be used interactively or as an interpreter to run script programs. It includes the capabilities of plotting two-dimensional and three-dimensional functions and data sets, making it useful for data analysis and visualization. MATLAB is a commercial product;[7] the free open source GNU Octave program behaves similarly and can be used to execute all the examples in this section. A number of other similar tools exist, such as Mathematica, LabVIEW, and Maple. The approach taken by some of these tools varies; for example, Mathematica is designed with a focus on symbolic mathematical operations, while MATLAB is focused on numerical analysis. However, the capabilities of all these software packages overlap, and the concepts discussed in this section are common to most mathematical software packages.

Figure 9.1 shows the standard MATLAB interface displayed when the program is started. It consists of three subwindows: a command window (right-side), a file listing (top-left side), and a command history (bottom-left side). MATLAB can also be started without a graphical interface as follows:

```
matlab -nodesktop -nojvm -nosplash
```

In this case, only the command window is shown. In either case, the command window is the primary window in which MATLAB commands are entered.

MATLAB can be used interactively, much like a shell. For example:

```
>> format compact
>> x=7
x =
    7
>> y=x*2
y =
    14
>> disp 'Hello from MATLAB'
Hello from MATLAB
>>
```

The >> symbols are the MATLAB command window prompt. After a command is typed at this prompt, the result is computed and displayed immediately. By default, MATLAB displays empty lines surrounding most output. The command

---

7. See www.matlab.com.

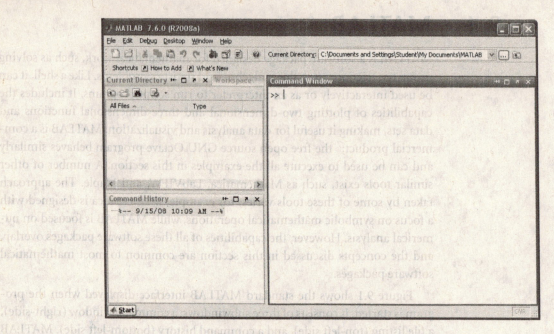

Figure 9.1   Standard MATLAB interface.

format compact suppresses the display of empty lines, allowing more text to be seen without scrolling. The display of output can be suppressed entirely by including a semicolon (;) at the end of a line. For example:

```
>> x=7;
>> y=-3;
>> z=x*y
z =
    -21
>>
```

After the last line, the result is displayed because the command did not end in a semicolon.

A MATLAB script is a list of MATLAB commands that is intended to be executed like a program. It can be written using any text editor. The MATLAB interface provides its own text editor that can be accessed from the main menu as File->New->M-File. By convention, MATLAB scripts are stored using a .m filename extension and are sometimes called M-files. The following code will be used to demonstrate the execution of a MATLAB script:

```
x=41;
y=3.3;
z=x/y;
disp (z);
```

Assuming this code is stored in a file named `intro1.m`, then it can be executed as follows:

```
>> run intro1
   12.4242
>>
```

It can also be run simply by typing its filename:

```
>> intro1
   12.4242
>>
```

Like a shell, MATLAB keeps track of its own current working directory. Standard Unix commands can be used to both print the working directory and to change it. For example:

```
>> cd /users/ahoover
>> pwd
ans =
/users/ahoover
>>
```

This section explains some of the basics of the MATLAB language and how it is used for programming. The goal is to familiarize the reader with the concepts that save programming time, and hence the type of work for which MATLAB scripting is an appropriate tool. There are a number of books that teach MATLAB more fully or serve as a reference. The interested reader is referred to *MATLAB: An Introduction with Applications*, 3rd ed,, A. Gilat, Wiley, 2008, ISBN 0470108770; or *Mastering MATLAB 7*, D. Hanselman and B. Littlefield, Prentice Hall, 2004, ISBN 0131430181.

9.4.1   Input/Output

The basic I/O functions for MATLAB are *disp* and *input*. For example:

```
% This is a comment
x=input('Enter a number: ');
y=input('Second number: ');
```

```
z=x/y;
disp('Their ratio is ');
disp(z);
```

If this code is stored in a file named io1.m, then executing it produces the following output:

```
>> io1
Enter a number: 7
Second number: 3
Their ratio is
    2.3333
>>
```

The percent symbol (%) is used to denote a comment. A pair of single quotes (') is used to enclose strings for display in either function.

The input function displays the given text and accepts a numeric value as input. If a nonnumeric value is given, then MATLAB tries to evaluate it as an expression. An expression can contain any defined variables, operators, or functions. For example:

```
>> io1
Enter a number: 3*2+1
Second number: z
Their ratio is
    3
>>
```

The first expression is evaluated as 7 and stored in the variable x. The second expression is evaluated as the value from the variable z, which was 2.3333 from the first execution of the program, and is stored in the variable y. The default behavior is to treat all data as mathematical expressions and evaluate them on-the-fly. This shortcut is designed to facilitate mathematical work. This can be contrasted with shell scripting, where the expected work is textual in nature and so the default behavior is to treat all data as strings.

The disp function can display only a single text or variable argument. A more complex output function is *fprintf*, which is modeled after the C programming function of the same name. For example:

```
>> fprintf('The ratio of %f to %f is %.4f\n',x,y,z);
   The ratio of 7.000000 to 2.333300 is 3.0000
>>
```

Most of the symbols available for formatting fprintf() statements in the C programming language are available in the fprintf statement for the MATLAB language, and they follow the same conventions.

Notice that the precision displayed in the previous example was six digits for the first two variables and four digits for the last variable. The exact number of digits displayed can be set precisely using fprintf formatting conventions, as shown. The default precision for the disp function can also be changed, using the *format* statement. For example:

```
>> format long
>> disp(y)
   2.333300000000000
>> format short
>> disp(y)
   2.3333
>>
```

Other options for the format statement include scientific notation and adding or omitting extra empty lines between output.

Files can be accessed using a family of functions including *fopen*, *fclose*, *fread*, *fwrite*, *fseek*, *fprintf*, and *fscanf*. These functions have similar syntax and behave similarly to the functions with the same names in the C programming language. For example:

```
>> fid1=fopen('data1.txt','w');
>> fprintf(fid1,'14\n11\n8\n5\n');
>> fclose(fid1);
>>
```

This creates a file data1.txt with contents as follows:

```
14
11
8
5
```

The fread and fwrite functions work at a byte level instead of processing all data as text.

There are a number of functions designed to simplify the reading of data files. For example:

```
>> a=importdata('data1.txt')
a =
      14
      11
       8
       5
>>
```

The *importdata* function is most commonly used to read data from a text file (although it can also read other types of files) into an array. Whitespace characters (space, tab, newline) are assumed to be delimiters. The function automatically determines the dimensions and extents of the array based upon the file contents. The *textscan* function works similarly but provides more control over how the data is to be interpreted. For example:

```
>> fid1=fopen('data1.txt','r');
>> b=textscan(fid1,'%1d');
>> b{:}
ans =
       1
       4
       1
       1
       8
       5
>> fclose(fid1);
>>
```

Using the textscan function, each line of the data file can be parsed using the formatting notation for the fprintf function. In this example, a series of one character integers were read, leading to a 6×1 cell array of data. The *xlsread* and *xlswrite* functions provide for the reading and writing of data to and from Microsoft Excel files. Their syntax can specify a specific worksheet within a file as well as the range of data on a worksheet. All of these file reading and writing functions provide convenient shortcuts for working with data files and support the nature of the work expected to be done with MATLAB.

9.4.2   Variables

All variables in MATLAB are arrays. The number of dimensions in the array, and the number of elements (size) of each dimension, are defined by the context of the operation creating the variable. For example:

```
>> a=2
a =
     2
>> b=[3 1 5]
b =
     3     1     5
>> c=[6 2; 8 3; 14 42]
c =
     6      2
     8      3
    14     42
>>
```

The variable *a* is a single value, but MATLAB stores it as a one-element array. The variable *b* was declared as a one-dimensional array holding three values. The variable *c* was declared as a two-dimensional array holding six values, organized into three rows by two columns. The semicolon (;) is used to separate rows of values during direct variable initialization.

The indices for arrays are labeled according to the conventions for matrix notation. For example:

```
>> b(3)=-2
b =
     3     1    -2
>> c(3,1)=b(3)+2.4
c =
     6.0000    2.0000
     8.0000    3.0000
     0.4000   42.0000
>>
```

Values for indexing start at one,[8] and dimensions are indexed in row, column order from the top-left.

There are several shorthand mechanisms for populating arrays with ranges of values. For example:

```
>> d=[0:0.2:1]
d =
          0    0.2000    0.4000    0.6000    0.8000    1.0000
```

---

8. This can cause problems when converting between C code, which indexes from zero, and MATLAB code, which indexes from one.

```
>> e=linspace(0,1,4)
e =

         0    0.3333    0.6667    1.0000
>>
```

The variable *d* was declared using a starting value (0), an ending value (1), and a delta (0.2) between consecutive values in the array. This results in a six-element one-dimensional array. The variable *e* was declared with the *linspace* function using a starting value (0), an ending value (1), and the number of elements (4) whose values are evenly distributed between the end points. This results in a four-element one-dimensional array. Other shortcuts for initializing an array include *diag*, *eye*, *ones*, *rand*, and *zeros*, all of which provide mechanisms for populating an array with values.

As with other scripting languages, variables in MATLAB do not need to be explicitly declared before being used. The MATLAB environment allocates space for a variable when it first sees its name, and manages the space required to store the variable throughout its usage in a program. The size of a variable can be adjusted in a number of ways. For example:

```
>> b
b =

     3     1    -2
>> b(6)=-12
b =

     3     1    -2     0     0   -12
>> b(2)=[]
b =

     3    -2     0     0   -12
>> b(2,1)=21
b =

     3    -2     0     0   -12
    21     0     0     0     0
>>
```

Typing a variable name reports its current value(s). Assigning a value to an index outside the current dimensions or bounds of the variable causes it to automatically expand to a rectilinear size capable of holding the new value. Assigning a value of [] (empty square brackets) to an index causes its deletion, with the other values collapsing to fill the void. There are several other mechanisms that can be used to adjust a range of values, to move a range of values, or to transpose array dimensions. All of these mechanisms provide shortcuts for dynamic memory management. In particular, they simplify the handling of tabular data.

9.4.3 Loops and Conditionals

The MATLAB language has the familiar *for* and *while* loop programming state-ments. For example:

```
for i=1:3,
    disp('Hello');
end
i=0;
while i<3,
    disp('Goodbye');
    i=i+1;
end
```

If this code is stored in a file named `loops1.m`, then executing it produces the following output:

```
>> loops1
Hello
Hello
Hello
Goodbye
Goodbye
Goodbye
>>
```

The for statement iterates a counter variable from a beginning value to an ending value by an optional delta amount (the default delta is 1). The while statement iterates as long as a condition is true. For both types of loop, all statements between the comma following the loop definition and the end statement are executed each iteration. The MATLAB language also contains *break* and *continue* statements that operate similarly to their C language counterparts.

When processing tabular data, a common loop operation is to perform the same operation on every element in a table. This is facilitated in MATLAB by matrix operations. For example:

```
>> a=[3 1 6]

a =

      3      1      6

>> b=[4 5 2]

b =

      4      5      2

>> c=a-b
```

```
c =
    -1   -4    4
>>
```

The last statement c=a-b is essentially a loop statement. It performs the subtraction on each paired element of a and b to create the c variable. Similar statements can be performed for matrix addition and multiplication. Other mechanisms provide for copying ranges of one matrix to another. Thus, matrix operations provide a convenient shorthand notation for processing tabular data.

The MATLAB language also has the familiar *if* conditional statement. For example:

```
for i=1:3,
  if i >= 2,
    disp('Hello');
  end
end
i=0;
while i<3,
  if i >= 2,
    disp('Goodbye');
  else
    disp('Oops - forgot something');
  end
  i=i+1;
end
```

If this code is stored in a file named if1.m, then executing it produces the following output:

```
>> if1
Hello
Hello
Oops - forgot something
Oops - forgot something
Goodbye
>>
```

The if statement tests a condition; if the condition is true, then the statements between the comma following the condition and the end statement are executed. The if statement can be paired with *else* and *elseif* clauses. MATLAB also has a version of the *case* statement that is similar to the C programming case statement.

When working with tabular data, conditional tests are often performed on an entire array. For example, given a sample of test grades, a programmer may want to find out how many are within certain grade ranges. In MATLAB, this sort of work is again facilitated by matrix operations. For example:

```
>> grades=[85 92 75 73 88 97 65 75]
grades =
    85    92    75    73    88    97    65    75
>> A=grades>=90
A =
     0     1     0     0     0     1     0     0
>> B=grades>=80 & grades<90
B =
     1     0     0     0     1     0     0     0
>>
```

When a variable is assigned to another variable using a conditional, the result variable contains a 1 at all indices where the condition was true, and a 0 at all indices where the condition was false. This is a shorthand notation for looping through all elements of the array and testing each one against the conditional. The *find* function performs a similar operation:

```
>> find(grades>=90)
ans =
     2     6
>>
```

The find function returns the indices of the values in the array for which the condition tested is true. Instead of having to write loop, test, and assignment code for every element in an array, the same set of operations can be accomplished by a single matrix operation.

9.4.4 Built-in Mathematical Functions

MATLAB provides a large number of built-in functions for performing various types of mathematical operations. For example:

```
>> a=[7 1 5 7];
>> sqrt(a)
ans =
    2.6458    1.0000    2.2361    2.6458
>> cos(a)
ans =
    0.7539    0.5403    0.2837    0.7539
>>
```

These functions perform the operation on every element in the array variable. Other functions return a single value for the array. For example:

```
>> sum(a)
ans =
    20
>> mean(a)
ans =
     5
>> std(a)
ans =
    2.8284
>>
```

Table 9.1 presents a list of some of the more commonly used functions. These functions all simplify coding for mathematical work.

Table 9.1 Some of the mathematical functions built into MATLAB.

Function	Description	Function	Description
Basic functions		**Basic functions**	
sqrt	square root	log	natural logarithm
exp	exponential	abs	absolute value
min	minimum value	max	maximum value
sum	sum of values	length	length of array
Trigonometric functions		**Statistics functions**	
cos	cosine	mean	mean of values
sin	sine	median	median of values
tan	tangent	var	variance of values
acos	inverse cosine	std	standard deviation
atan	inverse tangent	cov	covariance matrix
Rounding functions		**Order functions**	
ceil	round values up	sort	sort values
floor	round values down	issorted	test for sortedness
round	round to nearest integer	unique	eliminate copies

9.4.5   Plotting

MATLAB provides several functions for plotting data. The simplest is the *plot* function. For example:

```
x=0:0.01:1;
s=sin(x);
c=cos(x);
plot(s,c);
```

Executing this code produces the plot shown in Figure 9.2. This code computes a range of values from 0 to 1 in 0.01 increments, and then computes the sine and cosine of those values. The plot function creates a two-dimensional plot of the given data, using the values in the first array for the horizontal axis and the values in the second array for the vertical axis.

MATLAB opens a figure window to display the plot. The figure window has a menu that includes options to save the plot in various formats, zoom the view of the plot, and change various attributes of the plot, such as its legend. The plot function itself can also be given optional arguments to change how the plot appears. For example:

```
plot(s,c,'--k','LineWidth',4);
```

The '--' argument indicates the data should be connected with a dotted line. The 'k' argument indicates the line should be black. The 'LineWidth',4 arguments indicate that the line should be 4 points wide. Figure 9.3 shows the plot that

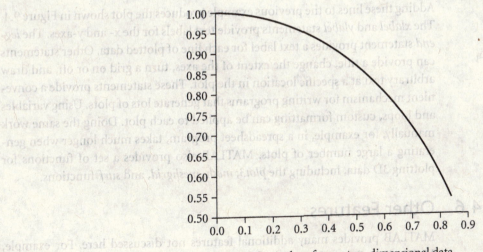

Figure 9.2 A plot of some two-dimensional data.

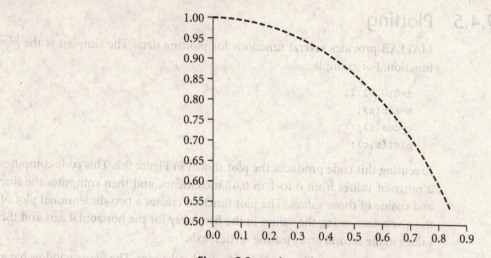

Figure 9.3 A plot with some custom characteristics.

results from this command. Other options include which symbol to use to mark a data point, and which colors to use for symbols and lines.

The format of a plot, such as the title, legend, and axis labels, can be changed manually through the menu interface of the plot window. However, they can also be changed using script statements. For example:

```
xlabel('sin(x)');
ylabel('cos(x)');
legend('turtle');
```

Adding these lines to the previous example produces the plot shown in Figure 9.4. The *xlabel* and *ylabel* statements provide text labels for the x- and y-axes. The *legend* statement provides a text label for each line of plotted data. Other statements can provide a title, change the extent of the axes, turn a grid on or off, and draw arbitrary text at a specific location in the plot. These statements provide a convenient mechanism for writing programs that generate lots of plots. Using variables and loops, custom formatting can be applied to each plot. Doing the same work manually, for example, in a spreadsheet program, takes much longer when generating a large number of plots. MATLAB also provides a set of functions for plotting 3D data, including the *plot3, mesh, meshgrid,* and *surf* functions.

9.4.6   Other Features

MATLAB provides many additional features not discussed here. For example, MATLAB can be used to solve systems of linear equations. MATLAB provides op-

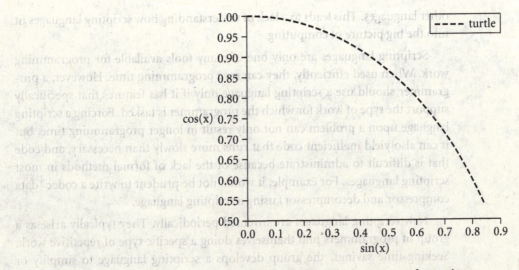

Figure 9.4 A plot with some custom formatting.

erations to fit functions to data sets, and to interpolate values in various manners. Symbolic expressions can be evaluated, for example, working analytically (as opposed to numerically) with mathematical functions. There are also a number of packages that can be added to basic MATLAB, providing additional functions and features. One of the more popular packages provides mechanisms for image processing. All of these features simplify working with mathematical or tabular data. If a task involves writing programs for this kind of work, writing MATLAB scripts generally takes much less time than writing the same programs using the C language.

9.5 • Discussion

Computing professionals are known for developing strong opinions on preferences for tools of the trade, such as operating systems, text editors, and code development environments. Scripting languages are no different. To some programmers, a particular scripting language is good for all programming work. This is of course a fallacy. This can be explained partly by the amount of experience a particular person may have with a specific language. As more and more shortcuts are learned within a scripting language, a programmer gains proficiency and realizes increased time savings. In reality though, overuse of a particular programming language usually comes from the opposite: inexperience with other languages. This leads to a lack of understanding how scripting languages fit into the big picture of computing.

Scripting languages are only one of many tools available for programming work. When used efficiently, they can save programming time. However, a programmer should use a scripting language only if it has features that specifically support the type of work for which the programmer is tasked. Forcing a scripting language upon a problem can not only result in longer programming time, but it can also yield inefficient code that runs more slowly than necessary, and code that is difficult to administrate because of the lack of formal methods in most scripting languages. For example, it would not be prudent to write a codec (data compressor and decompressor) using a scripting language.

New scripting languages are invented periodically. They typically arise as a group of programmers find themselves doing a specific type of repetitive work. Seeking time savings, the group develops a scripting language to simplify or automate parts of the work. It is highly likely that a computing professional will see several scripting languages throughout his or her career. Understanding their design goals and limitations helps one make good decisions about how to use scripting languages for programming work.

Questions and Exercises

1. What is the primary goal in using a scripting language for programming work?

2. What two things are commonly done to a script file in order to treat it as a program?

3. What shortcuts do scripting languages provide with respect to variables?

4. Write a shell program that renames all files in the current directory. It should remove all vowels from the filenames. For example, `apple.txt` should be renamed `ppl.txt`. If the resulting filename is an empty string, then the file should not be renamed.

5. Write a shell program that counts the number of files in a given directory. The directory should be specified as a command line argument. The program does not need to count files recursively in subdirectories; instead, it should not count subdirectories at all.

6. Write a shell program that parses a given file and counts all occurrences of words that contain one or more "e" letters. For example, the count of words containing one or more e's in this sentence is 6. Write the same program using the C lan-

guage. Compare how long it takes to write each program, and the length of the program code.

7. Write a Perl program that parses the source for a web page and outputs a list of any email addresses contained in the source. The program should use pattern matching to determine what is an email address, according to the form `name@place.place`, where place must be an alphanumeric string. For testing, most web browsers have an option to view and save the source of a web page.

8. Write a Perl program that backs up a directory of files. It should perform the backup by copying each file from the given directory to a backup directory. The program should take two command line arguments, one being the path of the directory to copy, the second being the name of the path in which to place the backup. If the backup is performed repeatedly, the program should recopy only those files that have been modified since the last time they were backed up. The program should ignore subdirectories; it needs to backup files only within the given directory.

9. Write a Perl program that automates the creation of a personal web page. The program should take as a command line argument the name of a file containing the following data in text format:

```
name
address
email

biographical sketch

web link #1
web link #2
.
.
.
```

The program should create a web page file according to the following format:

```
<TITLE>name's Web Page</TITLE>
name<P>
address<P>
email<P>
<HR>
<H2>Biography</H2>
biographical sketch<P>
<HR>
<H2>Favorite web links</H2>
```

```
<UL>
<LI> <A HREF="http://...web link #1...">
name of link #1</A><P>
<LI> <A HREF="http://...web link #1...">
name of link #2</A><P>
:    repeat for all web links
:
</UL>
```

The web page should be tested using any web brower to display it.

10. Write a Perl program that parses a text file and removes all occurrences of the following eight punctuation marks: ' " : ; , . ! ?. Write the same program using the C language. Compare how long it takes to write each program, and the length of the program code.

11. How do shell scripting and MATLAB differ in how data is stored and treated?

12. Write a MATLAB program that determines if one circle is entirely inside a second circle. The program should prompt the user for the center point and radius of two circles, and then perform the computation. The program should print out a text message declaring the answer, and plot the two circles for display.

13. Write a MATLAB program that reads a text file and displays a histogram of the occurrences of the 26 letters of the English alphabet. For example, the count of a's in this sentence is 2. That count should be computed for every letter. Counts should be case insensitive, and all other characters should be ignored. The counts should be displayed as a plot, with appropriately labeled axes and a title.

14. Write a MATLAB program to solve triangles. Follow the instructions in Exercise 7 in Chapter 8. After solving for a triangle, the program should display the triangle in a plot.

A

ASCII Table

The following tables provide the binary, decimal, and symbol codes or glyphs for the American Standard Code for Information Interchange (ASCII) bit model. The decimal values 0–31 and 127 are control characters and do not have visual glyphs; the others represent printable characters. For the nonprintable characters, a description is provided as well as a character escape code (not all nonprintable characters have escape codes) that can be used in C programming and other related languages such as Perl.

Control characters

Decimal	Symbol	Binary	Escape code	Description
0	NUL	00000000	\0	null character
1	SOH	00000001		start of header
2	STX	00000010		start of text
3	ETX	00000011		end of text
4	EOT	00000100		end of transmission
5	ENQ	00000101		enquiry
6	ACK	00000110		acknowledgment
7	BEL	00000111	\a	bell
8	BS	00001000	\b	backspace
9	HT	00001001	\t	horizontal tab
10	LF	00001010	\n	line feed
11	VT	00001011	\v	vertical tab
12	FF	00001100	\f	form feed
13	CR	00001101	\r	carriage return
14	SO	00001110		shift out
15	SI	00001111		shift in
16	DLE	00010000		data link escape
17	DC1	00010001		device control 1
18	DC2	00010010		device control 2
19	DC3	00010011		device control 3
20	DC4	00010100		device control 4
21	NAK	00010101		negative acknowledge
22	SYN	00010110		synchronous idle
23	ETB	00010111		end of transmission
24	CAN	00011000		cancel
25	EM	00011001		end of medium
26	SUB	00011010		substitute
27	ESC	00011011		escape
28	FS	00011100		file separator
29	GS	00011101		group separator
30	RS	00011110		record separator
31	US	00011111		unit separator
127	DEL	01111111		delete

Printable characters

Dec.	Symbol	Binary	Dec.	Symbol	Binary	Dec.	Symbol	Binary
32	[space]	00100000	64	@	01000000	96	'	01100000
33	!	00100001	65	A	01000001	97	a	01100001
34	"	00100010	66	B	01000010	98	b	01100010
35	#	00100011	67	C	01000011	99	c	01100011
36	$	00100100	68	D	01000100	100	d	01100100
37	%	00100101	69	E	01000101	101	e	01100101
38	&	00100110	70	F	01000110	102	f	01100110
39	'	00100111	71	G	01000111	103	g	01100111
40	(	00101000	72	H	01001000	104	h	01101000
41	)	00101001	73	I	01001001	105	i	01101001
42	*	00101010	74	J	01001010	106	j	01101010
43	+	00101011	75	K	01001011	107	k	01101011
44	,	00101100	76	L	01001100	108	l	01101100
45	-	00101101	77	M	01001101	109	m	01101101
46	.	00101110	78	N	01001110	110	n	01101110
47	/	00101111	79	O	01001111	111	o	01101111
48	0	00110000	80	P	01010000	112	p	01110000
49	1	00110001	81	Q	01010001	113	q	01110001
50	2	00110010	82	R	01010010	114	r	01110010
51	3	00110011	83	S	01010011	115	s	01110011
52	4	00110100	84	T	01010100	116	t	01110100
53	5	00110101	85	U	01010101	117	u	01110101
54	6	00110110	86	V	01010110	118	v	01110110
55	7	00110111	87	W	01010111	119	w	01110111
56	8	00111000	88	X	01011000	120	x	01111000
57	9	00111001	89	Y	01011001	121	y	01111001
58	:	00111010	90	Z	01011010	122	z	01111010
59	;	00111011	91	[	01011011	123	{	01111011
60	<	00111100	92	\	01011100	124			01111100
61	=	00111101	93	]	01011101	125	}	01111101
62	>	00111110	94	^	01011110	126	~	01111110
63	?	00111111	95	_	01011111			

Printable characters

Dec	Symbol	Binary	Dec	Symbol	Binary	Dec	Symbol	Binary
32	(space)	00100000	64	@	01000000	96	`	01100000
33	!	00100001	65	A	01000001	97	a	01100001
34	"	00100010	66	B	01000010	98	b	01100010
35	#	00100011	67	C	01000011	99	c	01100011
36	$	00100100	68	D	01000100	100	d	01100100
37	%	00100101	69	E	01000101	101	e	01100101
38	&	00100110	70	F	01000110	102	f	01100110
39	'	00100111	71	G	01000111	103	g	01100111
40	(	00101000	72	H	01001000	104	h	01101000
41	)	00101001	73	I	01001001	105	i	01101001
42	*	00101010	74	J	01001010	106	j	01101010
43	+	00101011	75	K	01001011	107	k	01101011
44	,	00101100	76	L	01001100	108	l	01101100
45	-	00101101	77	M	01001101	109	m	01101101
46	.	00101110	78	N	01001110	110	n	01101110
47	/	00101111	79	O	01001111	111	o	01101111
48	0	00110000	80	P	01010000	112	p	01110000
49	1	00110001	81	Q	01010001	113	q	01110001
50	2	00110010	82	R	01010010	114	r	01110010
51	3	00110011	83	S	01010011	115	s	01110011
52	4	00110100	84	T	01010100	116	t	01110100
53	5	00110101	85	U	01010101	117	u	01110101
54	6	00110110	86	V	01010110	118	v	01110110
55	7	00110111	87	W	01010111	119	w	01110111
56	8	00111000	88	X	01011000	120	x	01111000
57	9	00111001	89	Y	01011001	121	y	01111001
58	:	00111010	90	Z	01011010	122	z	01111010
59	;	00111011	91	[	01011011	123	{	01111011
60	<	00111100	92	\	01011100	124	|	01111100
61	=	00111101	93	]	01011101	125	}	01111101
62	>	00111110	94	^	01011110	126	~	01111110
63	?	00111111	95	_	01011111			

B

Common Shell Commands

The following table provides a list of commands commonly used in a shell. Many are built-in commands available on most shells, but some are actually system programs depending on the particular shell. A brief description or use for each command is provided. More information can be found in the man page for a specific shell, such as sh, bash, ksh, or tcsh.

Command	Description
ls	file listing
cd	change directory
pwd	print working directory
mkdir	make a new directory
rmdir	remove a directory
rm	remove a file
mv	rename a file to a new name
alias	create an alias for a command
unalias	delete an existing alias
fg	run a process in the foreground
bg	run a process in the background
kill	send a signal to a process (usually to terminate)
nice	run a process at the given priority
renice	change the priority of a process
time	display how long a command takes to execute

chgrp	change the group for a file
chmod	change the permission bits of a file
chown	change the owner of a file
umask	set the default permissions for a created file
echo	print the given message
set	display or give a value to a shell variable
unset	delete an existing shell variable

C

System Programs

The following table provides a list of system programs available on most Unix systems. A brief description of each command is provided. More information can be found in the man page for each program.

Program	Description
ar	create or extract files from an archive file
at	run command at a specified time
awk	text processing (pattern matching and substitution)
basename	display filename portion of a full pathname
bc	text-based calculator
cal	text-based calendar
cat	concatenate files and display to standard output
compress	compress a file
cp	copy a file
crontab	schedule periodic execution of commands
cut	display selected fields of each line of text
date	display the date and time
dd	copy and convert a file (limited conversions)
df	report the free disk space
diff	compare two files
dirname	display directory portion of a full pathname

du	display disk space usage
ed	text editor
eval	return the exit value of a command
exit	exit the shell
expr	evaluate simple expression, displaying the result
file	determine the type of file
find	find a file
grep	search for a text pattern
head	display the first part of a file
lex	generate a lexical analyzer
ln	link an existing file to a new filename
lp	send a file to a printer
lprm	remove a file from a printer's queue
lpq	print a list of files in a printer's queue
mail	text-based email program
make	build a program according to a makefile
man	display a manual page for a command or program
mkdir	make a new directory
more	display a file one screenfull at a time
patch	apply given changes to text files
ps	display a list of processes
rm	remove a file
rmdir	remove a directory
sed	text processing (stream editor)
sleep	pause for a specified amount of time
sort	sort one or more text files
strings	display text-portions of a binary file
strip	remove inessential portions of an executable file
tail	display the last part of a file
test	test a simple expression, returning the result
touch	update the access and modified times for a file
tr	transliterate characters in a text file
tty	display the terminal name
uname	display the system name
uncompress	uncompress a file

uniq	filter out repeated lines in a text file
wc	display line, word, and byte count for a file
who	display who is logged into the system
yacc	generate a parser

Index